# Student Engagement
## and
## Achievement
## in
## American
## Secondary Schools

# Student Engagement
# and
# Achievement
# in
# American
# Secondary Schools

*Fred M. Newmann*
*Editor*

**Teachers College, Columbia University**
**New York and London**

1992

This book was prepared at the National Center on Effective Secondary Schools and the Center on Organization and Restructuring of Schools, which were supported in part by grants from the Office of Educational Research and Improvement (Grant No. G-0086900007 and R117Q00005-91), by the Wisconsin Center for Education Research, and the School of Education, University of Wisconsin–Madison. Any opinions, findings, and conclusions or recommendations expressed in this publication are those of the authors and do not necessarily reflect the views of the supporting agencies.

Published by Teachers College Press, 1234 Amsterdam Avenue
New York, NY 10027

*Library of Congress Cataloging-in-Publication Data*

Student engagement and achievement in American secondary schools /
    Fred M. Newmann, editor.
        p.    cm.
    "Findings from five main projects in the National Center on
Effective Secondary Schools, which operated from December 1, 1985 to
February 28, 1991" — Acknowledgments.
    Includes bibliographical references (p.  ) and index.
    ISBN 0–8077–3183–8 (alk. paper). — ISBN 0–8077–3182–X (alk. paper:
pbk.)
    1. Academic achievement — United States.    2. High school students —
United States.    3. Classroom environment — United States.
    I. Newmann, Fred M.
    LB1062.6.S78    1992
    373.18′0973 — dc20                                                92-15727

ISBN 0–8077–3183–8
ISBN 0–8077–3182–X (pbk.)

Printed on acid-free paper
Manufactured in the United States of America

99  98  97  96  95  94  93  92    8  7  6  5  4  3  2  1

# Contents

# Acknowledgments

This book presents research findings from five main projects in the National Center on Effective Secondary Schools, which operated from December 1, 1985 to February 28, 1991. A shorter summary of findings is available in the *Final Report*, which includes a listing of all personnel and about 150 publications that they produced.[1] The work of the Center depended on financial and substantive contributions from dozens of organizations and thousands of individuals. We cannot mention all by name. Funding was provided by the Office of Education Research and Improvement, U.S. Department of Education, the Wisconsin Center for Education Research, and the School of Education, University of Wisconsin–Madison. Members of the National Advisory Panel and the High School Advisory Network offered yearly counsel on our plans and reactions to tentative findings. Researchers and practitioners nationwide provided useful reviews of manuscripts. A variety of educational organizations helped to disseminate information from the Center, particularly the federally sponsored Research Centers and Educational Laboratories, the American Federation of Teachers, the National Education Association, the National Association of Secondary School Principals, and the Association for Supervision and Curriculum Development. The authors owe an enormous debt to staff at the University of Wisconsin, especially the student assistants and secretaries who shouldered the burdens of intense work behind the scenes. Diane Randall provided exceptionally efficient and friendly administrative coordination for the Center, and she skillfully prepared the manuscript. Finally, we recognize the cooperation of the ultimate sources of the knowledge generated — the students, teachers, and school administrators in secondary schools from coast to coast.

## NOTE

1. National Center on Effective Secondary Schools, *Final Report on OERI Grant No. G-0086900007*, March 20, 1991, available from WCER Document Service, Room 242, 1025 W. Johnson St., Madison, WI 53706. Make check or purchase order to "Center Document Service." Cost is $12.75, which includes shipping, handling, and first class mailing.

# Introduction

## Fred M. Newmann

Since the early 1980s, America's high schools have been besieged with studies, critiques, and proposals for reform. Critics have exposed academically weak curricula, neglect of problem solving and higher-order thinking, inequitable effects of curriculum tracking, professionally demeaning working conditions for teachers, and, in many schools, drop-out rates that exceed 50 percent for poor minority students. Reports of national test scores and international comparisons continually announce low levels of high school student achievement.

Beginning in the 1970s research on "effective schools" (Brookover, Beady, Flood, Schweitzer, & Wisenbaker, 1979; Edmonds, 1979) tried to identify the variables through which some elementary schools enabled poor minority students to achieve at levels comparable to middle-class white students on standardized reading and math tests. Strong leadership by the principal, a school-wide instructional focus on basic skills with continuous monitoring of student achievement, and high expectations by teachers were some of the key factors.

Following a body of research that emphasized the dominant influence of social background on student achievement (Coleman, Campbell, Hobson, McPartland, Modd, Weinfeld, & York, 1966; Jencks, Smith, Acland, Bane, Cohen, Gintis, Heyns, & Michaelson, 1972), effective schools research offered hope that schools could make a difference. The slogan was quickly appropriated to educational research and practice that extended well beyond the original issue of how elementary schools serving poor minority students might enhance standardized test scores to middle-class levels. In 1985 the federal government funded two 5-year centers to conduct research on effective schools — one dealing with elementary schools (at Johns Hopkins University), and the other dealing with secondary schools (University of Wisconsin–Madison). Both centers studied middle

1

schools. This book presents major findings from the National Center on Effective Secondary Schools (henceforth the Center), which concentrated primarily on high schools, with two of the five main projects studying middle schools.[1]

The Center began with a mission broader than boosting the achievement of low-income minority students on standardized tests. Our mission extended the effective schools framework in four ways.[2] First, we were concerned with students who did not succeed in school, especially low-income students of color, who are disproportionately represented in this group. Ultimately, however, we were interested in increased success for all students.

Second, we believed that success in school should not be judged primarily by the tests conventionally used in large-scale assessments. Such tests measure only limited forms of human accomplishment, they fail to test much of what schools try to teach, and, when norm-referenced and standardized, they make it impossible for half the students to succeed. Other indicators of school success are important, such as reduced drop-out rates, increased enrollment in advanced coursework or in extracurricular activities, and projects that reflect more authentic forms of intellectual performance.

Further, we doubted that secondary schools could be improved simply by identifying a list of variables related to student achievement and persuading schools to work on each item in the list. Instead, we felt that educational interventions would be powerful only to the extent that they were grounded in coherent theory that explained how and why certain approaches to instruction, curriculum, and school organization were more likely than others to produce favorable student outcomes.

Finally, research literature on American secondary schools, along with our conversations with teachers, suggested to us that the effective schools literature, and indeed most of the rhetoric about school improvement, had neglected the most salient issue for both teachers and students each hour of the school day.

## ENGAGEMENT

The most immediate and persisting issue for students and teachers is not low achievement, but student disengagement. The most obviously disengaged students disrupt classes, skip them, or fail to complete assignments. More typically, disengaged students behave well in school. They attend class and complete the work, but with little indication of excitement, commitment, or pride in mastery of the curriculum. In contrast, engaged students make a psychological investment in learning. They try hard to learn what school offers. They take pride not simply in earning the formal indicators of success (grades), but in understanding the material and incorporating or internalizing it in their lives.[3]

For teachers, the challenge is how to get students to do academic work and to take it seriously enough to learn; for students, the challenge is how to cope with teachers' demands so as to avoid boredom, to maintain self-respect, and, at the same time, to succeed in school. As we explain further in several chapters, meaningful learning cannot be delivered to high school students like pizza to be consumed or videos to be observed. Lasting learning develops largely through the labor of the student, who must be enticed to participate in a continuous cycle of studying, producing, correcting mistakes, and starting over again. Students cannot be expected to achieve unless they concentrate, work, and invest themselves in the mastery of school tasks. This is the sense in which student engagement is critical to educational success; to enhance achievement, one must first learn how to engage students.

The point seems almost too obvious to mention, but too many of us (educators and parents) have learned the hard way that it cannot be taken for granted. Student disengagement posed less of a problem in earlier times when secondary schools served more select populations of students, when families offered more cohesive, sustained support for students' investment in schoolwork, and when youth had fewer opportunities for activities that now compete with schoolwork. Today, however, schools' ability to engage students is constantly tested by increased cultural diversity in the student body, by large proportions of students who need special forms of care that school staff traditionally have not been expected to offer, and by a host of powerful distractions that compete for students' time and emotional investment. (For many students these "distractors" involve substantial responsibilities for family care.)

Public concerns for education expressed in the mass media; in the debates of policy makers; in programs and mandates of districts, states, and professional organizations; and in the views of corporate leaders often focus on the "bottom line" — student achievement. What students actually know, what they can do, and the attitudes or other outcomes of schooling should, of course, receive substantial attention. But attempts to establish consensus on achievement outcomes for secondary school students on either a national or local level will continue to pose major issues in the United States. Concern with end results has often deflected attention from fundamental conditions of teaching and learning. Ultimately, we must craft policy, practice, and research to enhance student achievement, but until we learn more about the fundamental problem of how to engage students in schoolwork, there is no reason to expect improvements in achievement, however these outcomes may be defined.

To study how to enhance student engagement, the Center encouraged diverse perspectives and developed five projects to investigate the problem. Students at risk present the most visible symptoms of disengagement — numerous programs have tried to address them, and so one of the projects studied experiences and effects of alternative programs and policies to assist at-risk students. Concerned that the secondary school curriculum usually offers few opportunities for critical thinking or problem solving, and hypothesizing that challenging students to use their minds would enhance engagement, another project studied how to increase higher-order thinking in social studies. A third project developed a model of authentic instructional discourse that included criteria for the kind of writing, reading, and talking most likely to promote engagement and achievement. It examined the extent to which grouping and tracking policies affect student opportunities for authentic discourse. Recognizing that teachers have the most direct opportunities to affect student engagement, a project on teacher quality of worklife studied how organizational features of the school contribute to teachers' engagement and success in teaching. A final project studied high school mainly from the students' perspective to learn how engagement and achievement might be influenced by student experiences in four noninstructional settings — namely, the family, peer group, extracurricular activity, and part-time work.

The projects investigated different aspects of the engagement and achievement problems — through literature reviews, analyses of existing data sets, and new studies of students and staff in 32 middle and 62 high schools throughout the United States. Because research on the nature and measurement of student engagement has only just begun, and because of continuing controversy over what forms of achievement ought to be assessed and what forms can be assessed within reasonable costs, it was not possible or even advisable for all projects to use a common set of indicators of student engagement and achievement.

## ACHIEVEMENT

Before presenting results from each project, we wish to explain why the Center did not use a common set of tests or other indicators of student achievement across all projects. The simple reason is that a good set of indicators is not available. In spite of recent interest in national goals for student achievement, there exists no set of indicators for student achievement in American secondary schools that is considered valid by researchers and the public at large and that also can be used to compare the progress, from high school entry to exit, of students from different schools and with different educational needs.

Many indicators have been used to measure the accomplishments of students and schools: attendance (drop-out rates), credits earned, grades, and performance on several types of tests — standardized achievement tests; college admission tests; competency tests constructed by schools, districts, states, and the national assessment; and teacher-made tests for specific courses. Unfortunately, each of these indicators is deficient on one or more of the following grounds:

1. Failure to indicate what the student actually knows or can do
2. Neglect of important educational goals such as creativity, interpersonal sensitivity, psychological development, civic responsibility, or critical thinking
3. Perpetuation of cultural biases that unfairly restrict educational opportunity
4. Providing information that has little relationship to success beyond school
5. Failure to assess the specific curriculum taught within an individual high school

Indicators of achievement that avoid these faults cannot be constructed by specialists in testing and measurement alone. Such a project requires reexamination of the very goals of schooling, which, in a democracy, demands broad participation of educators and the public at large. The challenge is particularly perplexing in a society that now encounters two underlying and opposing social forces. On the one hand, we face the *homogenizing* aspects of modernization — accelerating centralization, nationalization, and globalization of experience. These, combined with a commitment to equity, suggest the need to evaluate educational achievement through common national or even international standards. On the other hand, in the United States we face the *diversifying* forces of increased cultural pluralism and economic polarization. These, combined with a long-standing commitment to preserve the autonomy of local communities to determine school goals, support the prospect of diverse, rather than common, educational standards across schools. As a nation, we are only beginning to address the question of what standards for secondary school achievement should be applied in common and what standards might be unique to different groups of students.

The press for national goals and tests should bring to the surface long-standing dilemmas, rarely discussed in public, about the proper aims of education. Dominant voices of corporate leaders and policy makers tend to emphasize utilitarian, economic outcomes for both individuals and the nation. But these are unlikely to silence historically persistent cries that education also serve the ends of civic welfare and personal fulfillment. Once the debate is ignited, we will see that the conflicts are more complex than arriving at relative priorities among vocational, civic, or personal goals. If faced honestly and openly, a host of other issues, both within and across these realms, will make it increasingly difficult to forge national consensus on the meaning of school achievement and how to measure it.

To give a sense of the contested territory, we list here only some of the issues.

1. To what extent should education focus on the transmission and reproduction of authoritative knowledge versus student construction, or production of students' own understandings?
2. How much emphasis should be given to development of abstract verbal and logical competence, in contrast to other forms of intelligence such as spatial, musical, bodily-kinesthetic, or personal?
3. What should be the balance between socializing students to accept and to "succeed" within existing social institutions versus developing the critical capacity, commitment, and competence to change those institutions?
4. In what ways should conceptions of education be anchored in visions of individual welfare and development as opposed to visions of communal or collective welfare and development?
5. To what extent should formal education help students to understand their historical and cultural roots; how are these to be identified and taught to a culturally diverse student population?
6. Is knowledge itself to be regarded largely as a body of conclusive truth discovered by impartial experts, or more as a set of provisional claims continually influenced by social–cultural values and designed to serve particular interests?

The contrasts posed by these issues are not intended to suggest that they be resolved by choosing one side or the other. What makes them controversial is that each side of the dilemma contains enough "truth" or "validity" to prevent its outright dismissal. Constructive resolution of the issues in schools, communities, and states can be expected to involve serious disagreement, strenuous intellectual work, sensitive efforts in communication, and political savvy.

It remains to be seen whether new standards for educational achievement become crafted through careful consideration of these issues. It is possible that the substance of issues will remain largely ignored by most of the participants in the education enterprise. Dominant regulatory groups that assume that these issues have already been resolved through existing tests and other indicators (e.g., grades, drop-out rates, or college attendance rates) may continue to prevail. The issues can also be avoided through the political strategy of allowing separate teachers, schools, districts, or states to "do their own thing." On the other hand, if all teachers and schools face high-stakes consequences for student performance on standard, highly specific tests and tasks, we can expect an explosion of interest in rethinking what we mean by student achievement.

Even using data from currently available tests, research is inconclusive on the size of achievement gains from high school entry to exit. Unfortunately, there is almost no information on gains in student achievement attributable to American secondary schools. The most systematically gathered information from a national sample recorded student performance only at the end of 10th and 12th Grade.[4] The tests included vocabulary, reading, writing, mathematics, science, and civics — all in multiple-choice format. The average magnitude of these two-year gains was only one to two items on tests ranging from 20 to 40 items.

In two years of school, students presumably spend about 2,000 hours, or the equivalent of fifty 40-hour weeks, on schoolwork.[5] Considering the amount of time that students spend in educational activity, we might conclude from these results that (1) high schools have no important impact on achievement; (2) they must have a far greater impact than what is measured by the tests; or (3) the impact is unclear unless we know more about the items on which progress is made. Learning four new words, for example, may be educationally insignificant, but perhaps learning how to solve just one algebraic equation reflects a major accomplishment.

Lacking a valid system of achievement indicators, realizing that current tests often reveal only marginal or inconclusive gains attributable to high school education, and believing that student engagement should be attacked directly as the most salient issue, we avoided Center-wide emphasis on a common set of tests or other indicators of student success. Instead, projects in the Center were encouraged to develop a variety of indicators and to learn from existing assessments used in schools. This strategy did not permit the projects within the Center to formally test a comprehensive theory of how specific school practices and policies improve student achievement through enhancing engagement. Each project has, however, produced findings that contribute to both the development of theory and the improvement of practice on the central problem.

## OVERVIEW OF THE CHAPTERS

We begin by explaining student engagement. Chapter 1 presents a definition of engagement in academic work, discusses its significance to learning, and outlines the major sources or causes of engagement that schools can deliberately try to promote. The theory of engagement is illustrated by examples from students' experiences. We then enter some classrooms to examine in Chapter 2 how high-quality conversation can engage students by taking their ideas seriously, and building upon them, rather than expecting students always to reproduce correct answers that have been prespecified by the teacher. The teaching of literature in 9th Grade revealed only rare examples of high-quality discourse, but high-quality conversation about literature did improve student understanding. Next we consider the hypothesis that student boredom is often due to an absence of intellectual challenge in the classroom. To explore this, Chapter 3 proposes a conception of higher-order thinking and a scheme for analyzing classroom thoughtfulness. In this study of social studies teaching, students reported more engagement in classes that challenged them to use their minds. The study explains how some high school departments succeeded far more than others, but all faced a number of barriers in developing thoughtful classrooms.

Chapters 4, 5, and 6 look well beyond the classroom for influences on student engagement and academic achievement. Chapter 4 focuses on the problem of engaging at-risk students, those with histories of low achievement who also confront other difficulties that inhibit their engagement in conventional schooling. The chapter studies this problem through two strategies. First, it draws conclusions about the keys to success from a number of novel, alternative school programs created to respond to needs of at-risk students in different locations. Then it examines a unique effort sponsored by a national foundation to restructure several entire school districts to respond to all students at risk in all the districts' schools. Isolated small alternative programs have found ways to engage at-risk students, but major issues in educational restructuring must be faced before these successes can be implemented systemically.

One major issue is how to develop schools that build teacher commitment to the engagement and achievement of all students. Chapter 5 deals with this issue by clarifying the conditions in schools and districts that promote and sustain teacher engagement, especially with low-income students, whom many teachers find so difficult to teach. This study of four innovative high schools with large proportions of low-income students found high levels of teacher engagement. By examining leadership, school culture, specific structural changes, and community context, the study explains how these schools have apparently broken the "iron law of social class" to attain high levels of teacher engagement.

To this point, the book looks to student experiences in school as major influences on student engagement and achievement. Chapter 6 reminds us that schooling occupies only a small portion of adolescents' lives. Through a study of students in nine high schools, it examines the influence of family, peers, participation in extracurricular activities, and part-time employment. Some of these influences are substantial, and the chapter discusses what might be done — by school authorities, parents, employers, students, and others — to minimize negative effects.

Finally, we offer an interpretive summary of the findings (Chapter 7) and their implications for engaging adolescents in academic work in both conventional and "restructured" schools. To accomplish major improvements on a systemic basis will require far more than teachers' understanding of what currently seems to "work," or the introduction of new tests, new curricula, or new organizational structures for schools and districts. Significant advances in student engagement and achievement will depend on communities and the nation as a whole confronting a number of controversial issues dealing with educational aims for children, the content of teacher education and professional development, redistribution of power and authority in the conduct of schooling, and public willingness to invest not only in innovative schooling, but in the building of more basic social support for children.

## NOTES

1. See National Center on Effective Secondary Schools (1991) for a more complete listing of Center activities and publications.

2. See Bliss, Firestone, and Richards (1991) for a more comprehensive discussion of effective schools research and practice.

3. Studies that document student disengagement include Cusick (1973), Eckert (1989), Fine (1991), Goodlad (1984), McNeil (1986), Powell, Farrar, and Cohen (1985), Sedlak, Wheeler, Pullin, and Cusick (1986), Weis (1990), and Weis, Farrar, and Petrie (1989).

4. This is the High School and Beyond (HSB) project of the National Center on Education Statistics (NCES), which tested sophomores and seniors from 1,000 high schools in 1980 with succeeding two-year follow-ups. By 1992, a more recent project of NCES, the National Education Longitudinal Study of 1988 (NELS:88)

will provide data on student gains over four years in high school. Better longitudinal data may also become available later in the 1990s from the National Assessment of Educational Progress.

5. Assuming 180 days (36 weeks) of school per year, five hours of classes per day, and three hours per week of homework.

## REFERENCES

Bliss, J. R., Firestone, W. A., & Richards, C. E. (Eds.). (1991). *Rethinking effective schools: Research and practice.* Englewood Cliffs, NJ: Prentice-Hall.

Brookover, W. B., Beady, C., Flood, P., Schweitzer, J., & Wisenbaker, J. (1979). *School social systems and student achievement: Schools can make a difference.* New York: Praeger.

Coleman, J. S., Campbell, E. Q., Hobson, C. J., McPartland, J., Modd, A. M., Weinfeld, F., & York, R. L. (1966). *Equality of educational opportunity.* Washington, DC: Superintendent of Documents, U.S. Government Printing Office.

Cusick, P. A. (1973). *Inside high school: The student's world.* New York: Holt, Rinehart & Winston.

Eckert, P. (1989). *Jocks and burnouts: Social categories and identity in the high school.* New York: Teachers College Press.

Edmonds, R. R. (1979). Effective schools for the urban poor. *Educational Leadership, 37,* 15–27.

Fine, M. (1991). *Framing dropouts: Notes on the politics of an urban public high school.* Albany: State University of New York Press.

Goodlad, J. I. (1984). *A place called school: Prospects for the future.* New York: McGraw-Hill.

Jencks, C., Smith, M., Acland, H., Bane, M. J., Cohen, D., Gintis, H., Heyns, B., & Michaelson, S. (1972). *Inequality: A reassessment of the effect of family and schooling in America.* New York: Basic Books.

McNeil, L. M. (1986). *Contradictions of control: School structure and school knowledge.* New York: Routledge.

National Center on Effective Secondary Schools. (1991). *Final report.* [WCER Document Service, Room 242, 1025 West Johnson St., Madison, WI 53706. $12.75 postpaid.] Madison, WI: Author.

Powell, A. G., Farrar, E., & Cohen, D. K. (1985). *The shopping mall high school: Winners and losers in the educational marketplace.* Boston: Houghton Mifflin.

Sedlak, M. W., Wheeler, C. W., Pullin, D. C., & Cusick, P. A. (1986). *Selling students short: Classroom bargains and academic reform in the American high school.* New York: Teachers College Press.

Weis, L. (1990). *Working class without work: High school students in a decentralizing economy.* New York: Routledge.

Weis, L., Farrar, E., & Petrie, H. G. (1989). *Dropouts from school: Issues, dilemmas, and solutions.* Albany: State University of New York Press.

CHAPTER 1

# The Significance and Sources of Student Engagement

## Fred M. Newmann, Gary G. Wehlage, and Susie D. Lamborn

A sense of engagement is conveyed by three high school students who told us about some positive kinds of involvement in school.

> I like the fact that I know that I'm challenging myself in school. . . . I like to work hard and that's the thing I value the most. There are always students and teachers that are there to challenge me. I like to be involved in sports and I like to have good times with my friends, pretty much like all teenagers my age, but I value those things, really getting involved and getting to know all kinds of people.

> I'm really happy with what they're teaching me because it's like I really have to use my head. I'm really enthused with what they're teaching me. I think it's really good.

> More than anything I would just advise them to be themselves. I don't think they should try to show anybody up or act cool. Just be yourself and people will respect you more for that than if you try to be cool and stuff. Just be yourself, strive for the best, don't quit or anything, be open to everyone, all the teachers, all your peers, students. I'd encourage them to get involved because I think you really get the most out of life then; it helps your studies, too.

Engagement stands for active involvement, commitment, and concentrated attention, in contrast to superficial participation, apathy, or lack of interest. In work, play, and social interaction, we may experience

11

varying levels of engagement as we talk, listen, observe, read, reflect, and use our bodies. The causes of human engagement and its results are complex and can be best understood in reference to specific activities and social contexts. We begin, therefore, by defining the concept as it applies to student engagement in academic work. Next we argue for its importance in building an agenda for educational reform. Finally, we suggest important sources of engagement in academic work that schools can deliberately try to promote.[1]

## WHAT IS ENGAGEMENT IN ACADEMIC WORK?

Academic work consists of the tasks, usually specified by teachers, that students are asked to undertake in order to master the knowledge, skills, and crafts that serve as the instructional objectives of schooling. The work can occur as part of classroom instruction, homework, or exams, and it may include different types of reading, writing, computing, participating in discussions, and individual and group projects. The boundaries for academic work should not be limited to tasks commonly pursued in the teaching of traditional school subjects of the liberal arts (e.g., mathematics, sciences, humanities, languages). A more adequate conception would recognize as academic work attempts to master any field of expertise that is based on a tradition of accumulated public knowledge and that, through activities of practitioners and/or researchers, continually strives to create advanced levels of understanding or performance in the field. In this sense the mastery of subjects as diverse as electronics, child care, modern dance, or cosmetology can involve academic work.

*We define student engagement in academic work as the student's psychological investment in and effort directed toward learning, understanding, or mastering the knowledge, skills, or crafts that academic work is intended to promote.* This definition requires elaboration and clarification on several points.

Engagement involves psychological investment in learning, comprehending, or mastering knowledge, skills, and crafts, not simply a commitment to complete assigned tasks or to acquire symbols of high performance such as grades or social approval. Students may complete academic work and perform well without being engaged in the mastery of a topic, skill, or craft. In fact, a significant body of research indicates that students invest much of their energy in performing rituals, procedures, and routines without developing substantive understanding (see Eckert, 1989; McNeil, 1986; Powell, Farrar, & Cohen, 1985; Sedlak, Wheeler, Pullin, & Cusick, 1986; & Weis, 1990).

Psychological investment and effort to master are not readily observable characteristics. Rather, engagement is a construct used to describe an inner quality of concentration and effort to learn. The student's investment in any given type of mastery should be viewed on a continuum from less to more, not as a dichotomous state of being either engaged or unengaged. Levels of engagement must be estimated or inferred from indirect indicators such as the amount of participation in academic work (attendance, portion of tasks completed, amount of time spent on academic work), the intensity of student concentration, the enthusiasm and interest expressed, and the degree of care shown in completing the work. All of these, however, can be misleading indicators of engagement, for at times they may represent a student's willingness to comply with school routines, rather than an actual investment in mastering, comprehending, or learning knowledge, skills, and crafts.

Tasks that students complete in order to succeed in school often involve meaningless rituals, mechanistic reproduction of knowledge, and trivial forms of learning that offer little opportunity for students to use their minds well or to develop in-depth understanding and critical, creative mastery. Ideally, we would like all forms of schoolwork to be more meaningful. However, our technical definition of engagement does not prescribe any particular arenas of knowledge to be understood, skills to be learned, or dispositions to be cultivated. It therefore leaves the fundamental question of educational aims unanswered. Deciding *what* kinds of knowledge students should be engaged in is another matter, one charged with controversy.

Engagement implies more than motivation. Academic motivation usually refers to a general desire or disposition to succeed in academic work and in the more specific tasks of school. Conceivably students can be motivated to perform well in a general sense without being engaged in the specific tasks of school. Engagement in specific tasks may either precede or presume general motivation to succeed. By focusing on the extent to which students demonstrate active interest, effort, and concentration in the specific work that teachers design, engagement calls special attention to the social contexts that help activate underlying motivation, and also to conditions that may generate new motivation.[2]

## WHY IS STUDENT ENGAGEMENT IMPORTANT TO LEARNING IN SCHOOL?

The importance of student engagement becomes clearer if we consider the relationship of teacher to student in contrast to professional–client relationships in other professions such as law, engineering, finance, management, and, in some cases, medicine. In other professions the client often recognizes a problem and voluntarily seeks the help of a professional. The professional is trusted to have important knowledge that will have clear benefits for the client, usually within a reasonably short period of time. The teaching of children, however, is more coercive. Children are told by society that they have a problem (ignorance) that must be solved regardless of whether they feel a need for education. They are subjected to a program of labor that the teacher prescribes. The benefits of this labor are rarely self-evident to the student, partly because they are projected far into the future. These circumstances seem to diminish student trust in the professional, which is necessary if the student is to invest the considerable effort required for learning. Client effort is also required in other professions, especially, for example, mental health fields, but teaching stands out as the profession whose success depends on exceptionally long-term committed participation of its clients.[3]

Other professionals focus on the unique needs of individuals, helping one person at a time, but teaching school usually requires the professional to serve the needs of groups, that is, to treat large numbers of clients (20–35 per class) simultaneously. Since individual students vary in the kinds of interaction and activities they find most engaging, teaching large groups magnifies the difficulty of eliciting student effort from everyone. As one student explained, "You want to talk a lot in class and sometimes your friends influence you . . . you find yourself holding a conversation while the teacher's up front trying to teach and that's a big problem, too."

Of course, students may give only token effort and still succeed in school. That is, they can tune out, complete some of the work with only minimal concentration, and even cheat. But if most of their learning is approached in this manner, it will yield only superficial understanding and short-term retention, unlikely to be applied or transferred beyond a few school tests. Meaningful cognitive demands of formal education cannot be mastered through passive listening and reading, nor through being entertained; they require an engaged student.

Students usually agree that learning requires work, but, as illustrated by the following four students, some explain this from a more positive perspective than others.[4]

> I like to work hard and I guess I'll just pound it into myself if I don't understand. If I don't understand something, I make sure that I work at it until I do understand, and I keep it up and I never give up. I'm not a quitter at all.

> I'd say like get serious about your work, right away. . . . You know, like do your homework every night and things like that.

And don't skip and stuff like that. I'd say also go out for a fall sport either way. 'Cause that's how you meet like a lot of people.

I like learning a lot of this stuff but I've been slack in a lot of classes. It happened in science courses before — biology and chemistry. I'd shift between B's and D's sometimes. Like the second or first day, a bad report card and I'll compensate for it this weekend but it's like it gets worse when I do that, like a snowball rolling, it gets bigger and bigger. I'm in a deep hole all of the time.

When you go home there's always something you can be doing with your friends besides homework so you just do enough to get a decent grade but you don't try to get your best grade, you do just enough to finish.

The social roles and developmental dynamics of adolescence pose roadblocks to engagement in academic work, as other concerns and activities occupy students' attention and energy. Interpersonal issues with parents and peers usually take on added significance, as do sexual relations. As we will see in Chapter 6, adolescents' expanded opportunities for social participation with peers and in the adult work force can interfere with engagement in academic work. In effect, teachers must compete for students' attention with parents, siblings, boyfriends, girlfriends, bosses, coaches, salespeople, media figures, and a host of others who touch adolescents' lives. One study found that adolescents spent only about 25 percent of their waking hours in classes or doing homework. The balance of their day was spent at home (41 percent of waking hours) or elsewhere (27 percent) in diverse activities unconnected to school learning: eating, running errands and doing chores, socializing with friends, pursuing hobbies or extracurricular activities, working at a part-time job, watching TV or relaxing, talking with family members, and so on.[5]

The marginal role of academic learning in students' lives was further illustrated when we asked students what they liked most about their time in school. The most common answers highlighted social life, not what they were studying or learning.

"Well, I don't know what I like best about school. Well, most of my friends are here. This is where I generally meet them. I don't have any friends in my neighborhood. So this is where I come to see if they want to goof around after school."

"Just that I'm around my friends. And just that friends are around."

"Well, the people maybe. Be with your friends."

"I hardly ever did my work in any [of my classes]. I failed like pretty much all of them. Mostly F's. I planned on quitting but I decided not to. I just came to see people."

When we asked what they liked least about school, the responses were more diverse and included too much homework, poor teachers, restrictive rules, unappetizing lunches, and disruptive or snotty peers.

Up to this point we have explained how student engagement is necessary to the learning of school subjects, but that engagement in academic work is often difficult to stimulate in high school. We have not yet demonstrated a strong quantitative connection between engagement and achievement. Using scales of engagement based on student surveys, we found only modest statistical associations between engagement and achievement. But these preliminary findings have not diminished our belief in the importance of student engagement to achievement.

First, as indicated in the Introduction, the measurement of achievement itself is problematic, which prevented the standardization of valid achievement measures across the many studies within the Center.[6] Second, student engagement has only recently been proposed as a variable deserving theoretical and empirical study. To measure it quantitatively, we experimented with different survey items, but it will take more research to develop valid survey indicators of student engagement.[7] Third, the lack of correlation between engagement and achievement could well be due to the fact that many low-achieving students are highly engaged because they find schoolwork difficult, and, conversely, many high-achieving students can succeed with low levels of engagement because their prior high achievement makes school success relatively easy. Finally, teacher testimony and our own observational evidence continue to suggest that for any given level of prior achievement or ability, the more engaged the student in the work expected by the school, the higher the level of achievement on indicators consistent with that work.

The problem of disengaged students can be viewed as an instance of the more general challenge of reducing alienation in modern culture.[8] Relations with other individuals, with objects, with the physical environment, with social institutions, with one's own labor, and even with the supernatural or divine can be construed on a scale or continuum. At one extreme, relations can be characterized by detachment, isolation, fragmentation, disconnectedness, estrangement, or powerlessness. These bespeak alienation. At the other extreme, relations represent more of a quality of attachment, inclusion, integration, unity, connectedness, or empowerment. Alienation literature does not identify a single term to characterize its opposite, but if one term were chosen, engagement seems to capture many of these missing qualities in relations to people, work, or the physical environment. In this sense, the promotion of student engagement should bring benefits to quality of life that are more fundamental than increases in school achievement.

## FACTORS THAT AFFECT ENGAGEMENT

What might schools do to promote engagement? To answer this, we first sought to clarify the factors that affect (or cause) engagement. A significant body of research has shown that students from different social and cultural backgrounds look at schooling in vastly different ways (see Eckert, 1989; Farrell, 1990; Weis, 1990). For example, students who identify with the conventional expectations of working hard at abstract verbal and mathematical tasks for credentials that bring future rewards are more likely to invest themselves in academic work than students who have little hope in the future rewards promised by the system, or students more interested in manual and physical competence. From this perspective, the social–cultural orientations that students bring to school are the most important factors affecting student engagement.

Students' beliefs, values, and orientations toward schooling are critical, and educators must take them seriously. Consideration of the social–cultural determinants of student engagement can, however, lead to conflicting interpretations of the role of schooling. One interpretation puts so much emphasis on the powerful influences of race, class, gender, family, and social experience outside of school that school practitioners are seen as having almost no effective means for enhancing student engagement in school. The other realizes that schooling may have minimal impact on students' present lives beyond school, but contends, nevertheless, that changing students' experiences within school can enhance engagement. The Center grounded its research more in the latter perspective.

To be most useful to practitioners, we restricted this analysis to factors affecting engagement about which schools could conceivably do something. Research on how schools might enhance student engagement in academic work is lacking, but scholarship in psychology, sociology, and studies of schooling suggest the importance of several factors. As indicated in Figure 1.1, we construe engagement in academic work to result largely from three broad factors: students' underlying need for competence, the extent to which students experience membership in the school, and the authenticity of the work they are asked to complete. This model does not attempt to offer a comprehensive guide to all the important things a school

**Figure 1.1**
**Factors That Influence Student Engagement in Academic Work**

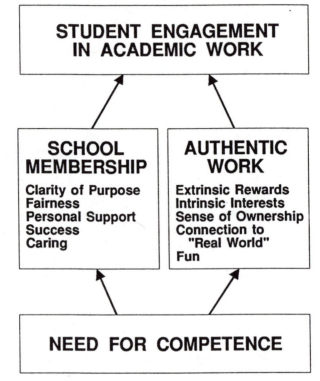

should do. We focus here only on critical aspects that have been neglected in both the research literature and reform efforts. The broad challenge for the school is how to generate membership and authentic work that channels the need for competence into academic success. The first step is to understand the importance of these foundations of engagement.

**Need for Competence**

> Being challenged really influenced me to strive for the best. So now I take courses that I think are challenging. . . . If I just keep the right attitude I think I can work around obstacles. I mean, there's always going to be problems, just got to go with them.

> I want to be an architect. I want to be really successful. I did really well in my architectural class. I don't think I got lower

than a B. And see I just love drawing, I just love it. When I sit
on the phone and I just sit there and I just draw.

Most people, especially children, have a powerful need to develop
and to express competence. Achieving cognitive understanding and skill
mastery—getting it right—are personally rewarding, especially as they
enable people to have some impact on the world. When efforts to act
competently are met with success, this generates continued investment,
and the cycle continues. The need for competence has been recognized as
one of the most powerful bases for human action and motivation. Researchers have considered it comparable in significance to sexual energy
or to such fundamental needs as autonomy and social affiliation.[9] Mastery
of schoolwork offers numerous opportunities for the development of competence, but competence can also be expressed through countless other
forms, such as interpersonal skills, physical development, entrepreneurial
projects, or excellence in arts, crafts, and hobbies, that schools rarely
develop. The question is, "What kinds of work must schools design so that
students' underlying need for competence will be channeled into academic
mastery?"[10] As indicated in Figure 1.1, this depends on the extent to which
students experience membership and authentic work in school.

## School Membership

If students are to invest themselves in the forms of mastery required
by schools, they must perceive the general enterprise of schooling as legitimate, deserving of their committed effort, and honoring them as respect-
ed members. Large numbers of students are so alienated from schools
that almost any activities that fall under school sponsorship are suspect
(Wehlage, Rutter, Smith, Lesko, & Fernandez, 1989; Wheelock, 1986).
For many students, schooling signifies institutional hypocrisy and aimlessness, rather than consistency and clarity of purpose; arbitrariness and
inequity, rather than fairness; ridicule and humiliation, rather than personal support and respect; and worst of all, failure, rather than success.
For others, the disaffection can seem less personally damaging—school is
seen as a theatre of meaningless ritual, unrelated to students' serious concerns. Before considering the problem of designing specific forms of academic work that engage students, we should first stand back and ask,
"What institutional conditions are necessary to get students to buy into
the general enterprise of trying to succeed in school?" The key is school
membership.

Building on the work of Merton (1953), Connell (1990) describes
engagement as involving commitment to both the institution's per-

ceived goals and the means it prescribes for members to pursue the goals. Wehlage et al. (1989) present another perspective of student bonding to schools that builds upon the work of Tinto (1987) and others. Bonding, or a sense of membership, develops when students establish affective, cognitive, and behavioral connections to the institution. To synthesize a diverse body of work on students' organizational commitment, we suggest that schools are most likely to cultivate a sense of membership in students if they demonstrate clarity of purpose, equity, and personal support, provide frequent occasions for all students to experience educational success, and integrate all of these features into a climate of caring.

Students touched on some of these qualities.

> I think I feel confident that you're in a good atmosphere. As far as school is concerned, you feel like you know everybody and you're comfortable. And that way you can concentrate on your schoolwork . . . because then you get to know the people around you a little bit better. And it feels like a family situation.

> Well, the coaches that I have, they emphasize at the beginning of meetings and stuff like that if you need any help, they can help you or find people to help you, like my swimming coach. I was having some trouble with algebra and stuff like that and he was an algebra teacher and he helped me out during practices and everything and for like a week or so I practiced half the time and then I'd do my schoolwork and he'd help me out with any questions I had. We have a lot of teachers who are pretty active outside of just teaching. You may not have them for a class but you can be really good friends with them because you know them through a club or something like that they are a leader of.

> In other classes, teachers didn't like me so I didn't do their homework. The teachers would just give you a hard time all the time. Just sort of make you stick out. Give other people privileges and not yourself. And she'd get on me right away if I tried to talk to anybody. But other people she'd just tell to be quiet.

### Clarity of Purpose

Identification with school can be cultivated partly through symbolic activity (school name, colors, songs) and through participation in a common agenda of activities (taking courses, eating lunch, attending athletic events). But the sense of membership needed for investment in mastery of academic work will be weak unless students' organizational affiliation is grounded in clear educational purposes. The "shopping mall high school" (Powell et al., 1985), for example, by attempting to serve all interests and tastes, and by even refusing to insist that any be pursued with vigor, offers no reason for adolescents to become engaged in academic mastery. It is hard to feel a strong sense of membership in organizations with ambiguous purposes. The success of "effective schools" has been attributed in part to clarity of school purpose (Purkey & Smith, 1983). One explanation of this success is that clarity of purpose builds a sense of membership that enhances engagement in work.

Clarity of purpose can be undermined both by hypocrisy (claiming to stand for goals that in fact are not pursued in practice) and by aimlessness, which results from failure to push for any goals in particular or from adopting (and pursuing) multiple goals that may conflict with one another. Comprehensive high schools with diverse student populations and with multiple demands from the community have a difficult time establishing purposes that are clear enough to enhance students' sense of membership. Sometimes this is accomplished more effectively through magnet schools or special programs within the school.

*Fairness*

A sense of fair treatment is critical to organizational bonding. In schools, fairness is often undermined both by violations of due process in disciplinary matters and by inequity in allocation of opportunities and rewards. Basic elements of due process include due notice of rules, consistent and uniform enforcement, a chance to defend oneself if accused, avenues of appeal, and reasonable punishments. Equitable allocation of opportunities entails nondiscrimination in access to courses and good teachers, to counseling and social services, and to participation in extracurricular activities. Blatant discrimination based on race, gender, or religion may seem rare, but in many schools, students of low social–economic status with poor records of achievement or deportment are subject to subtle, yet pervasive, inequity. Studies have shown that teachers communicate less interest in and lower expectations for these students, and that they receive lower-quality instruction and more disapproval from staff (see Gamoran & Berends, 1987; Goodlad, 1984; Oakes, 1990). Similarly, students of minority cultural backgrounds may feel excluded from membership when the curriculum and extracurricular activities fail to take account of their unique experiences.[11] In contrast, when schools strive for fairness through inclusion, equity, and due process, a heightened sense of school membership should advance student engagement in the work.

## Personal Support

Learning involves risk-taking; that is, trying to learn new material when chances for success are uncertain, making mistakes, and trying again. Unless one can trust teachers and peers to offer support for the hard work of making and correcting mistakes, the learning process can be too punishing to try. Especially in a competitive society, the social disrespect that often accompanies failure can suppress engagement in academic work and divert the need for competence to alternative, psychologically more comfortable activities. In short, if students are to build confidence and willingness to invest themselves, their participation in academic tasks must be accompanied by personal support from teachers and peers.[12] Support is most needed as security to fail in the short run so that success in the long run becomes more likely. In addition to support from teachers, cooperative learning among peers also offers forms of personal support to counteract alienating aspects of competitive learning. Personal support contributes directly to students' engagement in academic work; it also contributes indirectly, for it enhances student bonding to staff and to the organization, which, in turn, fortifies the students' investment in the organization's goals and means.

## Success

Our theory posits a basic need to develop competence as the foundation of student engagement in academic work. If the school is to nurture a sense of membership, its most important task is to ensure that students experience success in the development of competence. It is self-destructive to affiliate with an organization that offers experiences of repeated failure, but when the organization is seen as a site of opportunities for meaningful success, this invites membership. Sense of success will not be achieved by grade inflation or reducing the rigor of academic demands; students know the difference between meaningful achievement and merely completing busy work to earn points. Instead, the task for educators is to design schoolwork that presents significant challenges, that meets criteria for authenticity (discussed below), and that offers the kind of personal support just described, and to provide institutional recognition for the successes of all students (not simply the most distinguished). The enhanced sense of membership that comes from successful demonstration of competence will pay off through further engagement in the academic work sponsored by the school.

## Caring

There is more to life than academic achievement. Academic success must not, therefore, be the sole criterion for school membership. Students' moral worth and dignity must be affirmed through other avenues as well, such as nonacademic contact between staff and students — in athletics, music, outings, and personal advising. In short, to build membership, the separate features we identify (purpose, fairness, support, success) must be integrated within a more general climate of caring. Such a climate communicates that all students are worthy, important members of the school, that the school is serious about helping all to build new forms of competence, and that activities in pursuit of this mission will be discharged with fairness, personal support, and ample opportunity for success. Students are cared for as persons who represent multiple aspects of humanity, not simply as units to be processed through the official agenda of the school.[13]

Many students go through high school with a strong sense of membership — they are committed to the goals of schooling, and they experience sufficient support and success to master the school demands. But increasingly large percentages of students have experienced only alienation in schools. For these students, high schools will have to work hard to generate the commitment to clear purposes, fairness, personal support, success experiences, and climate of care that otherwise may have been taken for granted. Sense of membership can be further enhanced by making the schoolwork itself more authentic.

## Authentic Work

Assuming that conditions to nurture bonding and sense of membership can be established, how can academic work itself be designed so as to maximize student engagement? We use the term *authentic work* to characterize tasks that are considered meaningful, valuable, significant, and worthy of one's effort, in contrast to those considered nonsensical, useless, contrived, trivial, and therefore unworthy of effort. As explained below, work that entails extrinsic rewards, meets intrinsic interests, offers students a sense of ownership, is connected to the "real world" (i.e., the world beyond school), and involves some fun is more authentic and more likely to engage students.[14]

When students expressed enthusiasm for schoolwork, some of these qualities emerged.

> I like getting as much out of class as I can. . . . It's a good program here. I mean we're learning. I like to learn. My brother said it helps for college. . . . I like chemistry the best. Chemistry is more interesting and it's like more applying yourself instead of having to memorize all of these theories and formulas.

> I like to learn, but it's the teacher that really motivates someone to learn. I don't like a teacher to get in front of me and just talk. I like them to have a personality when they teach. Kind of try to make the subject fun, like show what it means in the real world instead of just in theory.

> I wish I could redo my freshman year. I was hyper, immature, didn't really think school was important. Skipped a lot of classes. I got injured between my freshman and sophomore year over the summer in a soccer game. I was amused by how the trainer wrapped my ankle and what he said was wrong with it. I decided I wanted a career in sports medicine. So I want to get good grades until the end of school to get into a medical program. . . . I just cracked down, kept my eyes in the book, paid attention as best I could in class.

## Extrinsic Rewards

Committed effort should increase if mastery of school tasks is accompanied by rewards such as high grades, admission to higher education, attractive jobs, increased income, and social approval and status. What may appear to be powerful extrinsic rewards for some students, however, may have no effect on or may actually decrease the engagement of others. Only when students value the rewards, perceive that academic achievement will lead to them, and believe that their own hard work will result in academic achievement, would we expect student engagement to increase.[15] Another problem is that some powerful extrinsic rewards, such as jobs and income, tend to be distributed for long-term, cumulative effort, rather than for engagement in short-term, daily tasks that lead to academic learning. This makes it difficult for teachers to offer impressive extrinsic rewards. Nevertheless, many instructional tasks can be designed to yield social approval, official credentials (grades), public displays of impressive accomplishment, and special privileges.

## Intrinsic Interest

Regardless of the level of extrinsic rewards, students may invest in or withdraw from learning depending on how interesting they find the material. Interest refers to the fact that some topics and activities are considered more stimulating, fascinating, or enjoyable to work on than others.[16] What will be interesting probably depends not simply on the subjects or topics, but largely on the way the topics are approached by the teacher, the student's prior experience with similar material, and other factors, discussed below.

Student interest will probably be enhanced when tasks permit expression of diverse forms of talent. Schooling concentrates primarily on abstract verbal and mathematical competence, to the neglect of aesthetic, interpersonal, intrapersonal, kinesthetic, and spatial competencies (Gardner, 1983). Students may be interested in developing competence in several of these dimensions. Limiting school tasks to a narrow range diminishes the opportunity to respond to students' intrinsic interests and to build their competence upon their prior knowledge.

Adult learners speak of the value and significance of academic study for reasons other than interest and extrinsic benefit. It may be considered worthwhile to understand the logic of mathematics, the process of scientific inquiry, or the foundations of culture, even when these subjects may appear less interesting or lead to less impressive extrinsic rewards than other subjects. The belief that mastery of certain topics, skills, or crafts is intrinsically valuable or worthwhile can also enhance engagement.

## Sense of Ownership

Engagement with and internalization of knowledge depend to a large degree on the opportunities students have to "own" the work. Rather than toiling always under predetermined routines to master skills and knowledge dictated arbitrarily by school authorities, students need some influence over the conception, execution, and evaluation of the work itself.[17] At a minimum this entails flexibility in the pace and procedures of learning; opportunity for students to ask questions and to study topics they consider important; and students' constructing and producing knowledge in their own language, rather than merely reproducing the language of others. There are, of course, important limits on the extent to which students can control the learning of academic subjects. Certain facts, definitions, concepts, algorithms, and processes of verification must be assimilated according to predetermined standards of the fields of knowledge to be taught. But even for this kind of learning, students' sense of ownership can be enhanced if learning tasks offer some autonomy in the way students study and apply the material.

## Connection to the "Real World"

Students often explain their disengagement by calling schoolwork irrelevant; that is, unrelated to issues, competencies, or concerns of the real world. Why devote effort to the mastery of knowledge that seems necessary to success only in school, but in no other aspects of life? The authenticity of schoolwork depends largely on its connections to work beyond instructional settings. We notice at least four qualities of adult work in the real world that are often missing in schoolwork: value beyond instruction, clear feedback, collaboration, and flexible use of time.[18]

### Value Beyond Instruction

One of most critical criteria for authentic work is that it has its value and meaning beyond the instructional context. To the extent that the messages students speak and write, the products they make, the performances they complete (music, dance, sports) make an impact on others and on students themselves, beyond certifying students' level of competence or compliance, these activities gain in authenticity. Writing to persuade a friend or to publicize one's views in a letter to the editor is more authentic than writing only to show a teacher that one is capable of organizing a coherent paragraph. Studying the habits of animals or fish when one is also responsible for their care is more authentic than learning about their behavior from texts. Remodeling a house, repairing a car, developing a computer program, and tutoring all involve application of knowledge in ways that can have value or use in the world beyond the instruction of the student who completes the work.

### Clear, Prompt Feedback

In the real world, feedback on the quality of one's work is often more clear and immediate than in school. Some activities, such as music, sports, or mechanical repair, provide almost instant and clear evidence of success or failure. It is not necessary to wait for a teacher's response to learn whether one got a hit in baseball, whether the sweater one knitted fits, or whether one remembered his or her lines in the play. In contrast, after completing abstract academic tasks, the feedback students receive is often much delayed and difficult to comprehend (What did I do wrong in this homework assignment, and why was it wrong?). To the extent that feedback is mystified and delayed, we would expect engagement to suffer.

## Collaboration

Achievements outside school often depend on the opportunity to ask questions of, to receive feedback from, and to count on the help of others, including peers and authorities. In contrast, typical activities in school require the student to work alone, often without access to books and other information-rich resources. Working together and access to published information are often prohibited, because they are seen as a form of cheating. It is important, of course, for students to learn to work on their own, rather than becoming overly dependent on others. But if opportunities to cooperate and to consult authoritative sources are consistently denied, this violates a critical process that adults, both expert and novice, consistently rely on for success.

## Flexible Use of Time

Meaningful achievements outside school often cannot be produced within rigidly specified time periods. Adults working to solve complicated problems, to compose effective discourse, or to design products rarely are forced to work within the rigid time constraints imposed on students, such as the 50-minute class or the two-hour examination period. Standard, predetermined time schedules that flow from bureaucratic procedures for managing masses of students in diverse course offerings, rather than from the time requirements of disciplined inquiry, can reduce the authenticity of students' work. Achievements in noninstructional tasks such as journalistic writing, interior design, or medical care do, of course, involve deadlines and time limits, but here the schedules tend to be determined more by the nature of the work than by the requirements of institutional management.

## Fun

In emphasizing qualities that help to generate serious effort and concentration on academic tasks, we must not overlook the importance of fun, play, and humor. Learning can be hard work, but to sustain engagement, the tasks should also provide opportunities for lighthearted interaction, for play-like and imaginative activity. Fun reduces the distress of intense pressure to succeed and the boredom of unchallenging, but perhaps necessary, routines. When it is unfeasible to arrange in advance for fun in specific academic tasks, it can be planned for other times during a lesson or the school day, and this should enhance student sense of bonding or membership in the school as a whole.

To summarize, we have indicated a number of guidelines for the design of academic work that should maximize student engagement. Ideally, plans for student assignments, projects, and classroom discourse should provide extrinsic rewards, cultivate intrinsic interests, permit a sense of student ownership, reflect aspects of work beyond school, and involve some fun. [19] At this point in the development of a theory of student engagement, we realize that several issues need further study. One is whether some of these guidelines are more fundamental than others, whether some are much harder to achieve than others, whether schools ought to place higher priority on working on some over others. Another is whether the guidelines might entail difficult contradictions; for example, structuring learning around extrinsic rewards could conflict with enhancing engagement based on intrinsic interest. We have not examined these problems in sufficient detail to make recommendations. Now that we have developed an argument for each of the criteria, it remains to be seen how they might be most productively implemented when instruction is designed more explicitly to promote student engagement.

## MARVIN

To illustrate the importance of membership and authentic work, consider Marvin, a 13-year-old African-American for whom low school achievement has become a normal pattern. Although a good student in elementary school (he even made the honor roll in 3rd Grade), Marvin appears to have lost interest in academic achievement. Now in 7th Grade, his semester report card recorded F's in language arts and science and D's in reading and math. Marvin is typical of a large number of students we observed in his school as well as in other urban schools that serve mostly economically disadvantaged students, both white and black.

Marvin's teachers complain that he won't do assigned work and that he often has to be disciplined for talking out or disrupting the class in some way. He quickly reached the maximum number of absences that, according to district decree, requires automatic failure, regardless of actual academic performance. Marvin has his own complaints about school and teachers. He says that school is boring and that his teachers don't teach. "They don't make classes interesting. They just preach."

## Marvin's Day at School

From 8:00 a.m. until 3:00 p.m. Marvin has eight class periods with only 30 minutes for lunch. He eats in a basement cafeteria with no chance to leave the building. This is the only time, except for brief passing periods between classes, when he can talk freely to his friends. Except for this time, almost all of Marvin's school day is spent sitting at a desk in a room full of adolescents constrained by rules intended to inhibit their natural inclination to move and speak. Although Marvin admits he puts out little effort to learn what his teachers offer, he still believes learning is important. He is not very explicit about how to improve school, but he notes that "there should be more learning and less fussing."

Marvin's day starts with language arts. Ms. Voss is a middle-aged African-American woman with a mixed reputation among the students. On this day, as always, she positions herself squarely in front of the class to take roll the moment the bell rings beginning the first period. Failing to get the attention she usually commands, today she announces, "When I'm in front, you close your mouths." Students quickly quiet down. Ms. Voss immediately moves into the planned lesson: "Today's lesson is about capitalization. Take out your papers."

Students spend the next 20 minutes inserting mostly single words or symbols on a worksheet to answer questions, correct capitalization mistakes, and place commas correctly in sentences. When the worksheets are completed, Ms. Voss requests volunteers to read their answers. In what is the liveliest part of the class, many students raise their hands, eagerly seeking to be chosen. Marvin, however, is not among them. As the work is reviewed, Marvin makes a few corrections on his paper. At one point Ms. Voss interrupts the recitation and addresses a small girl with her feet curled under her, "Elizabeth, watch how you're sitting. Ladies don't sit like that." This provokes a whisper from Marvin to a friend, "Hey, there goes Sister Voss." Ms. Voss eyes him and says, "Marvin, what are you talking about? You be quiet now!" A number of students turn toward Marvin with subtle gestures of approval.

Ms. Voss quickly restores order, and the class continues reciting from their worksheets. But a few minutes later Michael, apparently late to class, enters the room carrying a stainless steel bowl and a sponge. He ambles over to a cupboard behind Ms. Voss's desk to put the items away. Ms. Voss tells him that they do not belong in her room. He turns and slowly walks to the door while Ms. Voss tries to resume the lesson. But the students' attention is on Michael rather than their teacher. Becoming angry, Ms. Voss barks at him, "Michael, you leave this room right now and don't come back. I don't want to be disturbed by you anymore." After Michael leaves, she locks the door. A few minutes later someone knocks on the door. Ms. Voss initially ignores it, but finally opens it and admits a small boy who quickly goes to his seat. A minute later Michael knocks. Ms. Voss pulls him into the room by his shirt sleeve and seats him next to her. She then says to no one in particular, "This is why we can't teach. Interruptions! That's my main beef."

Later in the day, Marvin attends social studies class. By this time, the desks in the room have been pushed into irregular rows with some grouped facing each other. Paper and books are scattered on the floor. After taking roll, Ms. Stewart, a young white woman recently out of college, attempts to call the class to order with shouts of "Class, listen up." Although most of the students are seated, they continue to talk among themselves. Marvin and his friend Jimmy are among those who ignore Ms. Stewart's pleas for quiet. "Class, we have a quiz today on southern Europe. Take out a piece of paper."

Many students continue in subdued conversation. Ms. Stewart begins reading the questions aloud, but then interrupts herself with the admonition, "Students, you should listen to the questions. Let me repeat, for questions 1 through 4, name four of the seven southern European countries." After giving students a minute or so, she goes on. "Question 5: Spain and Italy are both peninsulas. Give me a definition of a peninsula. Remember, if you listen you'll hear a lot of clues." After five more questions, the students are told to exchange papers to correct during recitation. The questions are reviewed one by one with students volunteering answers, often incorrect, and marking the papers.

Thirty minutes into the class the correct answers to 10 questions have been pulled from the students, and the papers have been marked, collected, and placed on the teacher's desk. Ms. Stewart then tells the class to open their books to page 335. For the next assignment, students are to draw the outline of southern Europe and then indicate the origin of major products of this region on their map. Students may work in pairs if they choose, and Marvin and Jimmy move their seats together, slowly beginning to draw their outlines.

Several minutes into this activity, two white boys who have been generally quiet up to this point begin arguing. They both rise from their seats. The smaller of the two draws himself to full height, throws his shoulders back, puffs out his chest, and moves forward making frontal contact with his larger opponent. At first, Ms. Stewart does not seem to notice this confrontation, but when the smaller boy takes an awkward swing at the other boy, she swiftly intervenes. Ms. Stewart takes the smaller boy into the hall and then quickly returns to the room. She asks,

"Does anyone need any help?" By now most students are either talking excitedly or are out of their seats, some even dancing in the aisles. One boy says, "Ms. Stewart, this class is acting pitifully." The bell sounds shortly after this, and the students rush into the hall.

The last period of the day for Marvin is science, taught by Mr. Johnson, the only male teacher Marvin encounters. Mr. Johnson creates an impressive physical presence because of his apparent devotion to body-building activities. He is known for his no-nonsense approach to discipline, and students take their seats immediately on entering the room and engage in quiet conversations. Five minutes after the bell has rung Mr. Johnson rises from behind his desk, where he has been checking some papers, and calls roll. He then directs students to continue working on the assignment they started yesterday — a two-page worksheet on astronomy. The worksheet asks students to define terms such as refractor and reflective telescopes, celestial sphere, constellation, and pulsar. Mr. Johnson reminds the class that all answers to these questions can be found in their textbook. After this short introduction, he returns to his desk where he takes out some reading material.

A number of students, including Marvin and Jimmy, are working together, quietly looking up answers in the text. At one point they are uncertain about an answer, and Marvin raises his hand.

After a while, Mr. Johnson walks over to them. Marvin says, "We can't find pulsar." The teacher looks at their worksheets and asks rhetorically, "What have you guys been doing the last 15 minutes?" "We've been working," Marvin protests. "Well, you haven't been doing much." "Tell us, what's a pulsar?" Mr. Johnson turns away and says, "Look it up in your book. It's in the chapter." Jimmy says, "Well, we can't find it." "It's there. Just look harder. And stop messing around so much." As he walks away, Marvin mutters to Jimmy, "He never teaches us anything. All he ever does is tell us to look it up in the book."

Hearing the muttering, Mr. Johnson spins around, takes several giant strides, grabs Marvin by the shoulder forcefully, and says, "Hey, Marvin, have you got a problem?" "No! No!" is Marvin's quick and reassuring reply. Jimmy and Marvin continue quietly with the worksheet for the remainder of the period and complete about half of it.

## Exploring the Causes of Marvin's Disengagement

In what ways do Marvin's experiences reinforce a sense of membership and the opportunity to invest in authentic work? First consider the qualities that promote membership: clarity of school purpose, fairness, personal support, success, and caring.

It is doubtful that Marvin sees a clear purpose in mastering the work-sheet-style routines and fragmented exercises to which he is subjected in his academic subjects.

Fairness is another problem. Anthony, one of Marvin's classmates, was being picked on continually by another boy. One day Anthony was forced to fight in self-defense. The two boys were apprehended by school officials, and the punishment for Anthony and his tormentor was the same — four days of suspension from school and three days of school deten-tion. One of Anthony's teachers agreed that it was not fair, but saw no way out of the situation: "If you punish everybody you don't have to decide who's innocent and who's guilty. You just throw everybody into detention. That simplifies the problem for the staff."

What about personal support, academic success, and caring? During the 1989–90 school year, more than half Marvin's classmates in Grades 7 through 12 failed one or more courses, and about one sixth of the students were retained. Mr. Johnson's refusal to help Marvin and Jimmy and Ms. Stewart's willingness to allow two boys to ignore her quiz are indicative of teachers' indifference to some students. In a survey taken during the 1988–89 school year, 78 percent of the students at Marvin's school indicated that teachers expected them to know material after hearing it only one time. Despite this difficulty, 59 percent of the same group of students said that they rarely or never spoke with teachers about class problems.

Mr. Johnson and others establish a social distance between themselves and students, which makes it impossible for students to develop bonds of friendship and trust. In fact, 67 percent of Marvin's peers rarely or never speak to their teachers about outside-school activities.

Student engagement is inhibited not only by threats to membership, but also by the absence of authentic work. The work that Marvin was asked to complete failed most of the criteria for authenticity. Marvin perceived little or no extrinsic value associated with completing the work successfully. Marvin's getting A's rather than D's would not lead to a better job or higher wage. Filling out worksheets with one-word answers, most of which could be found by skimming a text, was of no intrinsic interest; it did not build on students' multiple "intelligences," capture their imaginations, or challenge them to think. The work, dictated entirely by teachers, offered no sense of ownership. Even if the work was completed according to teachers' expectations, it had no value beyond school, nor did it involve certain other important characteristics that can establish connections to the real world (e.g., collaboration and flexible use of time). Finally, the work was devoid of humor or playfulness.

As indicated earlier, we chose a perspective on student engagement that emphasizes schools' responsibility to respond constructively to the students they serve. This is not to neglect either the nonschool factors that affect student engagement or the personal responsibility students must take for their own success or failure. Many adults, having endured and succeeded in schools not too different from Marvin's, see the solution to disengagement more in terms of changing students and their families. The problem should be understood from both angles, but there is a long tradition in American education of blaming students for their own failure and marginalization. This perspective has led both educators and policymakers to ignore the contributions of the school itself to the failure of so many young people. It also has led educators and policymakers to ignore the positive role school can play in creating an educational environment that builds student membership and offers students authentic work that produces high levels of engagement and achievement.

## SUMMARY AND IMPLICATIONS

Dominant concerns in the educational reform movement have neglected one of the problems most critical to the improvement of high schools: how to engage students in academic work. Engagement is defined as the student's psychological investment in and effort to master the knowledge, skills, and crafts that academic work is intended to produce. The importance of engagement and the difficulty of stimulating it were clarified by discussing the relationship of professional to client in teaching versus other professions, social–psychological characteristics in adolescents' roles, and the more general problem of alienation in modern culture. Based on the assumption that all humans share a fundamental need to develop competence, educators can enhance student engagement in academic work by attention to two general factors: building a sense of student membership in the school at large, and designing academic tasks to maximize the authenticity of schoolwork.

The concepts of membership, authentic work, and criteria for each complement other research related to school improvement. For example, research on effective schools and on the bargains that teachers make with students suggests that teachers often need to raise levels of expectation and challenge. Our theory of engagement helps to explain *why* high expectations (no easy bargains) can improve learning. For example, high expectations and challenge can enhance membership by demonstrating clear goals, support, equity, and caring. If directed toward authentic work, high expectations are likely to enhance intrinsic interest and sense of ownership. All of this should promote engagement.

Our model proposes qualities for student experiences that can guide the conduct of instruction as well as other aspects of students' lives in school. Achieving membership and authentic work is, of course, easier said than done, because student experiences in school and the meaning that students attribute to them are affected by a host of factors, some of which cannot be easily controlled by individual practitioners or even an entire school staff. A comprehensive explanation of the nature of membership and work in a school, as well as programs for improvement, need to consider the impact of at least the following factors:

1. Students' personal and social backgrounds
2. The district and community context, whose norms and policies affect many aspects of life in school
3. School culture, reflected in beliefs and values of staff and students
4. School organization (size, structure, division of labor)
5. Curriculum
6. Teachers' background and competence
7. Teacher–student interaction, in and out of class.

These and other factors can both enhance and diminish membership and authentic work. Well-intended teachers, unaware of how students' social backgrounds affect their approach to schooling, may misinterpret their behavior. Organizational routines and curriculum mandates can reduce possibilities for authentic academic work. When the culture of schooling preoccupies itself with the maintenance of order, or competitive individualism, it deprives many students of a sense of membership. In short, schools' ability to enhance membership and authentic work for students depends on a complex ecology.

The Center's studies shed light on a number of these factors. Chapters 2 and 3 examine the nature of teacher–student interaction and how this may be affected by school organization and culture. Chapter 4 highlights the role of curriculum, school culture, and district–community context. Chapter 5 emphasizes leadership, school culture, organization, and district context. Chapter 6 focuses on noninstructional aspects of students' lives.

## NOTES

1. An earlier version of some material in this chapter appears in Newmann (1991a).

2. Syntheses of research on motivating students to learn (Brophy, 1987; Stipek, 1986) distinguish between motivation to perform and motivation to learn. Discussions of the latter include factors that we see as critical to engagement.

3. See Bidwell (1970) for useful analyses of client-serving institutions. The

need for serious effort on the part of the student has been demonstrated both by practitioners' claims and by analytic and empirical research (Cohen, 1988; Cusick, 1973; Powell, Farrar, & Cohen, 1985; Sedlak, Wheeler, Pullin, & Cusick, 1986). Carroll's (1963) widely cited model of school learning, for example, includes the variable of student perseverance, which is consistent with our engagement concept. Empirical studies have shown that variables such as student effort and involvement have effects on student achievement independent of student ability (Grabe, 1982; Grabe & Latta, 1981; Laffey, 1982).

4. Marshall (1988) observes that using the metaphor of work to describe learning can have unfortunate implications for how teachers relate to students and how students regard the process of learning. This is because the properties of adult work settings often involve lack of worker autonomy, labor for the profit of others rather than self-improvement, and other conditions that may inhibit meaningful learning. Our use of the term *academic work* is meant not to suggest that schools should replicate dominant conditions of adult labor, but instead to emphasize the point that meaningful learning requires serious effort by the learner, and further that the design of the work tasks themselves must aim toward enhancing engagement in mastery, rather than simply securing compliance in task completion. We would agree with Marshall that the characteristics of academic work that engages students would differ from characteristics in the typical work and recreational settings she discusses.

5. In this study Csikszentmihalyi and Larson (1984) had a sample of teenagers carry electronic beepers and record their location, activity, and companions at random times when they were "beeped." Farrell's (1990) detailed portrait of the lives of high school students at risk also illustrates the power of influences beyond the classroom to detract from school engagement.

6. Studies within the Center measured achievement through a variety of tests and also students' grade-point averages.

7. Examples of engagement survey items included: "How often in this class do you . . . Try as hard as you can? . . . Think what you are supposed to learn is interesting and worthwhile? . . . Find yourself concentrating so hard that time passes quickly? . . ." Responses on a five-point scale varied from "never" to "almost every day."

8. Newmann's (1981) study of the implications of philosophical, psychological, and sociological literature on alienation for high school reform offers a more detailed analysis of this topic.

9. See the original research on "effectance" by White (1959), the synthesis on competence by Smith (1968), DeCharms's (1984) discussion of agency, and Connell's (1990) analysis of motivation.

10. Dweck (1986) explained how students' social cognitions about their competence affect motivation to learn. Stipek (1986) described how particular classroom activities can affect these cognitions positively and negatively, and thereby affect engagement. Stipek's review of motivation research also supports our conclusions below related to intrinsic interests and student sense of ownership over work.

11. Students from minority cultures or low-status groups face special threats

to self-esteem from the dominant culture. Culturally responsive pedagogy is necessary to transform student alienation into membership (Erickson, 1987).

12. See Steinberg (1990) for a concise summary of some research showing how support and caring from teachers can enhance student engagement.

13. Moos's (1986) summary of literature on workplace conditions indicates that social acceptance and cohesion produce higher worker morale and less stress. Bryk and Driscoll (1988) present evidence on the advantages of communal features in high schools.

14. Newmann (1991b) conceptualized authentic academic achievement as the production (rather than reproduction) of knowledge, through disciplined inquiry, that has aesthetic, utilitarian, or personal value beyond demonstrating the competence of the learner. The criteria for authentic *work* developed in this chapter are consistent with those criteria for authentic *achievement*, but the criteria here are more elaborate, because they address the broader issue of the kind of work most likely to engage students.

15. Bishop (1989), for example, claims that job placement and salary levels offer few extrinsic rewards for academic engagement, because they are not tied to students' achievement levels in high school. He also argues that an economic system that provides only a competitive reward structure (a zero sum game where winners emerge only by creating losers) offers no incentive for students in the bottom half to become academically engaged. Ogbu (1974) also showed how students' perceptions of future economic opportunity affect engagement in school.

16. See Deci (1975) and Maehr (1984) for syntheses of research on intrinsic motivation.

17. The need for a sense of control over one's work has been established in the literature on alienation (Blauner, 1964; Braverman, 1974), motivation (Connell, 1990; DeCharms, 1984; Deci & Ryan, 1985) and self-management in the workplace (Hackman, 1986).

18. Resnick's (1987) analysis of learning in school versus more practical problem solving out of school reflects concerns similar to those that we address.

19. The factors are consistent with conditions that define a flow experience according to Csikszentmihalyi and Larson (1984). In these experiences a person concentrates on mastering a specific challenge that has usually been voluntarily chosen. The challenge demands extending one's skills to new levels of complexity, but not so far as to generate extreme anxiety. To meet the challenge, one must abide by certain "rules" of interaction or discipline, and the process entails concrete feedback on the degree of success.

## REFERENCES

Bidwell, C. (1970). Students and schools: Some observations on client trust in client-serving organizations. In W. R. Rosengren & M. Lefton (Eds.), *Organizations and clients* (pp. 37–69). Columbus, OH: Merrill.

Bishop, J. H. (1989). Why the apathy in American high schools? *Educational Researcher, 18*(1), 6–10.

Blauner, R. (1964). *Alienation and freedom: The factory worker and his industry.* Chicago: University of Chicago Press.

Braverman, H. (1974). *Labor and monopoly capital.* New York: Monthly Review Press.

Brophy, J. (1987). Synthesis of research on strategies for motivating students to learn. *Educational Leadership, 45*(2), 40–48.

Bryk, A. S., & Driscoll, M. E. (1988). *The high school as community: Contextual influences and consequences for students and teachers.* Madison, WI: National Center on Effective Secondary Schools, University of Wisconsin–Madison.

Carroll, J. B. (1963). A model of school learning. *Teachers College Record, 64,* 723–733.

Cohen, D. K. (1988). *Teaching practice: Plus ça change . . .* (No. 88-3). East Lansing, MI: National Center for Research on Teacher Education, Michigan State University.

Connell, J. P. (1990). Context, self and action: A motivational analysis of self-system processes across the life-span. In D. Cicchetti (Ed.), *The self in transition: Infancy to childhood* (pp. 61–97). Chicago: University of Chicago Press.

Csikszentmihalyi, M., & Larson, R. (1984). *Being adolescent: Conflict and growth in the teenage years.* New York: Basic Books.

Cusick, P. A. (1973). *Inside high school: The students' world.* New York: Holt, Rinehart & Winston.

DeCharms, R. (1984). Motivation enhancement in educational settings. In R. E. Ames & C. Ames (Eds.), *Research on motivation in education: Vol. 1. Student motivation* (pp. 275–310). Orlando, FL: Academic Press.

Deci, E. L. (1975). *Intrinsic motivation.* New York: Plenum.

Deci, E. L., & Ryan, R. M. (1985). *Intrinsic motivation and self-determination in human behavior.* New York: Plenum.

Dweck, C. S. (1986). Motivational processes affecting learning. *American Psychologist, 41*(10), 1040–1048.

Eckert, P. (1989). *Jocks and burnouts: Social categories and identity in the high school.* New York: Teachers College Press.

Erickson, F. A. (1987). Transformation and school success: The politics and culture of educational achievement. *Anthropology and Education Quarterly, 18*(3), 335–356.

Farrell, E. (1990). *Hanging in and dropping out: Voices of at-risk high school students.* New York: Teachers College Press.

Gamoran, A., & Berends, M. (1987). The effects of stratification in secondary schools: Synthesis of survey and ethnographic research. *Review of Educational Research, 56*(2), 195–211.

Gardner, H. (1983). *Frames of mind: The theory of multiple intelligences.* New York: Basic Books.

Goodlad, J. I. (1984). *A place called school: Prospects for the future.* New York: McGraw-Hill.

Grabe, M. (1982). Effort strategies in a mastery instructional system: The quantification of effort and the impact of effort on achievement. *Contemporary Educational Psychology, 7*, 327–333.

Grabe, M., & Latta, R. M. (1981). Cumulative achievement in a mastery instructional system: The impact of differences in resultant achievement motivation and persistence. *American Educational Research Journal, 18*(1), 7–13.

Hackman, J. R. (1986). The psychology of self-management in organizations. In M. S. Pallak & R. O. Perloff (Eds.), *Psychology and work: Productivity, change, and employment* (pp. 89–137). Washington, DC: American Psychological Association.

Laffey, J. M. (1982). The assessment of involvement with school work among urban high school students. *Journal of Educational Psychology, 74*(1), 62–71.

Maehr, M. L. (1984). Meaning and motivation: Toward a theory of personal investment. In R. E. Ames & C. Ames (Eds.), *Research on motivation in education: Vol. 1. Student motivation* (pp. 115–144). Orlando, FL: Academic Press.

Marshall, H. H. (1988). Work or learning: Implications of classroom metaphors. *Educational Researcher, 17*(9), 9–16.

McNeil, L. M. (1986). *Contradictions of control: School structure and school knowledge.* New York: Routledge & Kegan Paul.

Merton, R. (1953). *Social theory and social structure.* London: Free Press of Glendale.

Moos, R. H. (1986). Work as a human context. In M. S. Pallak & R. O. Perloff (Eds.), *Psychology and work: Productivity, change, and employment* (pp. 9–52). Washington, DC: American Psychological Association.

Newmann, F. M. (1981). Reducing alienation in high schools: Implications of theory. *Harvard Educational Review, 51*(4), 546–564.

Newmann, F. M. (1991a). Student engagement in academic work: Expanding the perspective on secondary school effectiveness. In J. R. Bliss, W. A. Firestone, & C. E. Richards (Eds.), *Rethinking effective schools: Research and practice* (pp. 58–76). Englewood Cliffs, NJ: Prentice-Hall.

Newmann, F. M. (1991b). Linking restructuring to authentic student achievement. *Phi Delta Kappan, 72*, 458–463.

Oakes, J. (1990). *Multiplying inequalities: The effects of race, social class, and tracking on opportunities to learn mathematics and science.* Santa Monica, CA: Rand Corporation.

Ogbu, J. U. (1974). *The next generation: An ethnography of an urban neighborhood.* New York: Academic Press.

Powell, A. G., Farrar, E., & Cohen, D. K. (1985). *The shopping mall high school: Winners and losers in the educational marketplace.* Boston: Houghton Mifflin.

Purkey, S. C., & Smith, M. S. (1983). Effective schools: A review. *The Elementary School Journal, 83*(4), 427–452.

Resnick, L. B. (1987). Learning in school and out. *Educational Researcher, 16*(9), 13–20.

Sedlak, M. W., Wheeler, C. W., Pullin, D. C., & Cusick, P. A. (1986). *Selling students short: Classroom bargains and academic reform in the American high school.* New York: Teachers College Press.

Smith, M. B. (1968). Competence and socialization. In J. A. Clausen (Ed.), *Socialization and society* (pp. 270–320). Boston: Little Brown.

Steinberg, A. (1990). Why kids give up on school—And what teachers can do about it. *Harvard Education Letter, 6*(5), 1–4.

Stipek, D. (1986). Children's motivation to learn. In T. M. Tomlinson & H. J. Walberg (Eds.), *Academic work and educational excellence.* Berkeley, CA: McCutchan.

Tinto, V. (1987). *Leaving college: Rethinking the causes and cures of student attrition.* Chicago: University of Chicago Press.

Wehlage, G. G., Rutter, R. A., Smith, G. A., Lesko, N. L., & Fernandez, R. R. (1989). *Reducing the risk: Schools as communities of support.* Philadelphia: Falmer Press.

Weis, L. (1990). *Working class without work: High school students in a de-industrializing economy.* New York: Routledge & Kegan Paul.

Wheelock, A. (1986). *The way out: Student exclusion practices in Boston middle schools.* Boston: Massachusetts Advocacy Center.

White, R. W. (1959). Motivation reconsidered: The concept of competence. *Psychological Review, 66,* 297–333.

# CHAPTER 2

# Taking Students Seriously

## Adam Gamoran and Martin Nystrand

Our colleagues have presented a conception of student engagement. We now face the problem of how to enhance it through instruction in a particular subject. Is there a set of specific pedagogical moves or student activities that are more likely to enhance membership and authentic work? To answer this question, one might synthesize research evidence on proposed interventions such as Madeline Hunter's mastery teaching, cooperative learning, the project method, the use of case studies, writing to learn, peer tutoring, and curriculum in specific subjects. Unfortunately, a review of this sort would probably give few clues on how to build membership and authentic work. First, empirical studies of such interventions have not usually given explicit attention to membership and authentic work. Second, logical analysis is most likely to conclude that the potential of any activity to promote membership or engagement will depend more on how it is implemented than on its inherent structure and function.

Instead of searching for the most effective generic techniques, we studied something more fundamental, something that most teaching activities have in common: conversation or discourse between teachers and students. Regardless of the activity in which students participate, discourse itself can offer a critical indicator of the extent to which school offers membership and authentic work. What kinds of discourse are most likely to communicate a sense of inclusion? What kinds of discourse are most likely to generate a sense of ownership and resemble the kinds of conversations that people value in the real world?

In studying the teaching of literature, we paid special attention to the kinds of questions that teachers ask students. In fact, we recorded and classified more than 20,000 questions, and developed a way of describing the pattern of questions in order to assess whether teachers were taking students seriously. When students' ideas are taken seriously, this tells the students that they are important members of a learning community, and the work of responding to teachers' questions is more authentic because the students can actually influence the course of the conversation. In this sense, questions that take students seriously promote engagement. In this chapter, we illustrate this way of looking at discourse in the teaching of literature in 9th Grade. We examine whether high-quality discourse occurs more frequently in some class situations than others (large versus small classes, high-ability versus low-ability groups), whether high-quality discourse seems to enhance students' engagement, and whether it seems to enhance their understanding of literature.

## THE QUALITY OF INSTRUCTIONAL DISCOURSE

Susan is like other 9th Grade girls we have met.[1] She gets along well enough in school, but doesn't find much excitement in her classes. In English class, for example, she does her homework most of the time, which she says takes her less than an hour each week. She finds some of the readings interesting, and reports that she generally has one or two things to say during class discussions. Susan says she often works as hard as she can, but rarely concentrates so hard that time passes quickly. We get the impression that she works as hard as she needs to.

Let's spend 50 minutes with Susan during one English class.

The period begins with the familiar ritual of attendance-taking. That accomplished, Mrs. Randolph, the teacher, reminds students that their silent reading period has begun. Mrs. Randolph is earnest, not especially dynamic but conscientious and well-organized. She projects a feeling of competence, but not much excitement or passion. Susan, who has been chatting with the girl in the next row, casually takes out *The Call of the Wild*, her assigned reading, eventually finds her place in the book, and begins reading. For the next 12 minutes, Susan sits quietly and reads, as if she were alone in a library.

Next, Susan dutifully takes her turn pointing out the grammatical errors planted for the students to find in sentences Mrs. Randolph has written on the blackboard. This activity takes 10 minutes, and half the period is over. The second half is occupied with students answering Mrs. Randolph's questions on *The Call of the Wild*. First, students write, on blank sheets, their answers to two questions that Mrs. Randolph reads aloud: "Why did Jack London give his novel the title *The Call of the Wild*?" and "What is London's message to his readers?" Mrs. Randolph collects these papers. Second, the students break into small groups to write answers to study questions. These questions check whether students have followed the narrative of the story; for example, "Briefly describe Buck's life at Judge Miller's" and "What important lesson did Buck learn from the man in the red sweater?" Finally, Mrs. Randolph reads the study questions aloud and calls on students to respond. Susan raises her hand a few times. The one time she is called on she responds correctly: "Explain why it took the team six days to travel 30 miles," reads Mrs. Randolph; "Because spring was coming and the ice was thin, so the team kept falling through," replies Susan.

Is this kind of instruction engaging? Although Susan does enough work to get by, she finds little reason to put more than minimal effort into it. Susan's class sessions, and her responses, accord with what many observers have said about instruction in American high schools: Teachers do most of the talking and almost all of the planning; controversies and complications are avoided; the tenor of instruction is devoid of passion. Teachers and students have made a "treaty" ("stalemate" might be a better word): Students go along with most demands, as long as they don't have to work too hard.[2]

What kind of instruction would be more engaging? How can the unspoken agreement of teachers and students not to expect much from one another be replaced by mutual engagement in learning? According to our theory of student engagement, instructional discourse that promotes membership and authentic work could make an essential contribution. In this chapter, we describe high-quality instructional discourse and explain how it makes students active partners in the instructional process, instead of passive respondents.

Like other forms of human interaction, instruction is governed by norms that guide the exchange of information. It would be hard to understand one another without certain conversational conventions: When to start from the beginning, and when to skip the details; when to explain ourselves, and when to make assumptions; and so on. Typically, though, talk between teachers and students bends these norms in odd ways. In ordinary discourse, someone asks a question because he or she wants to know the answer. Teachers, by contrast, already know the answers to most of their questions. They ask not to learn the answers, but to find out whether the *students* know the answers. Most teacher questions are essentially "test questions," which is not to say they are part of actual tests, but that their purpose is to test students' knowledge rather than to solicit new information.

What is being exchanged in such teacher–student interaction? There is little give-and-take in the *substance* of the discourse, compared with ordinary conversation. Susan, her classmates, and their teacher were not trading opinions and information back and forth, nor was the teacher seriously interested in what the students were thinking. Instead, exchange in classroom discourse typically has only a *procedural* basis: Teachers ask, and students answer. The content of a student's answer is not judged on its intrinsic merit, but on its conformity to a prespecified idea. In classes like Susan's, students are engaged in the procedures of discourse, but not in its substance. They pay attention and follow directions, but are not intellectually committed to issues of instructional content. And why should they be? They have little stake in it, for they are given little opportunity to contribute anything new to the conversation.

## High-Quality Instructional Discourse

Not all classroom discourse is like this. Sometimes, instead of test questions, teachers pose "authentic questions," which call for new information instead of prespecified knowledge. In place of the list of pre-ordained questions that dominates recitation, some teachers depart from the script to follow up on student responses, so that what students say influences the flow of discourse. This sort of follow-up, when teachers build on what students have said in framing subsequent questions, is called "uptake."[3] Sometimes the discourse flows so well that it is not even guided primarily by teacher questions, but moves among students and between students and the teacher like a real conversation. We call this "discussion," to distinguish it from ordinary question–answer recitation.

The following excerpt from another 9th Grade English class provides an example of a classroom conversation in which students are substantively as well as procedurally engaged.

> *The teacher asks a recitation question on a provocative topic:*
> *"Can you recall things from Huck Finn that seemed racist to*
> *you?" Students respond with a few examples. Then the teacher*
> *poses an authentic question, one for which the answer is not pre-*
> *specified.*

*Teacher:* How did that make you guys feel? I mean, what was your gut reaction to all that? . . .
*Student:* . . . everyone claims it's so historical, you can find that anywhere . . . "nigger," you know, you just hear that . . . and people always think . . . it's so historical.
*Teacher:* Like, oh, we wouldn't do that anymore.
*Student:* Yeah, like oh, we're not primitive, you know, and it's not, I mean, everybody does that, all the time. Well, not everybody, but people, people do that. . . . People can't get in[to] apartment buildings because they're black.

*Teacher:* Um-hm.

*Student:* They can't go to certain stores because they're black, or they're arrested because they're black . . . you know, it's just, I mean, everybody is always saying how historical it is, and it's right here, and it's right now . . .

*Teacher:* I like that comment, because do you remember . . . when I gave you that whole list of things that Twain is making fun of in the story? Well all of those things still exist, all right? Gullibility, religious convention, um, all kinds of things. Did this book stop being an accurate mirror of society? At any point? *[Students shake their heads negatively.]* I don't think so. . . . And we can look into this book as if we were looking into a mirror and saying, oh, OK, these are the things that are wrong with *me.*

This teacher has a point to make, but she does not simply state her views and move on. Nor does she restrict her questions to ones that call for summarizing the narrative of the story. Instead, she asks questions that move students to construct their own ideas about the topic. Moreover, she incorporates knowledge constructed by the students as part of instructional content. "What was your gut reaction *to all that*?" she asks, making the *students'* analysis of racism the subject of her next question. This question is an example of uptake and, as noted above, of authenticity as well. In the last part of the excerpt, the teacher and students move beyond question–answer to a discussion, a freer sharing of ideas. Again, the teacher builds on students' contributions to make her point. By taking students' ideas as serious and meaningful, this teacher engages students in the substantive content of literature.

Authentic questions, uptake, and discussion are characteristic of high-quality classroom discourse. Such discourse is inherently engaging for students because it offers them a real stake in its content. They play a role in determining its substance and direction. Their ideas are treated as primary information, indispensable to comprehending the meaning of literature itself. High-quality discourse takes students seriously.

Taking students seriously does not mean one must always *agree* with students or legitimize their opinions. Here is an excerpt from the same teacher in a different class, in which she exhibits respect for a student's view but argues against it.

*Student:* Well, we're talking about how white people are racist to black people, but blacks do that to us too.

*Teacher:* Um-hm, sure.

*Student:* I mean, just last night, we were on the bus, and we weren't even doing anything, all I was like looking out the window, and, and these,

these five black guys sitting right next to me . . . and then they start saying like they were going to start a fight. And we didn't even do anything . . .

*Teacher:* Helen, I go along with you . . . the thing is though, think about growing up, any of you . . . different from other people. . . . And, if you got people all of your life telling you that you're . . . nasty, and you're a drug dealer, and you can never amount to anything — you can't go to college, you can't do this and you can't do that. How do think you're going to start to act? *[Students murmur.]* You're going to act just like how people tell you to act, okay, that's called the self-fulfilling prophesy. And so, you're right, Helen, I know things like that happen, but . . . that doesn't come from anybody's skin color. That comes from hatred. That's' what hatred causes, and it's . . . a disease in our society.

What engages the student is the teacher's willingness to accept her point as meaningful, though incomplete. Unlike most descriptions of high school classes, these lessons are not "emotionally flat," and they do not avoid controversial or complicated issues. Instead, they promote engagement by incorporating students' contributions into the academic content.

Another feature of high-quality discourse is coherence among the various themes and activities of instruction. When reading, writing, and discussion activities have overlapping content and themes, instruction takes on a coherence that magnifies its capacity to enrich students' understanding. Observer accounts of contemporary high schools suggest that this type of coherence is relatively rare and that fragmentation rather than coherence is the norm (McNeil, 1986; Page, 1987).

## A STUDY OF INSTRUCTIONAL DISCOURSE IN 9TH GRADE ENGLISH

To learn more about instructional discourse and its relation to engagement and learning, we studied 54 9th Grade English classes located in nine high schools in the midwestern United States. The schools were chosen to vary in community context. Seven were public schools, including three in small-town and rural areas, one in a wealthy suburb and one in an upper middle-class urban neighborhood, and two in a working-class urban community. The other two were Catholic high schools with middle-class students. In the smallest schools, all 9th Grade English classes participated. In the others, representative samples of five to nine classes agreed to take part. Virtually all students in the participating classes (totaling about 1,100) were included in the study.

The description of Susan's class was drawn from one of the classes in one of the small-town schools, but the picture would not be much different in most classes in the other schools. The excerpts of high-quality discourse come from one of the Catholic schools. As will be evident, this type of discussion was far less common than the recitation in Susan's class.

We visited each of the 54 classes on four occasions. Observers recorded, both on audio-tapes and by typing into lap-top computers, all the questions asked during the class period. The questions were coded along dimensions that included authenticity and uptake. In addition, we noted the amount of time spent in activities such as seatwork, lecture, question–answer recitation, discussion, and small-group time. Students filled out tests and questionnaires in the fall and spring, and teachers also completed questionnaires in the spring.

## The Overall Quality of Discourse

In our study, the average class period was 50 minutes long, just like Susan's class. As Table 2.1 shows, about one third of the time was spent in question–answer recitation, the single most common activity. In this, too, the description of Susan's class is an apt characterization of the typical class. More free-flowing discussion, such as in the excerpts on racism, was exceedingly rare, averaging less than 15 seconds per day. Aside from recitation, class periods tended to be evenly divided among procedural matters, seatwork, lecture, and other activities.

Our results are consistent with the fragmentation that others have described. Students infrequently write about their readings or discuss what they have written: on average, these activities occur less than twice weekly. They have more opportunities to discuss their readings (average of 3.4 times per week). Overall, instructional activities are not tightly integrated with one another.

The findings for classroom discourse are slightly more encouraging than those for the structure and coherence of activities: Just over one quarter of teacher questions were authentic, and about the same proportion used uptake. Still, the large majority of questions called for conventional recitation and made little use of student contributions. Most teacher questions did not take students' ideas seriously, but consisted instead of what appeared to be preplanned lists of questions with prespecified answers.

## Differences Among Classes in the Quality of Discourse

Not all classes conformed to this profile of the typical class. For example, although 33 of the 54 classes had no discussion time at all, in four classes we observed more than a minute of discussion per day. Can instruc-

Table 2.1
Typical Classroom Discourse in 54 9th Grade English Classes

| Activities | Mean | Standard deviation |
|---|---|---|
| (observed minutes per day) | | |
| Procedures | 8.3 | 3.0 |
| Seatwork | 8.3 | 6.7 |
| Lecture[a] | 8.4 | 5.8 |
| Question-answer recitation | 17.6 | 6.6 |
| Discussion | 0.2 | 0.5 |
| Small-group work | 2.3 | 4.4 |
| Other[b] | 5.1 | 4.5 |
| Total observed minutes per day | 50.2 | 4.4 |
| | | |
| Coherence among activities | | |
| (teacher reported, times per week) | | |
| Students write about their readings | 1.5 | 1.3 |
| Students discuss their readings | 3.4 | 1.7 |
| Students discuss what they have written | 1.3 | 1.0 |
| | | |
| Nature of questions | | |
| (observed percentage) | | |
| Authentic teacher questions | 26.6% | 19.2 |
| Questions with uptake | 25.7% | 11.8 |

[a] Films, filmstrips, and teacher reading aloud were included under lecture.
[b] Other includes student presentation, students reading aloud, tests, and quizzes.

tional differences among classes be explained by their organizational contexts? We thought three conditions might be important. First, in eight of
the nine schools, students were divided into ability groups for English
class. These groups were easily identified by their names, such as "honors,"
"accelerated," "regular," "remedial," or "basic." Based on recent studies,
we expected to observe higher-quality discourse in the honors and accelerated classes, and more rigid, drill-and-worksheet instruction in remedial
and basic classes. Oakes (1985), for example, found that students in high-
track English classes had more opportunities for critical thinking tasks,
whereas low-track students more often engaged in memorization and
simple comprehension work. Similarly, Page (1987) described low-track
classes as "caricatures" of regular classes. Low-track classes deemphasized
academic concerns, she observed, and teachers did not take responsibility
for the learning of low-track students. Both authors also found low-track
instruction to be more fragmented, emphasizing small bits of information
instead of broad ideas. We expected these differences to be manifested in
our measures of instructional quality.

Second, we thought class size might affect the quality of instructional
discourse. Smaller classes might encourage closer personal relations, and
this could prompt teachers to incorporate students' ideas into the flow of
instruction. Thus, we expected to find greater use of authentic questions
and uptake in smaller classes. We further reasoned that teachers could
more easily carry on discussions in smaller classes. Finally, we hypothe-
sized that more experienced teachers would be more adept at leading
discussions. With fewer problems of classroom management, experienced
teachers might also be more willing to relinquish some of their control by
allowing students to influence the course of the lesson. On the other hand,
it seemed equally possible that experienced teachers would be set in their
ways, making even greater use of prescribed questions and predetermined
answers.

### Differences Associated with Ability Grouping

As it turned out, we found little evidence to confirm these expectations. High-ability classes devoted less time to seatwork and more time to
question–answer recitation, as expected, but there were no significant
differences in the amount of discussion time. Of the four classes averaging
more than a minute of discussion, two were honors-level, one was regular,
and one was remedial. Eight honors classes exhibited no discussion time at
all. Authenticity and coherence were highest in regular classes, and uptake
was highest in remedial classes, but these differences were small and statistically indistinguishable from zero.

*Differences Associated with Class Size and Teacher Experience*

Class size and teacher experience were also largely unrelated to discourse quality. Smaller classes spent less time on routine procedures, but more time on seatwork. For example, classes with fewer than 10 students averaged about 18 minutes per day of seatwork, while larger classes averaged just under eight minutes.[4] Experienced teachers allocated less time for discussion and reported fewer interrelations among activities. Otherwise, years of teaching experience was unrelated to our measures of instruction.

## Discourse Quality and Other Measures of Engagement

We think of high-quality discourse as substantively engaging because it draws students into the content of the lessons. In this sense, classes with more authentic questions, uptake, discussion, and coherent discourse may be seen as having more engaging instruction, compared with classes that generally lack these features. This notion, however, is not necessarily the same as students' views of engaging instruction. We expected students to report more interest and effort, and to exhibit more consistent participation, in classes with higher-quality discourse. Again, however, our expectations were largely frustrated. First, we constructed a scale from three questions posed on student questionnaires.

In English class, how often do you . . .
> Try as hard as you can?
> Think what you are learning is interesting and worthwhile?
> Find yourself concentrating so hard that time passes
> quickly?

This measure of engagement was essentially unrelated to the discourse quality of the class. We also examined student reports of assignment completion and homework time, as well as observed data on the proportion of students offtask. Again, we found no consistent relations between discourse quality and these participation indicators.

These findings reflect the complexity of measuring student engagement. As noted in Chapter 1, investment and effort in academic work are not easy to observe. One student could appear to be daydreaming, yet actually be thinking about the lesson topic. Another could seem to be hard at work, but not really be concentrating. Survey questions are also problematic. How accurately do students report their levels of effort and concentration? How sensitive are such reports to fluctuations in students' moods or in recent, as opposed to typical, classroom events? Moreover, positive responses to questions about effort and homework may reflect *procedural* engagement even when students' intellectual commitment to the material — that is, their *substantive* engagement — is attenuated. Weak correlations among indicators of engagement and engaging instruction probably result from both the unreliability of the measures and the fact that different indicators may tap different aspects of engagement.

## Discourse Quality and Literature Achievement

Which, if any, aspects of instruction and engagement are related to student achievement? To address this question, we must first consider what we mean by achievement. Given our focus on instruction that incorporates students' ideas into the academic content, we had little interest in conventional multiple-choice tests of vocabulary or reading comprehension. At the same time, we favored a test that was relevant to the actual content students had covered in class. To assess the effects of instruction and engagement, we reasoned, one should measure how much students learned from the material they were taught.

### A Test of Literature Achievement

These concerns led us to design our own test of literature achievement, which we administered in the spring. The teachers provided us with lists of all the novels, short stories, and plays students had been assigned to read over the course of the year. From these lists, we chose five representative selections for each class, and on the tests, we asked a series of questions about the selected readings. The questions ranged from simple recall (e.g., "Who were the main characters in [name of story]?") to ones calling for in-depth understanding (e.g., "Relate the theme of [name of story] to the main conflict and to the ending."). The questions were the same for each class, but the readings they asked about differed, depending on what had been read in each class. In addition, students were asked to write an essay about a character from any story they had read in school that year. With this procedure, we hoped to satisfy our dual goals of allowing students to speak with their own voices and of testing their knowledge of material they had been taught.[5]

Despite these advantages over conventional tests, our system has its own limitations. It is important to bear in mind that the test covered only literature achievement and did not assess learning in other areas, such as grammar, speech, specific writing skills, and so on. Literature was the one topic that was common to all 54 classes, but the classes did not all focus on literature to the same degree.

Another limitation is that we do not know the extent to which questions on the test elicited students' own syntheses of knowledge, or simply required them to restate conclusions that had already been provided in class. Whereas the open-ended question asking students to explain their admiration for some character was reasonably authentic, a question such as, "What is the main theme of *Great Expectations*?" may or may not be an authentic question, depending on whether and how the issue was treated in class. Although we believe our test provides better measures of authentic learning than conventional paper-and-pencil tests, we acknowledge ambiguity about the extent of authenticity elicited by our test.

To measure the effects of instruction and engagement on achievement, we carried out a regression analysis. This technique statistically adjusts for differences among students in order to rule out spurious associations caused by preexisting conditions. For example, if uptake is associated with higher achievement, regression analysis may show whether the relation occurs because previously higher-achieving students receive more uptake, or because uptake leads students to obtain higher achievement. The regression technique estimates the effect of each variable while statistically holding constant each of the other variables. Instead of assessing the relation of each condition to achievement one at a time, we measure the effects of all our predictors simultaneously. Our analysis controls for the effects of background variables (sex, race, ethnicity, family socioeconomic status) and prior achievement (fall tests of reading and writing skills).[6] The complete regression results are displayed in Table 2.2.

*Effects of Psychological and Behavioral Engagement*

Our results suggest that psychological engagement as measured by the scale described earlier had no effect on literature achievement. This finding is, of course, subject to the measurement problems noted above. Behavioral indicators of procedural engagement, both student-reported and observed, were more closely tied to achievement. Students who completed all their reading and writing assignments scored about two points higher on the test than students who finished two thirds of their work.[7] This represents a moderate impact: It would move a student from the 50th to the 58th percentile. Similarly, students whose classes averaged 10 percent of students offtask scored about 1.2 points lower than those whose classes typically had no students offtask. With these items controlled, homework time had no additional impact.

*(continued on p. 54)*

Table 2.2

Effects of Instruction and Engagement on 9th Grade Literature Achievement

Dependent variable: Spring literature achievement (mean = 21.82, s.d. = 7.66).

N = 971 students, $R^2$ for regression = .52.  (*p<.05, **p<.01.)

| VARIABLE | MEAN | STANDARD DEVIATION | REGRESSION COEFFICIENT | STANDARD ERROR |
|---|---|---|---|---|
| Background variables | | | | |
| Sex (female = 1) | .51 | .50 | 1.47** | .37 |
| Race (black = 1) | .07 | .26 | -.46 | .72 |
| Ethnicity (Hisp = 1) | .09 | .28 | -1.56* | .65 |
| SES | -.02 | .80 | .44 | .25 |
| Fall reading | 31.88 | 5.34 | .40** | .04 |
| Fall writing | 5.71 | 1.28 | .90** | .15 |
| Ability groups | | | | |
| Honors/accelerated | .24 | .43 | .25 | .96 |
| Basic/remedial | .10 | .30 | -1.09 | 1.13 |
| Other[a] | .09 | .29 | .57 | 1.16 |
| Psychological engagement | | | | |
| Engagement scale[b] | 2.42 | 1.40 | -.02 | .14 |

| Behavioral engagement | | | | |
|---|---|---|---|---|
| Writing completed | 87.88% | 19.68 | .03** | .01 |
| Reading completed | 83.04% | 24.62 | .03** | .01 |
| Homework time (hrs/wk) | 1.27 | 1.27 | .19 | .15 |
| Offtask in class | 3.22% | 3.27 | -.12* | .06 |
| | | | | |
| Instructional discourse | | | | |
| Authentic questions: | | | | |
| In honors classes | 24.30% | 11.41 | .10** | .03 |
| In regular classes | 28.13% | 18.81 | -.02 | .01 |
| In remedial classes | 27.40% | 18.86 | -.09** | .04 |
| In other classes | 36.90% | 26.03 | -.20** | .03 |
| Uptake | 25.90% | 11.26 | .09** | .02 |
| Discussion | .24 | .48 | -.18 | .40 |
| Coherence[c] | 13.01 | 7.07 | -.12** | .03 |

[a] Other classes include two classes in a school-within-a-school program, and two classes in a heterogeneously grouped school.

[b] Engagement scale based on student responses to the following questions, coded on a weekly scale:

In English class, how often do you . . .
Try as hard as you can?
Think what you are learning is interesting and worthwhile?
Find yourself concentrating so hard that time passes quickly?

[c] Coherence measure based on teacher responses to the following questions, coded on a weekly scale:

About how often do students in your class write about (or in response to) things they have read?
About how often do you discuss writing topics with your students before asking them to write?
About how often do you and your class discuss the readings you assign?
When you ask students about their reading assignments in class, how frequently do you attempt to do each of the following: Ask them to relate what they have read to their other readings.
About how often does your class relate its discussion to previous discussions you have had?
About how often do you and your class discuss things students have written about?

*Effects of Instructional Discourse*

Discussion time failed to exert a significant impact in the regression analysis. However, both uptake and discourse coherence offered positive contributions. Classes in which 40 percent of the questions used uptake produced about 1.3 additional points on the test, compared with the typical class in which 25 percent of questions followed up on student responses. Achievement was about 1.6 points higher in classes in which activities were well-connected (coherence one standard deviation above the mean) compared with classes in which instructional activities rarely related to one another (coherence one standard deviation below the mean).

The analysis of authenticity revealed some surprising results. Initially, authentic teacher questions appeared to exert zero or even negative effects on achievement.[8] Exploratory analyses suggested that authenticity had different effects in different kinds of classes. Upon closer inspection, we discovered that authenticity had moderate *positive* effects in high-ability classes, and similarly sized *negative* effects in low-ability classes. Honors classes with 20 percent more authentic questions (one standard deviation) produced two additional points on the test, but remedial classes with 20 percent more authenticity *reduced* achievement by almost the same amount. Authentic questions had no impact at all in regular classes.

To interpret these findings, we posed the following question: Do the varying effects of authenticity result from teachers asking different types of authentic questions in different sorts of classes, or from students in varied classes responding differently to teachers' authentic questions?

## Authenticity in High- and Low-Ability Classes

A closer look at the data revealed that teachers in honors and remedial classes were not talking about the same issues when they asked authentic questions. Much more often in remedial classes, we found strings of authentic questions about topics unrelated to literature. One example was a discussion of test-taking skills and attitudes: "How do most of you feel about tests?" "What would your parents say if you got an A on next week's test?" Another was a brainstorming session: "What things would you associate with lying in the sun?" Another set of authentic questions emerged in a lesson on note-taking: "Do you ever have to take notes?" "Do you ever get lost because you fall behind?"

In another low-ability class, we observed that the teacher posed authentic questions when talking *about* literature generally, but more conventional recitation when asking about the actual texts studied. Here we observed two lessons on literary devices (e.g., symbolism) in which students had opportunities for original contributions (e.g., by inventing their own metaphors). Yet when this teacher asked students about a particular text, the vast majority of questions called for summarizing and clarifying what happened in the story.

By contrast, authentic questions in high-ability classes generally focused on the ideas and issues embedded in literary texts. For example, in a discussion of *Great Expectations*, a teacher in an accelerated class asked questions such as, "Do you think Pip could ever really be happy?" "You say 'No'; why not?" "What could Stella tell Pip to make him happy?" "Do you think she really does want to marry him?" Questions like these take students into the novel, leading them to see the characters' motivations from the inside. Indeed, at one point the teacher had students assume the identity of the characters: "Stella, what would *you* tell Pip to be happy?"

Another example of the type of authentic questions teachers asked in honors classes comes from a discussion of Chekhov's story "The Bet": "Do you think the sacrifice was worth it, to gain that much self-knowledge?" "Can you expand on that?" This teacher also gave student voices a prominent place in determining the interpretation of the text. Our impression that authentic questions in honors classes more often concerned the texts at hand is supported by a tally of authentic questions: 68 percent of authentic questions in honors classes were about a specific piece of literature, whereas this could be said of only 25 percent of authentic questions in remedial classes.

These findings suggest that the reason authenticity had positive effects in honors classes and negative effects in remedial classes is that honors teachers more often asked authentic questions about literature, which was, after all, the subject of the test. Our results do not show that authentic questions have no effect in low-ability classes; nor did we find that low-track teachers ask fewer authentic questions. Instead, we discovered that the kind of authentic questions asked in low-ability classes failed to pay off for literature achievement.

On the one hand, one could argue that our test was unfair: Had we tested students on the topics emphasized in remedial classes, we might have come up with different results. On the other hand, we think it is significant that students' ideas about literature received less emphasis in low-ability classes. Page (1987) claims that low-track teachers have relinquished responsibility for their students' learning. Our results are consistent with the argument that in low-ability English classes, academic content is not taken seriously.

## RAISING THE QUALITY OF INSTRUCTIONAL DISCOURSE

As others have found, our study shows that most classroom discourse is recitation. The dominant feature of instruction is the transmission of information. Teachers mainly play the role of examiner, and they treat learning as the recall of transmitted information. In pursuing these goals, most teachers ask questions that test student knowledge rather than elicit original interpretations or help students formulate their own ideas. The authentic questions teachers did ask, we found, tended to help students understand literature only in the high-track classes, though this seems to be because in low-track classes teachers' authentic questions tended to be about things other than literature; the proportion of authentic questions about literature was nearly three times as great in the high-track as in the low-track classes. In addition, teachers usually do not follow up on student answers. We found, in short, that high-quality discourse rarely occurs in 9th Grade literature instruction.

Instruction dominated by recitation trivializes important bodies of knowledge in the form of superficial, decontextualized facts that students recite in fill-in-the-blank and short-answer questions for homework, and in recitation during class. If student learning is to consist of more than short-term memorization of these snippets — if students are to have more than a superficial familiarity with broad domains of knowledge, if they are to think critically and originally about this information, and especially if they are themselves to develop in-depth understandings — then they must be involved in a far different and more substantial kind of discourse. Rather than merely recite other people's ideas and information, they must entertain and develop ideas of their own, and they must argue original points of view; they must learn to interpret, not merely recall. To accomplish these goals, teachers must approach students not as "rememberers" and memorizers; rather they must take students seriously as thinkers. They must elicit students' thoughts, listen carefully to what they have to say, and skillfully help them elaborate their ideas.

When instruction proceeds in this way, recitation gives way to something more conversational. In this sort of discourse, as in conversation, all the participants, not just the teacher, potentially affect the course of interaction. As in conversation, there is a reciprocal exchange of information, not merely a continuous evaluation of whether students have learned all the right facts and main points.

Bringing about such discourse is not a simple task. Unhappily, we found no simple answers or "magic bullet" for accomplishing it. We found, for example, that quality of discourse is not consistently related to class size, ability group, or teacher experience. Improving the quality of

instructional discourse is subtly complicated by many fundamental prem-
ises about the nature of knowledge, curriculum, and instruction and the
role and preparation of the teacher. We believe that the most fundamental
recommendation for improving literature instruction relates to the latter:
Teachers must first have a strong undergraduate preparation in and sensitivity for literature. They must understand that a literary text is fundamentally different from a news report, involving more than information
of the sort that is covered adequately through recitation and short-answer
study questions concerning who, what, when, where, and why. Because
of this, effective literature instruction must do more than teach basic textual information related to character, plot, setting, theme, and so on.
Effective preparation of prospective English teachers must teach them
how to read literature and respond to the idiosyncratic features of literary
texts (Fish, 1980; Purves, 1991).

Skilled readers read nonfictional texts such as newspaper and magazine articles for the main point, and they remember those points of information they are able to relate to the main point as they understand it
(van Dijk & Kintsch, 1983). But they read novels and short stories quite
differently; they read literature aesthetically by "living through" the narrative, especially in terms of their own experience, savoring "the qualities
of the structure ideas, situations, scenes, personalities, emotions called
forth, participating in the tensions, conflicts, and resolutions as they un-
fold" (Rosenblatt, 1988, p. 5).[9] For these reasons, learning how to read
and fully experience literature involves personal response, and it is just
this process that authentic teacher questions tend to promote. In contrast,
classroom discourse confined to recitation misses the character of literature. Unless teachers have themselves experienced ample literature selections in this way, unless they value literature and can respond to its idiosyncratic qualities themselves, and unless they are prepared to model
mature responses to literature and elicit students' own personal responses,
there is little chance they will succeed in teaching literature effectively.
Literature teachers who merely "cover the main points" trivialize literature instruction into sets of poor reading lessons.

From this perspective, it should be clear that multiple-choice tests
and short-answer questions foster inappropriate ways of reading and understanding literature, and thereby stifle high-quality classroom discourse.
Effective literature instruction is, however, enhanced by regular, open-
ended questions probing student responses, which they must develop into
extended pieces of written prose. These writing assignments are most effective, moreover, when teachers read them not as examiners but as trusted
adults (cf. Britton, Burgess, Martin, McLeod, & Rosen, 1975) seeking to
draw out and develop students' interpretations of what they have read.

If teachers are to engage students in such substantive conversations, the literature curriculum they teach must not be overspecified with long lists of facts, points, and obligatory principles to teach. Curriculum guides should guide more than dictate, and teachers must have ample latitude to address major curricular aims in ways that are best for them. For each class, the teacher must have the freedom to work out the curriculum with respect to the interests and capabilities that individual students bring to class. Schools might attract more effective teachers by considering only candidates with undergraduate majors in literature.

Unless teachers have a more than a superficial understanding of the titles they teach, they may avoid asking authentic questions simply because the answers to such questions are often unpredictable. When teachers ask authentic questions and engage their students in substantive conversations, they must be prepared to move with an unfolding discussion that they will not always be able fully to anticipate before class begins and that cannot be repeated from class to class; for any given class, they will not always be able to anticipate just which aspects of the text they may need to discuss. They must also be prepared to deal with the personal responses of their students. The more fully students respond to the text, the more comprehensive, in-depth, and fast-paced the discussion will be. In this sort of discussion, therefore, teachers must have a supple yet firm grasp of the text and be prepared to think quickly on their feet.

Staff development can no doubt help teachers develop many of these skills. We have found that some teachers benefit quickly when they discuss the importance of authentic questions and uptake. Some have found new confidence in their own teaching after learning from our research about the importance of such questions. Some teachers have also used our analytic scheme to assess and reflect on the quality of their classroom discourse. Since most school learning in fact occurs in classroom discourse — what Cazden (1988) calls "the language of learning" — staff development on these matters has great potential to improve instruction.

This kind of classroom discourse, if it is to be pedagogically effective, requires teachers to deftly negotiate an instructional path somewhere between a Scylla of correct answers and a Charybdis of free student response. As Harker (1991) explains, teachers must ask "not only those questions firmly anchored to textual evidence, but those which permit students to explore and develop an awareness of their responses to literature in an environment which permits and encourages individual risk-taking and self-exploration" (p. 72). He continues,

> Seen in this way, the classroom becomes a collaborative social system in which students' responses are extended and refined under the guidance

of their teachers and in collaboration with their peers. It is not that teachers arbitrarily impose their own interpretive strategies on their students or that students' individual responses are given totally free play. Rather, it is that students' responses are taken as points of departure for their further development, initially in collaboration with teachers and peers, but ultimately with growing independence in the minds of students themselves as instruction moves . . . towards more inclusive interpretations at higher levels of literary competence. In this sense, the direction of instruction is from collaborative, public reading involving students with their teachers and peers, to more private, independent reading carried on by students themselves. (p. 72)

The lively nature of substantive conversation makes it a somewhat risky enterprise. It is not for tired teachers or the faint of heart or for teachers who don't read literature — though it certainly has the potential to be more interesting as well, for both teacher and students. Teachers engaging in such classroom discourse escape the mind-numbing routine of having to teach exactly the same lesson to several classes. Instead, they gain opportunities to use literature to enrich their lives.

## NOTES

Additional support for this chapter came from the first author's Spencer Fellowship at the National Academy of Education. The authors are grateful for research assistance from Mark Berends, John Knapp, and James Ladwig, and for the cooperation of the teachers and students who participated in the study.

1. All names in this chapter are pseudonyms. Information about Susan's class came from a student questionnaire and a classroom observation. The description of Susan is a composite picture of students in the class, representing the experiences of a typical student.
2. Such descriptions are provided by the National Commission on Excellence in Education (1983); Goodlad (1984); Powell, Farrar, and Cohen (1985); McNeil (1986); and Sedlak, Wheeler, Pullin, and Cusick (1986).
3. "Uptake" is a term used by Collins (1982) and Cazden (1988).
4. The use of seatwork may have been more effective in smaller classes because teachers could work individually with more students.
5. The tests were scored holistically on a variety of dimensions such as recall, depth of understanding, understanding of character motivations, and so forth. Each test was scored by two readers, and the scores were averaged. The two readers' scores correlated at .82. We found a multiple correlation of .60 of the spring literature test with the fall tests of reading and writing skills.
6. Sex, race, and ethnicity were identified with dummy variables from stu-

dent questionnaires. Family socioeconomic status (SES) was indicated by an unweighted additive composite of father's and mother's education, the higher of either parent's occupational status, and a list of home resources, as reported on student questionnaires. Fall reading skills were measured by a multiple-choice test of reading comprehension, and fall writing skills were measured by a holistically scored writing sample. Further details on the background variables and achievement controls are provided by Gamoran and Nystrand (1991).

7. This inference is derived as follows: Students who completed 33 percent more of their reading (as in the comparison of those who completed all their work with those who completed two thirds of their work) scored, on average ($33 \times .03) = .99$ point higher (.03 is the coefficient for completion of reading from the regression results in Table 2.2). The same coefficients appear for completion of writing, adding another .99 point, for a total of about a two-point difference between those who complete all their reading and writing and those who do only two thirds of it.

8. This finding was surprising not only because it contradicted our expectations, but because in a similar study of 8th Grade literature achievement, we earlier found a small positive effect of authentic teacher questions (Nystrand & Gamoran, 1991).

9. As Rosenblatt (1978, 1988) explains, learning to read literature requires learning to distinguish between *efferent* and *aesthetic* readings: Hence, we read newspaper reports "efferently," for example, carrying away with us "the bottom line" or what psychologists call the gist of the text. By contrast, reading "aesthetically" requires "living through" and experiencing vicariously the "story world."

## REFERENCES

Britton, J., Burgess, T., Martin, N., McLeod, A., & Rosen, H. (1975). *The development of writing abilities: 11–18.* London: Macmillan.

Cazden, C. (1988). *Classroom discourse: The language of teaching and learning.* Portsmouth, NH: Heinemann.

Collins, J. (1982). Discourse style, classroom interaction and differential treatment. *Journal of Reading Behavior, 14,* 429–437.

Fish, S. (1980). *Is there a text in this class? The authority of interpretive communities.* Cambridge, MA: Harvard University Press.

Gamoran, A., & Nystrand, M. (1991). Background and instructional effects on achievement in eighth-grade English and social studies. *Journal of Research on Adolescence, 1*(3), 277–300.

Goodlad, J. I. (1984). *A place called school: Prospects for the future.* New York: McGraw-Hill.

Harker, W. J. (1991). Reader response and the interpretation of literature: Is there a teacher in the classroom? *Reflections on Canadian Literacy, 8*(2,3), 69–73.

McNeil, L. M. (1986). *Contradictions of control: School structure and school knowledge*. New York: Routledge & Kegan Paul.

National Commission on Excellence in Education. (1983). *A nation at risk*. Washington, DC: U.S. Department of Education.

Nystrand, M., & Gamoran, A. (1991). Instructional discourse, student engagement, and literature achievement. *Research in the Teaching of English, 25*(3), 261–290.

Oakes, J. (1985). *Keeping track: How schools structure inequality*. New Haven: Yale University Press.

Page, R. N. (1987). Lower-track classes at a college-preparatory school: A caricature of educational encounters. In G. Spindler & L. Spindler (Eds.), *Interpretive ethnography of schooling: At home and abroad* (pp. 447–472). Hillsdale, NJ: Erlbaum.

Powell, A. G., Farrar, E., & Cohen, D. K. (1985). *The shopping mall high school: Winners and losers in the educational marketplace*. Boston: Houghton Mifflin.

Purves, A. C. (1991). Indeterminate texts, responsive readers, and the idea of difficulty in literature learning. In A. C. Purves (Ed.), *The idea of difficulty in literature* (pp. 157–170). Albany: State University of New York Press.

Rosenblatt, L. (1978). *The reader, the text, the poem: A transactional theory of the literary work*. Carbondale: Southern Illinois University Press.

Rosenblatt, L. (1988). *Writing and reading: The transactional theory* (Tech. Rep. No. 13). Berkeley, CA: The Center for the Study of Writing.

Sedlak, M. W., Wheeler, C. W., Pullin, D. C., & Cusick, P. A. (1986). *Selling students short: Classroom bargains and academic reform in the American high school*. New York: Teachers College Press.

van Dijk, T., & Kintsch, W. (1983). *Strategies of discourse comprehension*. New York: Academic Press.

CHAPTER 3

# Higher-Order Thinking and Prospects for Classroom Thoughtfulness

**Fred M. Newmann**

National panels have increasingly called on American schools to teach reasoning, problem solving, critical thinking, and creative use of the mind.[1] Consistent with this movement, the model of instructional discourse presented in Chapter 2 urged teachers to aim beyond student reproduction of authoritative knowledge. It explained how teachers can empower students by helping them to integrate formal knowledge in ways that enhance the meaning of their personal experience. Nystrand and Gamoran found that this sort of discourse rarely occurs, unhappily supporting the findings of other studies that document the low level of cognitive work in most secondary school classrooms (Cuban, 1984; Goodlad, 1984; Hoetker & Ahlbrand, 1969; McNeil, 1986; Powell, Farrar, & Cohen, 1985).

This chapter extends the inquiry on classroom discourse. To engage students it is necessary not only to incorporate their own ideas into conversation about the subject, but also to challenge them to think. Higher-order thinking is both a means to student engagement and a central aim of education. Injunctions for schools to put more emphasis on thinking are plentiful, but implementing them is problematic, partly because of multiple, confusing, and unworkable conceptions of the term. Therefore, I first propose a conception of higher-order thinking that can guide teaching, together with a framework for observing the extent to which it is promoted in classrooms. Second, I report on a study to determine whether it is actually possible for high school teachers to teach students to use their minds well, and to depart from the familiar path of passing on numerous fragmented bits of information that students try to memorize but soon

62

forget. Is classroom thoughtfulness determined completely by the commitment and competence of individual teachers, or can it be institutionalized throughout a department? If some departments are more successful, what accounts for their success in contrast to the apparent difficulties faced by the majority?

Based on a study of 16 high school social studies departments, I summarize findings on the association between student engagement and higher-order thinking, overall levels of classroom thoughtfulness, and differences due to teachers, departments, and student characteristics. Next I suggest factors in teachers' thinking, school leadership, and organization that seem critical to success. Finally, I outline important barriers that must be addressed by leadership, staff development, and school restructuring.

## WHAT IS HIGHER-ORDER THINKING?

### A Definition

Higher-order thinking signifies challenge and expanded use of the mind; lower-order thinking signifies routine, mechanistic application, and constraints on the mind.[2] Challenge or expanded use of mind occurs when a person must interpret, analyze, or manipulate information, because a question to be answered or a problem to be solved cannot be resolved through the routine application of previously learned knowledge. The explorer trying to travel successfully over unknown terrain illustrates the idea that previously acquired knowledge (e.g., about map and compass use, weather, and survival techniques) must be applied in a new situation to reach the destination. Success requires considerable knowledge, but, because of the novelty of the task, *how* to apply the knowledge poses a significant challenge. In contrast, lower-order thinking generally involves repetitive routines such as listing information previously memorized, inserting numbers into previously learned formulae, or applying the rules for footnote format in a research paper.

Challenging problems can appear in many forms, in all curriculum subjects. They may lead to single, correct, and well-defined answers or to multiple, ambiguous, conflicting solutions. The challenges may involve different kinds of inquiry (logical, empirical, aesthetic, ethical), different forms of expression (oral, written, nonverbal), and different types of intelligence (verbal, mathematical, kinesthetic, interpersonal).

No particular question or problem, however, necessarily leads to higher-order thinking for all students. For one person, trying to understand and follow a bus schedule may require higher-order thought, but for another the same task will be routine. In this sense, higher-order thinking is relative: To determine the extent to which an individual is involved in higher-order thinking, one would presumably need to know much about the person's history. Furthermore, to assess the extent to which an individual is participating in the analysis, interpretation, and manipulation of information, one would want to "get inside" the person's head or experience his or her subjective state of thought.

This definition poses an operational problem. It is difficult to determine reliably the extent to which a person is involved in higher-order thinking. Teachers who interact with several students at once have little opportunity to diagnose students' individual mental states. Instead, they must make assumptions about the prior knowledge of groups of students and about the kinds of mental work that particular tasks are likely to stimulate. The teaching of thinking, therefore, is a rather imprecise enterprise. The best we can do is to engage students in what we predict will be challenging problems, to guide their manipulation of information to solve problems, and to support their efforts.

This conception of higher-order thinking has several positive features.

1. It assumes that any person, young or old, regardless of experience, can participate in higher-order thought. Students will differ in the kinds of challenges they are able to master, but all are capable of confronting a challenge in the interpretation, analysis, and manipulation of their knowledge.
2. It encompasses problem solving in a wide range of school subjects as well as in nonacademic areas.
3. It does not require acceptance of any particular theory of cognitive processing or rely on a restrictive pedagogy. This is an advantage, because solid knowledge on the best techniques for the promotion of thinking does not exist. The effectiveness of technique will probably depend on the nature of the mental challenges presented and the kinds of students exposed to them. Furthermore, this conception is hospitable to providing students with three important resources for thinking that are recognized widely in the literature: content knowledge, intellectual skills, and dispositions of thoughtfulness.

## The Need for Knowledge, Skills, and Dispositions

Merely presenting students with higher-order challenges will not necessarily help them develop the competence to meet the challenges successfully. Research on the nature of thinking (summarized by Walsh & Paul,

1987) indicates that for students to cope successfully with higher-order challenges, they need a combination of in-depth knowledge, intellectual skills, and attitudes or dispositions of thoughtfulness. These three components are the core of a curriculum focused on higher-order thinking, but how much emphasis to give to each is widely disputed. Consider a teacher trying to help students answer the question, "Were the American colonists justified in using violence to secure their independence from England?" To enhance students' success in addressing this problem, how much attention should teachers give to developing students' knowledge, skills, and dispositions? Building on a previous review of literature (Newmann, 1990a), we summarize here key arguments that can be made for each of these critical resources.

## The Knowledge Argument

Regardless of what side the student takes, a successful answer to this question demands in-depth knowledge of the circumstances of colonial life under British rule, including colonial grievances, British responses, principled arguments dealing with inalienable rights, taxation without representation, and ethical reasoning related to the destruction of property and the taking of human life. Beyond substantive knowledge about the historical period, students will need analytic knowledge; for example, on elements of a well-reasoned argument, distinctions between empirical and normative issues, and criteria for judging the reliability of evidence. Metacognitive knowledge may also be important, such as having a systematic approach for organizing one's thinking or an awareness of how one's thought processes and perceptions of others in a discussion might lead to error. The behavioral manifestations of some of these points might be labeled skills or dispositions, but they may all be considered knowledge in the sense that they all can be represented as cognitive beliefs. Skills and dispositions may facilitate the application of knowledge, but these points suggest that knowledge itself is the most critical foundation of understanding.[3]

## The Skills Argument

Knowledge is undoubtedly important, but for the purposes of the teaching of thinking, skills are critical, because they are the tools that permit knowledge to be used or applied to the solution of new problems. Some skills may be specific to the domain under study, and others may be more generic. To intelligently address the problem above, for example, one must be able to detect bias in the documents of colonial history and logical fallacies in inferences and arguments over the justification of the American Revolution. One must be able to distinguish relevant from irrelevant information, to anticipate and respond to arguments in opposition to one's own, and to state one's views clearly and persuasively. Skills themselves may be construed or labeled in a variety of ways, but the main point is to recognize their role as cognitive processes that put knowledge to work in solving problems. In practice, knowledge is usually transmitted from teacher to student without an expectation that the student will manipulate the knowledge to solve higher-order challenges. Unless the essential processes of using knowledge (i.e., skills) are stressed as central goals of education, higher-order thinking is likely to be neglected and the knowledge transmitted to remain inert. Perhaps for this reason many educational reformers prefer to advocate not the teaching of thinking, but instead the teaching of thinking *skills*.[4]

## The Dispositions Argument

Without dispositions of thoughtfulness, neither knowledge nor the tools for applying it are likely to be used intelligently. If raising questions about the justification of the war for American independence threatens patriotic feelings, this could jeopardize critical inquiry. Some people may avoid almost any argument to protect themselves from uncomfortable feelings of conflict. Those who emphasize the importance of dispositions suggest several traits: A persistent desire that claims be supported by reasons (and that the reasons themselves be scrutinized); a tendency to be reflective — to take time to think problems through for oneself, rather than acting impulsively or automatically accepting the views of others; a curiosity to explore new questions; and the flexibility to entertain alternative and original solutions to problems. Thoughtfulness thereby involves attitudes, personality or character traits, general values, and beliefs or epistemologies about the nature of knowledge (e.g., that rationality is desirable; that knowledge itself is socially constructed, subject to revision, and often indeterminate; and that thinking can lead to the understanding and solution of problems). Without dispositions of thoughtfulness, knowledge and skills are likely to be taught and applied mechanistically and nonsensically. Of the three main resources, dispositions have attracted the least attention in professional literature, but a good argument can be made that dispositions are central in generating both the *will* to think and in developing those artistic, ineffable qualities of judgment that steer knowledge and skills in productive directions.[5]

It is important that teachers design instruction explicitly to help students acquire and use in-depth knowledge, skills, and dispositions, but there appears to be no clear ordering of priorities among the three re- sources. The observation scheme presented next attempts to capture teach- ers' efforts to develop knowledge, skills, and dispositions, without giving center stage to any one resource.[6] Neither does it prescribe the precise kinds of knowledge, skills, and dispositions that should be promoted for the teaching of a particular subject. The reasoning behind this choice is explained as we introduce a framework for assessing classroom thoughtful- ness.

## A FRAMEWORK FOR ASSESSING CLASSROOM THOUGHTFULNESS

The overall goal of our research project was to search for social studies departments successful in promoting higher-order thinking and to learn from their work. Rather than concentrating primarily on differences among individual teachers, this study explored the problem of institution- alization: What is required for department-wide promotion of higher- order thinking? The strategy was to identify exemplary social studies de- partments (that is, those that make a serious department-wide effort to emphasize higher-order thinking) and then, by contrasting these depart- ments with others, to draw inferences about barriers and opportunities for success.

This called for a method for assessing classroom interaction that would provide comparative indicators of the extent to which higher-order thinking was promoted in classes that studied a variety of social studies subjects (e.g., U.S. history, world history, geography, government, sociol- ogy). Since it was logistically impossible to examine the actual thinking of individual students during the lessons, we needed a tool for describing thoughtfulness in the lesson as a whole. But how specific should the crite- ria be?

Interviews with history and social studies teachers indicated that highly specific lists of knowledge, skills, and dispositions were unlikely to generate widespread consensus. Instead, social studies teachers are likely to support a plurality of types of thinking, but even these will be grounded primarily in the teaching of their *subjects*. Thus, a broad conception of thinking, adaptable to a variety of content and skill objectives, is more likely to generate serious interest among a diverse population of high school teachers.

Rather than translating thinking into specific knowledge problems, skills, and attitudes for students, we began by asking what observable qualities of classroom activity would be most likely to help students achieve depth of understanding, intellectual skills, and dispositions of thoughtfulness. Thus, we moved from consideration of the nature of thinking in individual students to consideration of qualities that promote thoughtfulness in classrooms. Promoting classroom thoughtfulness requires both presenting students with higher-order challenges and helping them apply knowledge, skills, and dispositions to solve them. Emphasizing general qualities of classroom talk and activity rather than highly differentiated behaviors helps avoid the danger that in teaching a host of isolated thinking skills, one can actually undermine productive thinking.[7] A more general approach may also hold more promise both for students to solve new problems and for teachers to promote thinking across diverse lessons.

A broad set of criteria can strike at the heart of an underlying malady identified by many studies. At best, much classroom activity fails to challenge students to use their minds in *any* valuable ways; at worst, much classroom activity is nonsensical or mindless. The more serious problem, therefore, is not the failure to teach some specific aspect of thinking, but the profound absence of thoughtfulness in classrooms. Our general conception of thinking can address this basic issue. Ultimately, of course, teachers must focus on the content-specific activities that enhance understanding of their subjects, but the point here is to arrive at a general framework through which classrooms studying diverse subjects can be interpreted as promoting or undermining higher-order thinking.

In devising indicators of classroom thoughtfulness responsive to the points above, we initially rated lessons on 15 possible dimensions of classroom thoughtfulness, summarized in Table 3.1. Each was used to make an overall rating of an observed lesson on a five-point scale from 1 = "a very inaccurate" to 5 = "a very accurate" description of this lesson. After observing these qualities in 160 lessons in five "select" social studies departments and further examining them from a theoretical point of view, we chose the six main dimensions described below as most fundamental.[8]

1. *There was sustained examination of a few topics rather than superficial coverage of many.* Mastery of higher-order challenges requires in-depth study and sustained concentration on a limited number of topics or questions. Lessons that cover a large number of topics give students only a vague familiarity or awareness and thereby reduce the possibilities for building the complex knowledge, skills, and dispositions required to understand a topic.

2. *The lesson displayed substantive coherence and continuity.* Intelligent progress on higher-order challenges demands systematic inquiry that builds on relevant and accurate substantive knowledge in the field and that works toward the logical development and integration of ideas. In

contrast, lessons that teach material as unrelated fragments of knowledge, without pulling them together, undermine such inquiry.

3. *Students were given an appropriate amount of time to think, that is, to prepare responses to questions.* Thinking takes time, but often recitation, discussion, and written assignments pressure students to make responses before they have had enough time to reflect. Promoting thoughtfulness, therefore, requires periods of silence when students can ponder the validity of alternative responses, develop more elaborate reasoning, and experience patient reflection.

4. *The teacher asked challenging questions and/or structured challenging tasks (given the ability level and preparation of the students).* By our definition higher-order thinking occurs only when students are faced with questions or tasks that demand analysis, interpretation, or manipulation of information; that is, nonroutine mental work. In short, students must be faced with the challenge of how to use prior knowledge to gain new knowledge, rather than the task of merely retrieving prior knowledge.

5. *The teacher was a model of thoughtfulness.* To help students succeed with higher-order challenges, teachers themselves must model thoughtful dispositions as they teach. Of course, a thoughtful teacher would demonstrate many of the behaviors described above, but this scale is intended to capture a cluster of dispositions likely to be found in any thoughtful person. Key indicators include showing interest in students' ideas and in alternative approaches to problems; showing how he or she thought through a problem (rather than only the final answer); and acknowledging the difficulty of gaining a definitive understanding of problematic topics.

6. *Students offered explanations and reasons for their conclusions.* The answers or solutions to higher-order challenges are rarely self-evident. Their validity often rests on the quality of explanation or reasons given to support them. Therefore, beyond offering answers, students must also be able to produce explanations and reasons to support their conclusions.

The six dimensions were combined into a single scale (CHOT) that served as the indicator of classroom thoughtfulness for an observed lesson.[9] How often do high school social studies classes reflect the criteria of thoughtfulness just mentioned? How much do teachers differ? How much do departments differ? To what extent does the level of thoughtfulness observed depend on student background characteristics of the class? To answer these questions we conducted a study of high school social studies departments according to the design described below.

*(continued on p. 72)*

**Table 3.1**
**Nature of Discourse in 287 High School Social Studies Lessons (16 High Schools)**

Classes were rated from 1-5. 1 = "very inaccurate" description of class; 5 = "very accurate." Findings are reported as the percent of lessons receiving each rating.

| | 1 | 2 | 3 | 4 | 5 |
|---|---|---|---|---|---|
| *1 FEWTOP — In this class, there was sustained examination of a few topics rather than superficial coverage of many. | 8 | 17 | 24 | 26 | 24 |
| *2 SUBCOH — In this class, the lesson displayed substantive coherence and continuity. | 8 | 26 | 29 | 26 | 11 |
| *3 TIME — In this class, students were given an appropriate amount of time to think, that is, to prepare responses to questions. | 0 | 1 | 8 | 36 | 54 |
| 4. TCONS — In this class, the teacher carefully considered explanations and reasons for conclusions. | 25 | 37 | 23 | 12 | 4 |
| *5. TCHAL — In this class, the teacher asked challenging questions and/or structured challenging tasks (given the ability level and preparation of the students). | 4 | 19 | 25 | 29 | 23 |
| 6. TSOC — In this class, the teacher pressed individual students to justify or to clarify their assertions in a Socratic manner. | 53 | 32 | 11 | 2 | 3 |
| 7. TORIG — In this class, the teacher tried to get students to generate original and unconventional ideas, explanations, or solutions to problems. | 38 | 37 | 18 | 4 | 3 |

| | | | | | |
|---|---|---|---|---|---|
| *8. TMOD | In this classroom, the teacher was a model of thoughtfulness. (Principal indications are: The teacher showed appreciation for students' ideas and appreciation for alternative approaches or answers if based on sound reasoning; the teacher explained how he (she) thought through a problem; the teacher acknowledged the difficulty of gaining a definitive understanding of the topic.) | 4 | 24 | 36 | 24 | 11 |
| 9. SCRIT | In this class, students assumed the roles of questioner and critic. | 19 | 25 | 25 | 16 | 15 |
| *10. SEXPL | In this class, students offered explanations and reasons for their conclusions. | 20 | 21 | 25 | 23 | 13 |
| 11. SORIG | In this class, students generated original and unconventional ideas, explanations, hypotheses, or solutions to problems. | 12 | 17 | 49 | 20 | 2 |
| 12. SARTI | In this class, student contributions were articulate, germane to the topic, and connected to prior discussion. | 2 | 16 | 29 | 36 | 16 |
| 13. TALK | What proportion of students were active participants? | 0%<br>54 | 0-25%<br>4 | 25-50%<br>15 | 50-75%<br>35 | 75-100%<br>47 |
| 14. DISC | What proportion of time did students spend engaged in thoughtful discourse with each other? | 0%<br>54 | 1-25%<br>30 | 25-50%<br>8 | 50-75%<br>6 | ≥75%<br>2 |
| 15. INVO | What proportion of students showed genuine involvement in the topics discussed? (Cues include raising hands, attentiveness manifested by facial expression and body-language, interruptions motivated by involvement, length of student responses). | | 25%<br>19 | 25-50%<br>28 | 50-75%<br>26 | ≥75%<br>24 |

*These variables are considered minimal requirements for a thoughtful lesson.

## STUDY DESIGN AND METHODOLOGY

Between Fall 1986 and Spring 1990, the project conducted almost 500 lesson observations, and in-depth interviews with teachers, social studies department chairs, and principals in 16 demographically diverse high schools. Through national searches that involved nominations, phone interviews, and site visits, we identified three different sets of social studies departments: (1) those that place special emphasis on higher-order thinking, but that organize instruction according to familiar patterns in the comprehensive high school (henceforth the five "select" departments of Phase I); (2) those that make no special department-wide efforts toward higher-order thinking and are also conventionally organized (henceforth the seven "representative" departments of Phase II); and (3) those that involve a departmental emphasis on higher-order thinking and, in addition, have made significant changes in the organization of instruction (henceforth the four "restructured" departments of Phase III). Initial evidence of departmental emphasis on higher-order thinking was drawn from phone interviews with the department chair, examination of course syllabi, and classroom observations and teacher interviews completed in a one-day, two-person site visit.

Since we sought an estimate of the highest levels of classroom thoughtfulness, the strategy was to concentrate on those teachers in each department who emphasized higher-order thinking the most. But we also wanted evidence of opportunities for thoughtfulness for all students, not just the high achievers. The department chair at each school selected three main courses, taught by different teachers, to be observed at least four times over the school year. The three classes were to illustrate as much higher-order thinking as possible, but they were to include (1) a class with a substantial proportion of lower- and middle-achieving students; (2) a history course with a diverse range of students; and (3) any other class that best illustrated an emphasis on higher-order thinking (which usually comprised high achievers). Our analyses are based on four lesson observations from each of these three classes, plus six other lessons observed in each department drawn from at least two additional teachers. Within scheduling constraints, teachers were encouraged to select for our observation those lessons that placed most emphasis on higher-order thinking. In addition to recording ratings on the five-point dimensions, observers also wrote descriptive notes, especially to elaborate on high-scoring dimensions.[10]

Teachers, department chairs, and principals completed at least two hours of interviews.[11] These probed their written responses to questionnaires that explored their conceptions of and commitment to higher-order thinking as an educational goal, the factors they perceived as necessary to accomplish it, the barriers that stand in the way, and the kind of leadership devoted to it within the school.

Students were interviewed and/or surveyed about the kind of instruction they found engaging and challenging. In the representative and restructured schools students also took a test that called for higher-order thinking: writing a persuasive essay on a constitutional issue. The relationship between classroom thoughtfulness and student performance is discussed elsewhere;[12] the emphasis here is on the promotion of thoughtfulness in social studies classrooms.

## STUDENT ENGAGEMENT AND COGNITIVE CHALLENGE

Are students more engaged when they are challenged to think? A number of findings suggest that they are.

1. Observers rated both the level of thoughtfulness and the level of student engagement for each lesson. The correlation between the two was .57.[13]
2. Students indicated how engaged they were in their social studies class and how much it challenged them. The correlation between these ratings was .55.[14]
3. Comparing the top 25 percent with the bottom 25 percent of the classes on observer-rated engagement, we found that students in the top classes reported more cognitive challenge. Conversely, comparing the top 25 percent with the bottom 25 percent of the classes on observer-rated classroom thoughtfulness, students in the more thoughtful classes reported more engagement.[15]
4. When students indicated which subjects (English, social studies, science, math) they found most engaging and most challenging, the correlations ranged from .60 to .69.[16]
5. In open-ended interviews students were asked to identify a really engaging lesson or assignment in social studies and then asked if they were required to think very hard in that lesson or assignment. About three quarters of the students said they were. They were also asked to identify questions or tasks within a lesson that they found interesting, as well as questions or tasks that made them think or really use their mind. About half of the examples were identical.[17]
6. When students were asked to identify, independently, the most interesting and worthwhile class taken in the past year, and the class that made them think the hardest, almost 60 percent named the same class. This association was especially strong among students from lower socio-

economic groups. When students were asked to identify the class in which they put forth the most effort and the one they found most mentally challenging, over two thirds of the students nominated the same class.

7. Students were asked to rate the degree of interest and degree of difficulty they encountered when their social studies teacher engaged in certain pedagogical behaviors (e.g., solving problems where there is no single correct answer; questioning or criticizing arguments of other students). Correlations between interest and difficulty on four of five items ranged between .42 and .55.

These diverse findings indicate that students are more likely to try, to concentrate, and to be interested in academic study when they are challenged to think. The correlations do not prove that intellectually challenging classes necessarily cause higher student engagement. It is possible, for example, that teachers respond to engaged students by promoting more thinking, and this issue will be addressed later. Having found an association between classroom thoughtfulness and student engagement, we will next report on how often and under what conditions students are challenged to think.

## LEVELS OF CLASSROOM THOUGHTFULNESS AND DIFFERENCES DUE TO TEACHERS, DEPARTMENTS, AND STUDENT BACKGROUND

### Overall Levels

How much thoughtfulness was actually observed across all schools? Table 3.1 presents frequencies on 15 dimensions. Some dimensions occurred very rarely, especially Socratic reasoning (6), teacher encouraging originality (7), and students participating in thoughtful discourse with each other (14). Others showed high frequencies, such as teachers allowing enough time for students to respond (3) and students participating in class (13). Frequencies on the six minimal dimensions of thoughtfulness showed considerable variance, except for time, which was consistently high. Using the six minimal dimensions as a scale of classroom thoughtfulness, the mean of 287 lessons was 3.40 on the five-point scale.[18] The mean of the four highest-scoring departments was 3.92. We conclude that even among the more successful teachers and departments there is considerable room for improvement.

## Teacher Differences

Teachers varied from a high mean of 4.63 to a low of 2.21, and several teachers were represented at different points in the distribution. Of the 48 teachers observed, only 12 averaged above 4, but 12 averaged below 3. Teachers were reasonably consistent in the degree of thoughtfulness found in the four or more lessons observed. The research did not assess the consistency of individual teachers in different types of classes such as advanced placement, "regular," or "basic" tracks, but later we will see that higher-ability classes generally showed higher levels of thoughtfulness. In short, teachers vary considerably from one another in the levels of classroom thoughtfulness they promote, and most teachers are rather consistent in the extent to which they promote thoughtfulness across several lessons within a class.[19]

## Departmental Differences

Even with considerable variation among teachers, is it possible that some social studies departments have more thoughtful lessons than others? If so, analysis of the properties of the more successful departments might reveal strategies that would enhance thoughtfulness in others. Department totals varied considerably. Departmental means, summarized graphically in Figure 3.1, ranged from 2.88 to 4.05. The mean of the highest four departments (3.92) far exceeded the mean of the lowest four (2.92). As indicated in Figure 3.1, there was overlap among the three groups of select, representative, and restructured departments, but in relative terms the means of these groups also differed considerably.[20] The actual significance of departmental differences on lesson thoughtfulness, however, may depend in part on the influence of background features of each class.

## Student Background Features of the Class

Would teachers assume that older students are more capable of complex thought and therefore emphasize higher-order thinking more frequently in 12th Grade than 9th Grade classes? Would classes with a preponderance of high-achieving students offer consistently higher levels of thoughtfulness than classes with large numbers of low achievers? Would the proportion of African-American students in a class be associated with the level of thoughtfulness? Are elective courses more likely to promote thoughtfulness than required courses? We examined these issues by regressing CHOT on the relevant variables.

**Figure 3.1**
**Distribution of Departmental Means on Classroom Thoughtfulness (CHOT = 1–5)**

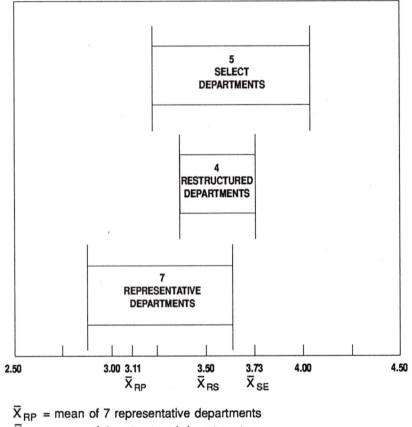

$\overline{X}_{RP}$ = mean of 7 representative departments
$\overline{X}_{RS}$ = mean of 4 restructured departments
$\overline{X}_{SE}$ = mean of 5 select departments

Results indicated that when these background factors were simultaneously controlled, the ability level of the class (and only this variable) had a sizable association with lesson thoughtfulness.[21] If a causal relationship were to be inferred, the hypothesis of teacher expectations would make sense: Teachers perceive higher-ability groups as more capable of participating in thoughtful discourse, and therefore they offer such groups more opportunities. This finding was expected and is further evidence that classes with higher percentages of low-achieving students are deprived of educational opportunities.[22] On the other hand, it can be considered good news that when class ability level was held constant, neither race nor age of the students seemed to determine the degree of thoughtfulness, and that the variance in lesson thoughtfulness explained by all background features together was less than 10 percent. This supports the more hopeful prospect that other variables (perhaps unmeasured) have far more impact than student background.

We found, for example, that departmental differences in classroom thoughtfulness had at least twice the association with the thoughtfulness of lessons than did class ability level. The strong impact of the department in relation to background features offers hope, because, in contrast to background characteristics of students (age, race, prior school achievement), features of departments can conceivably be changed for the better. Within the group of select departments, student background features had no effect, which indicates that some departments are successful not only in promoting classroom thoughtfulness, but also in delivering it equitably to classes of students with different background characteristics.

## QUALITIES CRITICAL TO SUCCESS

Differences in thought and practice between the most and least successful teachers and departments can suggest possible factors that need to be changed to increase classroom thoughtfulness. First we compare the thinking of individual teachers, and then we compare the kinds of leadership and institutional contexts that appear to promote thoughtfulness.

### Teachers' Thinking

Onosko (1989, 1991a) studied differences in the thinking of teachers whose lessons scored in the highest one fifth versus the lowest one fifth on classroom thoughtfulness. While the sample was small — 10 teachers in each group — interesting differences emerged in teachers' instructional goals, their thoughts on the problem of depth versus breadth of content coverage, and their conceptions of thinking.

In contrast to lower scorers, high scorers were more likely to identify student thinking as their highest priority goal, and they found the development of students' thinking more interesting than exposing students to subject matter content. When asked what gave them satisfaction as a teacher, they tended (more than lower scorers) to identify student behaviors closely associated with thinking (e.g., "seeing students start to make connections," "students wrestling with values and making links," "teaching students to generalize from data"). High scorers' open-ended goal statements were lengthier and more detailed, with a more impassioned focus on thinking.

On the issue of depth versus breadth of content coverage, both groups felt persisting conflict, but high scorers were more likely to identify coverage as detrimental to students' thinking. High scorers were more likely to attribute the pressure to external sources such as state tests, curriculum guidelines, and the department chair, whereas lower scorers said the main pressure came from within themselves. Lower scorers, including some who had taught advanced placement U.S. history courses, felt that broad coverage was important, but high scorers believed that breadth of coverage inhibited thinking. Larry, a lower scorer, explained,

> We really have to sacrifice depth to introduce the students to the areas we feel are important. . . . We are a survey course; we want to introduce the student to the areas and we encourage them to take other courses later on if they are interested.

Harold, a high scorer, felt too much coverage pressure from the state curriculum guidelines and tests.

> I do not preoccupy myself with finishing the curriculum. Instead, I attempt to teach whatever I teach well and select classroom topics and materials very carefully. . . . I don't emphasize content coverage. It's ludicrous to attempt to cover 100 years of history in a month or two. I focus on concepts or ideas.

Teachers were asked two questions to explore their conceptions of thinking: Do you have a conception of thinking that guides your teaching (If so, summarize its main aspects)? Consider your best thinkers; what distinguishes them from other students?

Higher scorers had more to say about the nature of thinking. They included points of clarification and subtle distinctions between their own views and possible alternative conceptions. For example, Hans challenged the notion that Bloom's cognitive skills should be viewed hierarchically, Hilary argued that students' intellectual curiosity should not be equated with inherent cognitive capacity, and Hanson asserted that the development of students' thinking should not be divorced from the development of students' values. Elaboration of this sort was missing in the brief statements of lower scorers.

In contrast to lower scorers, higher scorers identified a greater variety of dispositions and thinking skills. Hugh illustrates the importance of dispositions.

> A good thinker isn't afraid if someone challenges a position . . .
> is willing to take a look at someone else's hypothesis or theory
> even if it's 180 degrees apart from his own. . . . I'd like kids to
> always be questioning, to always be probing. You should always
> be on edge, never comfortable, no matter how well you've di-
> gested the material.

The main skills mentioned by higher scorers dealt with understanding, analyzing, manipulating, and generalizing from data; understanding the relevance of data to a central theme, formulating hypotheses and conclusions; and relating learning to one's own life experience or to current affairs.

Even if differences in teachers' thought are associated with differences in practice (i.e., in their levels of classroom thoughtfulness), this alone does not establish a causal link from thought to practice. Nevertheless, these findings are consistent with previous research that highlights a connection between teachers' thought and practice, and they suggest that it may be useful to help teachers reflect more systematically on their goals, conceptions of thinking, and management of the dilemma of depth versus coverage. Other strategies for helping individual teachers to promote higher-order thinking are summarized in Newmann, Onosko, and Stevenson (1990).

## Leadership

The main purpose of our study was to understand the extent and determinants of differences at the school or departmental level. Having found that departments do in fact differ in the levels of classroom thoughtfulness they promote, we asked about the extent to which differences in school leadership and organizational structure might account for differences in classroom thoughtfulness. We defined the most successful schools as those scoring more than one standard deviation (.38) above the mean for all schools (3.40). These included three select schools: Grandville, Carlsberg, and Arnold. The least successful were those scoring more than one standard deviation below the mean, which involved four representative schools: Erskine, Downing, Wadsworth, and Pierce.

Based on observations and staff interviews dealing with the nature of departmental and principal leadership, we found differences between the top-scoring and bottom-scoring schools related to goals, curriculum, pedagogy, and school culture.[23] In the top schools, department chairs, with support from principals, worked to develop a focus within the social studies department on the goal of promoting students' thinking. The three top schools varied considerably in their approach to higher-order thinking, but in contrast to the bottom schools — all of which lacked a coherent departmental focus on thinking — social studies departments in the top schools each aimed toward a common vision for promoting students' thinking. Grandville used a modified version of Bloom's taxonomy to structure generalizations, concepts, and themes in all courses. Carlsberg adopted a common procedure for each lesson: first, posing a central question at the beginning to focus student thinking, and second, structuring teacher-centered discussion to answer the question. Arnold also presented students with a central question or issue that framed each unit and asked them to create metaphors, analogies, and other sources of evidence and insight to achieve understanding.

The common goals were reinforced and implemented by the department heads' active participation in curriculum development with colleagues in the department who often worked in teams of teachers who taught the same course. The top departments varied in resources allocated for curriculum development, but all three schools worked on curriculum during the school year and/or summers. The main objective was not simply to update course content, but to do so in ways that would operationalize the department's approach to developing students' thinking. At two of the top schools, principals provided special support for curriculum development. In contrast, low-scoring schools participated in curriculum development, but it tended not to be focused on a common departmental vision of thinking.

Department heads in the top three schools made special efforts to comment in considerable detail on their colleagues' teaching and to support peer observation and discussion of specific pedagogy that promotes thinking. At Carlsberg, the department head taught demonstration lessons, with colleagues observing and criticizing afterward. Department meetings there have been used to view videotapes of colleagues' teaching and to jointly plan lessons. The principal at Carlsberg also took an active role in detailed observation and clinical supervision of teaching. In the lower-scoring schools, department heads' and principals' attention to pedagogy involved only perfunctory required visits for formal evaluation.

The efforts of department heads and principals in the high-scoring schools to shape goals, curriculum, and pedagogy toward an emphasis on thinking seem to have nurtured the kind of collegial faculty culture in these schools that has been found in other research to contribute to school effectiveness (e.g., Bryk, Lee, & Smith, 1990; Rosenholtz, 1989). These schools show how leaders can build such a culture by helping teachers develop and keep their sights on a common instructional mission, by directing technical assistance both from within and outside the system on this goal, and by providing material and emotional support for teachers to help one another approach the work critically.

## Organizational Features

Some teachers may be committed to the promotion of higher-order thinking, but find too many obstacles in the existing organizational structure of high schools. Discussions on the restructuring of education suggest that major organizational changes may be needed to assist teachers in the promotion of higher-order thinking; for example, increased opportunities for team planning among teachers to generate curriculum oriented toward thinking; smaller classes and reduced student load to allow teachers to respond more thoughtfully to students' work; changes in the scheduling of instruction to allow for more sustained inquiry than is possible in short class periods. How important are structural features such as these?

To investigate the importance of organizational features, we examined four social studies departments that we perceived in the selection process to indicate a sincere emphasis on higher-order thinking but that also operated in schools with organizationally innovative structures along the lines just mentioned. Each of the four used extensive team planning, and in three of the schools this occurred across different subjects. Three of the four included classes well below 25 students, and three of the four included scheduling changes that permitted flexibility in the conduct of instruction.

Information in Figure 3.1 shows that although the restructured departments scored above the representative departments and above the overall mean, none of the restructured departments scored highly enough on classroom thoughtfulness to be included in the top group. Furthermore, the highest-scoring schools did not differ substantially in structural features from the lowest-scoring ones, except that in two of the three highest-scoring schools, the department chair taught only one class per semester — a structural feature that allowed considerable time to exercise program leadership. How might we explain the finding that innovative structural features do not seem critical to achieving high levels of classroom thoughtfulness?

In examining the influence of organizational features on higher-order thinking, Ladwig (1991) distinguishes between organizational structures and organizational programs. Structures include the amount of time available to teachers for planning and sharing ideas with colleagues; the amount of time that teachers and students work together in classes and the degree of flexibility in how the time is spent; the number of students in a class and the total number taught by teachers; and the degree of authority teachers have individually and collectively to make important decisions about curriculum and teaching. Organizational programs could include departmentally coordinated curriculum design and revision; staff development activities using both outside authorities and collegial expertise to develop common goals and curriculum; and an organized program of peer observation and critique of individual teaching.

Organizational structures and programs are logically independent of one another. That is, having innovative structures does not necessarily entail having any particular instructional program. One would expect the highest levels of classroom thoughtfulness to occur in schools that combined a strong programmatic focus on higher-order thinking with the innovative organizational structures that seem to facilitate such a focus. The restructured schools we studied, however, did not manifest strong organizational programs aimed at promoting higher-order thinking. These departments expressed a clear interest in the goal and worked to implement it in several classes. In this sense they distinguished themselves from and scored higher than the representative schools. On the other hand, their programmatic efforts for higher-order thinking were not as focused nor as comprehensive as those in the highest-scoring three departments located in conventionally organized schools.

The select high-scoring departments in conventional schools had focused programmatic agendas for higher-order thinking. In contrast, staff in the restructured schools were involved in several programmatic activities at once that usually encompassed a number of educational goals beyond the promotion of higher-order thinking; for example, individualizing and personalizing school experiences for students; empowering faculty to develop curriculum and school policy; reducing negative consequences of tracking and ability grouping; creating interdisciplinary curricula; building special experiences for students at risk; and developing new methods of assessment. It is possible that having to deal with such a variety of issues tended to dilute the programmatic concentration that might otherwise have been channeled to the promotion of higher-order thinking.

Within the group of restructured schools, it is interesting to note that the two highest-scoring departments were part of efforts to restructure the entire school, the next was a restructured program within a traditionally structured school, and in the lowest scoring of these departments, restructuring occurred primarily within individual courses. The sample is too small to allow generalization about the process of restructuring in a larger, more diverse set of schools, but this finding suggests that school-wide efforts to restructure may offer more potential for reinforcing organizational programs for higher-order thinking than restructuring aimed only at schools within schools or within courses. School-wide initiatives could offer more of the support that teachers need from administrators and colleagues to emphasize student thinking and depth of understanding, rather than absorption of knowledge fragments and coverage of information.

The relative position of restructured schools (in Figure 3.1) illustrates several points: (1) Innovative structural features alone offer no advantages; strong program design may be more important. (2) Conventional school structures do not preclude reasonably high levels of classroom thoughtfulness. (3) Schools that combine significant restructuring with a strong programmatic emphasis on higher-order thinking may conceivably achieve levels of classroom thoughtfulness higher than we have yet been able to observe. In short, the keys to success seem to be strong organizational programs aimed at teachers' thinking and practice; and if these are supported through restructuring, we might well expect even higher levels of classroom thoughtfulness.

## CONFRONTING THE BARRIERS

In our search for thoughtful classrooms and for characteristics that distinguish between more and less successful departments, we have been struck by persistent and deeply rooted obstacles — within teachers, schools, and the larger society — that inhibit the promotion of higher-order thinking for students. Although we have identified some patterns of leadership and organizational features that seem to facilitate success, we have not discovered proven strategies for changing weak departments into strong ones or for improving the performance of the more successful.

Observations and interviews have convinced us, however, that leadership, staff development, and restructuring activities should aim directly at reversing or reducing the negative impact of four major barriers.

(1) The dominant conception of education as transmission of items of knowledge covering a broad range of topics, rather than the development of thinking; (2) The belief that students are incapable of or uninterested in higher order thinking; (3) Insufficient time for teachers to work with individual students and to plan instruction; and (4) A culture of professional isolation that prevents teachers from helping one another to achieve the difficult goal of teaching for higher order thinking. (Onosko, 1991b)

Unless improvement strategies within and out of schools attack these problems directly, little progress will be made. The following elaboration on these barriers can guide leadership, staff development, and restructuring in this area.

Although the promotion of thinking is widely endorsed as the ultimate end of education, it is persistently undermined by the effort to transmit information on countless topics to ensure that children possess basic (cultural, scientific, mathematical, economic, and civic) "literacy." Learning new information is, of course, critical for education and for thinking, but the pressure to cover material leaves little time to reflect on what is learned and to develop understanding and the capacity to use knowledge in creative ways to answer unforeseen questions. As a result, most of the time students receive only superficial exposure to countless items of knowledge that low-achieving students rarely learn and that high-achieving students remember only long enough to succeed on tests.

The pressure to transmit broad surveys of information is intense. It comes from interest groups — professional, political, economic, and other — who influence curriculum guidelines, textbooks, tests, and the education of teachers in universities. Teachers, administrators, and others will need a lot of help in bringing to curriculum more balance between the legitimate need to transmit a variety of information, on the one hand, and, on the other, the necessity of excluding material so that some topics can be studied in sufficient depth for students to develop understanding, the capacity to master higher-order challenges, and the intellectual empowerment that this brings.

One of the first steps is to help educators develop rationales for education that include well-reasoned conceptions of thinking applicable to all students. As we have indicated, in-depth knowledge is required to master higher-order challenges, but so are intellectual skills and dispositions of thoughtfulness. Research has indicated that students of all ages are capable of complex thought; that the more experience one has with a subject, the better the quality of thought; and that high-quality thinking about a problem does not necessarily require prior memorization of large quantities of information. Information is necessary to meet higher-order challenges, but information can be accessed through methods other than memory (e.g., having books and computers available to consult), and large quantities of information are not always needed — the amount and type of information needed depends on the nature of the problem. In order to develop informed staff commitment to the promotion of thinking, teachers will need time to study and carefully consider conceptions of thinking, the role of information in it, and the actual capacities of children. The points just mentioned will challenge assumptions and deeply held beliefs of many teachers, and so it is important to examine these matters within a supportive climate of open dialogue.

If teachers are to stress depth of understanding as much as vague awareness, and if they are to help students manipulate knowledge to solve new problems, rather than only to absorb knowledge and reproduce it, changes will be needed in curriculum content, instructional materials, teaching techniques, and tests. While some exceptional teachers manage to promote high levels of thoughtfulness in conventionally organized schools, we believe that most will need more time during the school day for planning, for responding to students' individual work, and for getting help from colleagues on how to traverse new, unknown, and often formidable educational territory.

Several organizational barriers stand in the way, especially the small amount of time that teachers have for these activities and the way teachers' time is organized. Planning periods of 50 minutes per day are inadequate, especially when teachers are responsible for more than 100 students daily and must prepare two or more different courses. Preparation periods are rarely scheduled to permit departmental colleagues to observe and confer with one another about the teaching of common courses. Staff development time, offered only a few half-days per year, is usually unrelated to any long-term agenda such as the promotion of thinking in social studies. When students are instructed in classes of 30 that meet 50 minutes per day, there is little opportunity to develop sustained inquiry—how often do adults solve problems in 50-minute blocks scheduled at the same time each day? The dominant mode of large-group instruction deprives students of feedback from both teacher and peers on their individual work.

To attack these problems, schools should reconsider not only increasing the amount of time available and reducing the number of students per teacher, but, more important, reorganizing the time; for example, by arranging for common planning time among teachers, by clustering both planning time and instructional time into longer continuous blocks, and by devoting more of the instructional time to small-group and individual study to allow more students to participate in thoughtful dialogue.

Suppose many of these suggestions were followed, and that teachers actually received technical help in understanding the nature of thinking and how to teach it, and administrators reorganized schools to allow more productive interaction among teachers and students. We suspect that increased technical and organizational assistance would not be enough to ensure the promotion of higher-order thinking for all high school students. In spite of paying lip service to the ideal for years, most students, parents, teachers, civic leaders, and other citizens have consistently made the cultivation of thoughtfulness a low priority among educational aims. Why?

The question leads to the hypothesis that the powerful forces of human personality, social structure, and cultural values may stand in the way of committed implementation of these otherwise reasonable proposals.

Higher-order thinking often calls for the resolution of conflicting views, tolerance for uncertainty and ambiguity, self-criticism, independence of judgment, and serious consideration of ideas that may challenge conventional wisdom. In this sense, thinking involves difficult mental work that can be personally unsettling, because it disrupts cognitive stability, order, and predictability. For many, it is psychologically more comfortable not to think too deeply about anything.

Critical thinking also increases the probability of youth challenging adult authority and of citizens challenging economic and political centers of power. Thus, thinking can be considered subversive and socially dangerous by dominant interests whose legitimacy is questioned. Some would argue that the very survival of certain social institutions (e.g., advertising, hierarchies of labor within corporations, capitalism) depends on limiting the opportunity to think to a small segment of the population.

Finally, cultural orientations that prescribe certain forms of interpersonal relations, religious and artistic expression, and play and recreation can minimize the importance of the kind of cognitive activity promoted here as higher-order thinking.

Our findings indicate that it is possible for high school departments to promote higher-order thinking and that students are more engaged in thoughtful classes. If those committed to the promotion of thinking in education are to confront the fundamental issues just raised, however, they will need to view this as a long-term project. To begin, it will be necessary to break down barriers of professional isolation, especially evident in secondary schools, in which teachers take pride in and are rewarded primarily for working alone. Collegial networks must be cultivated to provide emotional and technical support for teachers trying to work with students in new ways, and also to build a political base from which to confront resistance in the society at large. In short, transforming education into critical use of the mind involves far more than absorbing new research knowledge, adopting new programs, or changing a few teaching methods. Instead, it must be seen as a complex, long-term, and risky adventure in social change.

## NOTES

Major contributions to this work have been made by Dae-Dong Hahn, Bruce King, James Ladwig, Cameron McCarthy, Joseph Onosko, Francis Schrag, Robert Stevenson, and the cooperative staff and students in sixteen high schools.

1. Examples of national reports emphasizing thinking include American Association for the Advancement of Science (1989), Committee for Economic Development (1985), National Council of Teachers of Mathematics (1989), and Quality Education for Minorities Project (1990).

2. Material in this section is discussed in more detail in Newmann (1990a).

3. Various points in the argument for the centrality of knowledge have been made by Glaser (1984), McPeck (1981), and Nickerson (1988).

4. Various points in the argument for skills as the most central resource have been made by Beyer (1987); de Bono (1983); Herrnstein, Nickerson, De Sanchez, and Swets (1986); and Marzano et al. (1988).

5. Various points in the argument for dispositions as a central resource have been made by Cornbleth (1985), Dewey (1933), and Schrag (1988).

6. Those who emphasize interaction and interdependence among these resources include Bransford, Sherwood, Vye, and Rieser (1986); Ennis (1987); Greeno (1989); Perkins and Salomon (1989); and Walsh and Paul (1987).

7. The high degree of specificity that can occur in the naming of thinking skills is illustrated in Marzano et al. (1988), which notes 21 different core thinking skills, including such items as defining problems, setting goals, observing, ordering, inferring, summarizing, and establishing criteria.

8. The development of these indicators and selection of the six most critical are described more fully in Newmann (1990a, 1990b). See also Schrag (1987, 1989).

9. Items on the scale have a reasonably high level of internal consistency (Cronbach alpha = .82). Exploratory factor analysis and LISREL modeling also identified these dimensions as a distinct construct of thoughtfulness. Such analyses for a sample of select departments were reported in Newmann (1990b). Analyses for the entire sample of lessons showed similar results.

10. To estimate inter-rater reliability, 87 lessons were observed independently by different pairs of raters drawn from a team of six researchers. Considering the six dimensions in the CHOT scale, each scored from 1 to 5, the two observers agreed precisely in 64 percent of the ratings, they differed by one point or less on 96 percent of the ratings, and the overall average correlation between two raters was .76.

11. Principals in the representative schools were interviewed for one hour.

12. Newmann (1990c) describes the test. Newmann (1991) initially found a positive association between classroom thoughtfulness and student performance, but the relationship disappeared after controlling for student scores on a rigorous pretest. Since none of the observed teachers concentrated instruction either on constitutional understanding or on persuasive writing, and since our indicators of classroom thoughtfulness were so general (i.e., not derived from the specific understandings and skills measured in the tests), these results were predictable. Effects of these qualities of classroom thoughtfulness on students' thinking would best be investigated through performance tasks designed to assess the unique goals of each teacher. In this study it was logistically impossible to conduct such an assessment.

13. Based on 479 observed lessons in all 16 schools.

14. To assess engagement and challenge, we created two scales. For engage-

ment, students were asked, "In this social studies class, how often (from never to almost every day) do you . . . Try as hard as you can? . . . Think what you are supposed to learn is interesting and worthwhile? . . . Find yourself concentrating so hard that time passes quickly?" Challenge was measured by asking students, "How often in this social studies class do you . . . Feel yourself challenged to think hard and use your mind? . . . Have to explain to the teacher how you got your opinion? . . . Have to show that you *really understand,* not just give the right answer?" The correlation is based on student surveys in the 11 schools of Phases II and III (N = 1,315). The alpha reliability for the engagement scale was .59 and for challenge it was .65.

15. The findings are based on classes observed in Phases II and III. Differences in student-perceived challenge and engagement amount to about one point on a nine-point scale, which is about half a standard deviation. Student ratings of engagement and cognitive challenge were based on their perceptions of the entire class throughout the year, which included homework, tests, and other activities. Observer ratings were based only on approximately four lesson observations. This may account for the lack of a stronger relationship between engagement and cognitive challenge in this type of analysis.

16. This question was asked only of students who were interviewed in Phase III (N = 48).

17. Findings in points 5,6, and 7 are taken from Stevenson (1988) and based on student interviews (N = 45) in Phase I schools.

18. The standard deviation was .82, indicating that about 64 percent of the lessons ranged between 2.58 and 4.22.

19. Differences between teachers accounted for 51 percent of the total variance among lessons.

20. The difference between the top and bottom quartiles was 2.6 times the overall departmental standard deviation (.38) or 1.2 times the overall standard deviation among lessons (.82). The difference between the select and representative departments was about 1.4 times the overall departmental standard deviation; the restructured–representative difference was about 1 standard deviation; and the difference between the select and restructured department was about .6 of the overall departmental standard deviation. These differences accounted for about 21 percent of the total variance in thoughtfulness among lessons.

21. Ability level was measured as the teacher's estimate of the percentage of students whose grade-point average placed them in the lowest (1), middle (2), and highest (3) one third of the school achievement distribution. On average, a one-point increase in class ability level (scaled from 1 to 3) would be associated with about a one third point increase in classroom thoughtfulness for the lesson (scaled from 1 to 5).

22. In calling attention to teacher expectations (an unmeasured variable here) as a way of explaining the correlation between class ability and classroom thoughtfulness, I do not mean to underestimate the actual difficulties teachers face in promoting higher-order thinking with low-achieving students.

23. This analysis of leadership is based on McCarthy and Schrag (1990) and King (1991).

## REFERENCES

American Association for the Advancement of Science. (1989). *Science for all Americans: A Project 2061 report on literacy goals in science, mathematics and technology.* Washington, DC: Author.

Beyer, B. (1987). *Practical strategies for the teaching of thinking.* Boston: Allyn & Bacon.

Bransford, J., Sherwood, R., Vye, N., & Rieser, J. (1986). Teaching thinking and problem solving. *American Psychologist, 41*(10), 1078–1089.

Bryk, A. S., Lee, V. E., & Smith, J. B. (1990). High school organization and its effects on teachers and students: An interpretive summary of the research. In W. Clune & J. Witte (Eds.), *Choice and control in American education: Vol. 1. The theory of choice and control in American education* (pp. 135–226). Philadelphia: Falmer Press.

Committee for Economic Development. (1985). *Investing in our children.* Washington, DC: Author.

Cornbleth, C. (1985). Critical thinking and cognitive processes. In W. B. Stanley (Ed.), *Review of research in social studies education: 1976–1983* (pp. 11–63). Boulder, CO: ERIC Clearinghouse for Social Studies/Social Science Education.

Cuban, L. (1984). *How teachers taught: Constancy and change in American classrooms: 1890–1980.* New York: Longman.

de Bono, E. (1983). The direct teaching of thinking as a skill. *Phi Delta Kappan, 64*(10), 703–708.

Dewey, J. (1933). *How we think.* Boston: D.C. Heath.

Ennis, R. H. (1987). A taxonomy of critical thinking dispositions and abilities. In J. B. Baron & R. J. Sternberg (Eds.), *Teaching for thinking.* New York: Freeman.

Glaser, R. (1984). Education and thinking: The role of knowledge. *American Psychologist, 39*(2), 93–105.

Goodlad, J. I. (1984). *A place called school: Prospects for the future.* New York: McGraw-Hill.

Greeno, J. G. (1989). A perspective on thinking. *American Psychologist, 44*(2), 134–141.

Herrnstein, R. J., Nickerson, R. S., De Sanchez, M., & Swets, J. A. (1986). Teaching thinking skills. *American Psychologist, 41*(11), 1279–1289.

Hoetker, J., & Ahlbrand, W. (1969). The persistence of recitation. *American Educational Research Journal, 6*(2), 145–167.

King, M. B. (1991). Leadership efforts that facilitate classroom thoughtfulness in social studies. *Theory and Research in Social Education, 19*(4), 366–389.

Ladwig, J. G. (1991). Organizational features and classroom thoughtfulness in secondary social studies departments. *Theory and Research in Social Education, 19*(4), 390–408.

Marzano, R. J., Brandt, R. S., Hughes, C. S., Jones, B. F., Presseisen, B. Z., Rankin, S. C., & Suhor, C. (1988). *Dimensions of thinking: A framework for curriculum and instruction.* Alexandria, VA: Association for Supervision and Curriculum Development.

McCarthy, C., & Schrag, F. (1990). Departmental and principal leadership in promoting higher order thinking. *Journal of Curriculum Studies, 22*(6), 529–543.

McNeil, L. M. (1986). *Contradictions of control: School structure and school knowledge.* New York: Routledge & Kegan Paul.

McPeck, J. E. (1981). *Critical thinking and education.* New York: St. Martins.

National Council of Teachers of Mathematics. (1989). *Curriculum and evaluation standards for school mathematics.* Reston, VA: Author.

Newmann, F. M. (1990a). Higher order thinking in social studies: A rationale for the assessment of classroom thoughtfulness. *Journal of Curriculum Studies, 22*(1), 41–56.

Newmann, F. M. (1990b). Qualities of thoughtful social studies classes: An empirical profile. *Journal of Curriculum Studies, 22*(3), 253–275.

Newmann, F. M. (1990c). A test of higher order thinking in social studies. *Social Education, 54*(6), 369–373.

Newmann, F. M. (1991). Classroom thoughtfulness and students' higher order thinking: Common indicators and diverse social studies courses. *Theory and Research in Social Education, 19*(4), 409–431.

Newmann, F. M., Onosko, J., & Stevenson, R. B. (1990). Staff development for higher order thinking: A synthesis of practical wisdom. *Journal of Staff Development, 11*(3), 48–55.

Nickerson, R. S. (1988). On improving thinking through instruction. In E. Z. Rothkopf (Ed.), *Review of Research in Education, 15* (pp. 3–57). Washington, DC: American Educational Research Association.

Onosko, J. (1989). Comparing teachers' thinking about promoting students' thinking. *Theory and Research in Social Education, 17*(3),174–195.

Onosko, J. (1991a). *Differences in teacher thought between the most and least successful in promoting classroom thoughtfulness.* Paper presented to the annual meeting of the American Educational Research Association, Chicago.

Onosko, J. (1991b). Barriers to the promotion of higher order thinking in social studies. *Theory and Research in Social Education, 19*(4), 340–365.

Perkins, D. N., & Salomon, G. (1989). Are cognitive skills context-bound? *Educational Researcher, 18*(1), 16–25.

Powell, A. G., Farrar, E., & Cohen, D. K. (1985). *The shopping mall high school: Winners and losers in the educational marketplace.* Boston: Houghton Mifflin.

Quality Education for Minorities Project. (1990). *Education that works: An action plan for the education of minorities.* Cambridge: Author, Massachusetts Institute of Technology.

Rosenholtz, S. J. (1989). *Teachers' workplace: A social organizational analysis.* White Plains, NY: Longman.

Schrag, F. (1987). *Evaluating thinking in school.* Madison, WI: National Center on Effective Secondary Schools.

Schrag, F. (1988). *Thinking in school and society.* London: Routledge & Kegan Paul.

Schrag, F. (1989). Are there levels of thinking? *Teachers College Record, 90*(4), 529–533.

Stevenson, R. B. (1988). *Engagement and cognitive challenge in high school: A study of student perspectives.* Unpublished doctoral dissertation. University of Wisconsin-Madison.

Walsh, D., & Paul, R. W. (1987). *The goal of critical thinking: From educational ideal to educational reality.* Washington, DC: American Federation of Teachers.

# CHAPTER 4

# Building New Programs for Students at Risk

## Gary G. Wehlage and Gregory A. Smith

Thus far our colleagues have examined how authentic instructional conversation and promoting higher-order thinking can help to engage students. Teachers, parents, and students tell us, however, that even with the "best" teaching, some students are more likely to be engaged in school than others. They say that students at risk of school failure are far more difficult to engage than others. Youth can be "at risk" in different ways and for different reasons. An adolescent girl can be at risk of pregnancy; a boy can be at risk of drug abuse. And the presence of one risk factor can lead to others. This chapter focuses on students who are at risk of school failure and dropping out. Although definitions and estimates vary, we think at least 30 percent of the students in American secondary schools are at risk in the sense that they have only marginal prospects for succeeding in school.[1]

The causes of failure and dropping out are complex. Students' social class and family background are most often cited. Coming from a single-parent home, for example, is considered to be a risk factor, and the number of students coming from such homes has been increasing for several years. The former "typical" home of parents and their two children has almost vanished in the United States. Hodgkinson (1991) pointed out that the "Norman Rockwell" family of a working father, housewife mother, and two children now constitutes only about 6 percent of American homes.

Hodgkinson also described the economic, health, and educational consequences of changes in family structure and welfare. Trends at the end of the 1980s indicated that single mothers who have never been married were raising about 4.3 million children (about 10 percent of the K–12 student population), and that about 50 percent of the nation's youth will spend some time before age 18 being raised by a single parent. Currently 15 million children are being raised by single mothers whose incomes are near or below the poverty line. About 25 percent of pregnant women receive no medical care during the first trimester of their pregnancy. Although the United States is often seen as a land of opportunity, its young people are actually more vulnerable to poverty, divorce, homicide, infant mortality, and teen pregnancy than children in other industrialized nations.

We see two implications of the escalating proportions of youth at risk. One is that social policy in the society as a whole must confront more directly the challenge of rebuilding social capital. This will be discussed in Chapter 7. The second is that in spite of the difficulties of building social capital through institutions beyond schools, schools must assume immediate responsibility for the success of at-risk youth. In Chapter 1, in the case of Marvin, we saw how schools undermine membership and authentic work for at-risk students, thereby *increasing* the likelihood of school failure and dropping out. Other research, such as that dealing with retention in grade, the quality of instruction in low-track classes, and schools' relationships to low-income minority parents, further documents the schools' contributions to increasing failure rates for at-risk students.[2]

On a more positive note, we have studied individual schools that avoid these problems and find ways to increase engagement and achievement of students at risk. We have also studied entire school districts that have launched ambitious programs to improve education for at-risk students in many schools at once. This chapter reports what we have learned from both individual schools and entire districts that have taken responsibility for building new programs for students at risk.

## FOUR EXEMPLARY SCHOOLS

A growing body of literature provides descriptions of schools that actively nurture and support at-risk students in ways that produce school success (Foley & McConnaughy, 1982; Schorr, 1988; Slavin, Madden, & Karweit, 1989; Wehlage, Rutter, Smith, Lesko, & Fernandez, 1989). When teachers take on the role of mentor, friend, and confidant as well as instructor; when schools modify their policies in ways that acknowledge the difficult circumstances often encountered by students in their day-to-day lives; and when classrooms come to be characterized by learning activities that are meaningful for students and demand their active involvement, alienated students can develop a high level of engagement that results in achievement. In this section, we describe four schools that have provided this environment.

The schools were among 14 schools selected during Spring 1986 in a study of schools effective with at-risk students. Selection of schools was based on five criteria. A school had to

1. Serve students who could be identified as at risk of dropping out
2. Enroll a range of age, racial, and/or ethnic groups
3. Use a variety of intervention strategies and innovative practices
4. Show a record of some success with at-risk students, such as raising attendance rates or reducing drop-out rates
5. Demonstrate potential for serving as a model adaptable to other schools.

Schools were selected from nominations made by sources knowledgeable about schools serving dropouts and potential dropouts. Final selections were based on written information, phone interviews, and site visits to nominated schools.

Included in the study were two large comprehensive inner-city schools with all-minority populations, several schools serving largely white working- and lower-middle-class youth, an alternative junior high school in a medium-sized city, several small alternative programs located within comprehensive high schools, and specialized alternative schools such as one serving pregnant and mothering teen girls. Thirteen of the schools were in urban settings; one was located in a rural county. In studying these schools, a variety of data was gathered. Measures of academic achievement were obtained in reading, writing, and mathematics. Self-esteem, locus of control, and social bonding were among the social-psychological dimensions measured. Field researchers spent at least three weeks during the school year in each school observing classes and interviewing students and teachers.

The study provided concrete examples of how teachers and school administrators were able to promote membership and provide authentic student work. Here we describe four of the programs that were among the more effective and that represented quite different contexts and strategies. Despite differences among these schools and the wide variety of students they served, we found that all successfully developed school membership and authentic work that led to student engagement. The schools are: Sierra Mountain High School in Grass Valley, California; the Media Academy in Oakland, California; the School-Within-a-School at Memorial High School in Madison, Wisconsin; and the New Futures School in Albuquerque, New Mexico.

## Sierra Mountain High School

Sierra Mountain High School is a small "school of choice" that serves approximately 90 to 100 9th and 10th Grade students who share patterns of poor attendance and an unwillingness to cooperate with the behavioral standards and procedures of conventional schools.

Sierra Mountain's program is distinguished by its informality and the strong sense of community among students and staff. The school is especially successful with students who respond positively to increased attention from adults. Teachers consciously present themselves as potential friends and confidants as well as academic instructors. As one teacher reported,

> I tend to treat the kids with respect and come straight across
> with them. I have expectations of what their behavior should be
> and what their achievement should be in my classes, and I put
> that out without any conditions to my respect other than respect
> returned. I think that I put out affection for these kids. I feel real
> protective of them. They're my kids. I think that helps. Treating
> the kids with a feeling that they are your kids, the kids sense
> that. They sense that I care about them and what happens to
> them.

Most classes in the school are structured as workshops in which student and staff interaction is frequent and ongoing. Teachers use a variety of instructional strategies but tend to emphasize lessons that demand active involvement. Because of frequent communication and cooperative participation, relations between teachers and students can achieve a degree of intimacy and concern generally absent in more traditional educational settings.

Given the support and care students encounter at Sierra Mountain, they become willing to take the risks that allow them to extend their own range of competency, a critical step for students who may have experienced little encouragement and regular failure in their previous schools. As the physical education teacher at the school noted,

> Typically, the students we deal with hit the wall and stop. They
> spend so much energy trying to find a way around it instead of
> climbing it, but once they do climb it, they feel successful, and
> they'll go to the next one and it may be bigger, and it may be
> tougher, but they'll start up it. But you've got to be there to keep

them going because if you don't, they'll fall down and you'll see them going back to the same old pattern of trying to find a way around and spin and spin and spin their wheels.

The dynamics of this process of challenge and encouragement can be seen in the following vignette drawn from a drama class:

> This class focuses on the concept and experience of personal boundaries and the dramatic meaning of crossing. After presenting a variety of exercises designed to encourage students to recognize the way that space communicates meaning, the teacher chooses a boy and girl to enact a scene set in 1736 between a prosecuting attorney and a woman charged with murdering a nobleman. The woman, a former prostitute who has recently converted to Quakerism, is six months pregnant.
>
> The teacher has the students initially read the play. The acting is stilted. Dissatisfied, he takes away the play books and asks the students to improvise, asserting that "you can't say a wrong word if you become the person and go for your objectives." After a few minutes, the boy objects, saying, "I can't do this." The teacher responds, "How can you say you can't do this when you are doing it." He insists that they continue. When the boy stumbles again, the teacher hands him a book to use as a prop. With something in his hands, the boy relaxes and suddenly assumes the role of the lawyer. At one point, he crosses over to the girl with a pointed accusation. She backs away naturally, demonstrating the essence of the lesson. The teacher stops the students with a brief statement of praise, "You've peaked there."

This scene demonstrates how support and challenge can encourage students to transcend self-imposed limits and achieve more than they believe is possible. The girl involved in this scene observed that before she came to Sierra Mountain, she had been satisfied with lower grades because " . . . they [teachers] didn't really care. They just looked at you as an individual." It was her impression that teachers felt that if students "messed up," it was their own fault. At Sierra Mountain, she was earning A's and B's, largely because the attention of teachers had kindled her own ambition. "I'm doing good," she said, "and I'm going to go higher."

## The Media Academy

The Media Academy in Oakland, California similarly offers students the support, encouragement, and coaching needed to take the risks associated with academic success. Approximately 120 primarily African-American and Hispanic students are enrolled in the program for three years of high school. There, they major in print and electronic media and participate in the production of the school's publications: a newspaper, a yearbook, a Spanish/English community newspaper, and a teen magazine. After their sophomore year, coursework not associated with journalism or social studies is taken in the regular high school. The Media Academy succeeds in providing curriculum and instructional activities that are both extrinsically and intrinsically valuable for students.

Students' three-year stay in the Academy allows them to form personal ties to both their teachers and peers. As was the case at Sierra Mountain, this can contribute to higher levels of student achievement. A boy who had transformed his grades from C's and D's to A's and B's stated, "I had never experienced this before — where teachers are close and encourage me." What seems particularly important about learning in the Media Academy is that such success is seen as a vehicle for advancing not just the welfare of individuals, but also the welfare of all students in the program. Some minority students are quick to charge peers who do well in school with "acting white," but at the Media Academy the directing of academic efforts to *group* products frees students from fear of being condemned by their friends. As one girl observed, "No one is put down for doing well in subjects."

Within this socially supportive and academically focused setting, students who might be overlooked and neglected in conventional classrooms become willing to step forward to assert themselves and share their talents in ways that encourage further involvement and engagement. The following scene, for example, took place in the transmission studio of the Harbor Bay Teleport, a satellite communication system used by international businesses. The teleport is operated by one of the many community sponsors who serve on the Media Academy's advisory committee. On this visit to the teleport, Academy students interviewed via satellite John Drury, a television news anchorman at a San Francisco station.

Maria, a recent immigrant to the United States from Mexico, has stepped to the microphone to ask a question. Because her English is still halting, coursework at the Media Academy has been difficult. In preparation for the interview, she worked closely with the Academy's lead teacher to make sure that her questions were phrased in correct English. Carefully measuring her words, she asks, "Does one have to pass a government examination to become a television reporter?" After hearing Mr. Drury's answer, Maria continues with a follow-up question. "Is a college degree in journalism required for one to be a television reporter?" As she returns to her seat, she glances at her teacher, who raises his hand in a well-done signal.

Near the conclusion of the 45-minute session, other students cluster around the microphone taking turns to ask more questions. Maria, who had been sitting at the back of the room, has edged her way through her classmates to the microphone. Although time is almost gone, she asks one more question. "Does television make more people do things like taking hostages because they know television will be there?"

Through the Media Academy, students like Maria gain access to a world that may have previously seemed inaccessible. With the support and encouragement of their teachers as well as the example of their bolder classmates, they are presented with opportunities to explore their own potential and take on the role of adults successful in the broader society. The self-confidence that can come from such experiences can have an invaluable impact on students' conception of their own futures. What may have seemed impossible in the past, given their own backgrounds, now becomes approachable.

The link between schooling and desirable jobs is underscored by the Academy's effort to expose students both to media professionals and to different forms of work within various media establishments. Teachers in the program strive to introduce their students to reporters, cartoonists, and editors who have grown up in similar neighborhoods. Internships and summer jobs are also available in local newspapers and radio and television stations. This is all to demonstrate that skills learned in the Academy can be translated into meaningful work.

Students do not have to wait until they finish school to put into practice the skills they are learning in journalism classes. Their work on school publications requires them to take on the role of photographers, reporters, editors, lay-out artists, and advertisement solicitors. Not only do such activities give students the opportunity to act as media professionals in training, but they also give them the chance to cultivate and share talents and interests that may be intrinsically valuable to them. Because of their long-term relationship with the Academy, students are able to develop an increasing level of competence, and with this competence they earn the right to share in important decisions related to production activities. Novice students know that as they acquire the requisite skills they will be able to take on the jobs of their older colleagues. They know as well that they are responsible for and "own" the results of their efforts. Teachers at the Academy consciously facilitate rather than manage, avoiding tight direction and supervision. They are willing to delegate the choice of news articles and editorials to their students and to accept the results. This offers fresh and expanding opportunities for students to turn their growing confidence and ability into the exercise of responsibility, leadership, and commitment. The validation that comes from engagement becomes in itself the source of further engagement.

## Madison Memorial School-Within-a-School

The School-Within-a-School at Memorial High School in Madison, Wisconsin has also developed a curriculum and instructional practices that emphasize students' active involvement in tasks that are socially and personally meaningful. Established in 1984 in an effort to reduce the drop-out rate among older high school students seriously deficient in credits, the program is small, enrolling no more than 64 students, about equally divided between the junior and senior classes.

One of the strongest elements of the School-Within-a-School is its work experience program. A central concern of teachers in this alternative school is helping students master both the academic and social skills they will need to make a transition to employment after earning their diplomas. To assist with this transition, staff have devised a series of vocational units required of all juniors. Scheduled during the afternoon after a morning of primarily academic coursework, three of these units take place outside the school for a nine-week period each. In one, a team of approximately 16 students works with a community organization that renovates older houses. In another, students assist in day-care centers. During the third vocational experience, students work in different health care institutions. In each case, juniors in the program work with adults outside the school on projects that have important effects in the broader community. The final unit for juniors is taught within the school and focuses on business skills. Seniors take classes in either food services or marketing and are placed in paid positions in these areas. The goal of these placements is to help students gain extended experience in a single job site while retaining the support of school staff when and if problems arise.

The work experience program at the School-Within-a-School leads to higher levels of student engagement in a number of ways. First, students are given the chance to learn new skills that can lead to positive, quickly realized, and obvious accomplishments. As at Sierra Mountain and the Media Academy, their growing competence can enhance their self-esteem and self-confidence. Second, student work is infused with social meaning. Houses that are renovated with the help of School-Within-a-School students are sold to low-income families who might otherwise not be able to afford a home. The personal rewards of working with young children or the elderly are even more immediate and clear. Finally, in nearly all the work environments in which School-Within-a-School students are placed, they have the opportunity to interact with adults who often treat them as fellow workers, rather than children. For adolescents who often perceive themselves to be outside the society of adults, the attention and recognition they receive at job sites also contributes to their growing sense of competency and worth. The following scene shows how these experiences can increase students' involvement with school-related activities:

> The work site is an older but well-built, two-story home on Madison's east side. The interior remains largely gutted, but new exterior siding is already in place, giving the house a finished quality. The work looks professional. Students arrive close to 1:00 p.m. via bus or personal cars. Bruce, the supervisor, greets them and begins to assign chores. Karen, Margo, and Serena are sent to the living room, where they are shown how to putty over finishing nails and then stain the putty. Bruce emphasizes how important not marring the wood and removing all the putty will be if they want the job to look right. Ken and David are sent downstairs to paint the bathroom. Bruce accompanies Lauren, Teresa, and Nate to the attic, where they are given the task of installing a second layer of insulation and additional two-by-fours to keep the insulation in place.
>
> Bruce works in the attic most of the time, patiently answering the recurrent question, "What do I do next?" He takes time to show Nate how to use an electric drill to place holes and set screws. The girls are already skilled in using hammers and take delight in their strength and ability. The work is taxing, sticky, and dirty, but even when Bruce leaves to check on how the other students are doing, the attic crew stays on task. When students make mistakes in their measurements or drilling, Bruce encourages them to try again and get it right the second time around. When the insulation and new two-by-fours are in place, Teresa stands back and looks at their handiwork. "This place looks a lot nicer," she says. Her friends nod in agreement and then head down the stairs to take on another job.

At the School-Within-a-School students learn in an environment where they are helped to acquire skills that have obvious economic worth. But often their work becomes its own reward as they take pleasure in the completion of tasks they know are of value to others. Repairing and remodeling of homes is authentic and lacks the make-work quality of many of the activities that go on in most schools. Students' internship experiences can play an important role in helping them learn the persistence and care needed to succeed not only on the job but also in their classes. Although not all students in the School-Within-a-School transfer what they learn on their job sites to English or math, acquiring habits deemed valuable by employers offers them important preparation for the work they will face as adults.

## New Futures School

The New Futures School is an alternative public school for pregnant and mothering girls from 12 to 21 years old. Its comprehensive program offers the 250 girls typically enrolled health care, parenting classes, day care for 75 children, academic classes, and a jobs program. New Futures is distinguished by its comprehensive approach to teenage motherhood. Its staff see students as capable of being good mothers, good students, and successful adults. This positive outlook helps the girls adjust to their pregnancies and accept the responsibilities of motherhood. Small classes and attentive teachers help the girls improve their academic performance, which further boosts their self-esteem and belief in future possibilities. Regular interactions with counselors also promote self-reflection, goal setting, and problem solving. Students frequently credit New Futures as essential to their finishing high school, considering postsecondary schooling, and going on with their life plans.

One of the most powerful elements of the program for engaging students is the way that issues related to pregnancy and motherhood have been woven into the curriculum. Three special parenting classes, for example, deal specifically with diet, exercise, anatomy, growth of the fetus, labor and delivery, child development, and the care of toddlers. These topics are covered in depth, with the aim of preparing girls for the demands of labor and parenthood. As one girl noted, "When I went into labor, I knew *everything* that was going to happen to me." A companion agreed, "You learn the name of every part of you and what's happening. You know *so much*."

The courses related to child development and parenting involve typical classroom instruction as well as hands-on experience in the school's nursery. Students not only learn what to anticipate in regard to their infants' needs and development, but they are given the chance to apply their knowledge while caring for their classmates' children. As in the three other programs described above, teachers build student involvement into the very nature of assigned activities.

At one meeting of the sixth-hour child development class, 11 girls gather in the school's infant nursery. Dressed in blue jeans or corduroy pants and loose-fitting smocks, they are led by their teacher to a sink where they are instructed to carefully wash their hands with soap and a soap brush. Evaluation in this class is tied to the care they demonstrate in personal hygiene and other tasks.

Gerry, the Hispanic woman who oversees the nursery, then takes the girls to a changing table where she has arranged for a more experienced student to demonstrate how to bathe and diaper a baby. Details such as remembering to place the pins outside the baby's reach and different techniques for diapering boy and girl babies are emphasized. Gerry makes a point of telling the students that mothers expect expert care, saying that "little things mean a lot to a mother." She goes on to relate a story about a mother who was upset one day when she discovered that her baby had been scratched by a diaper pin and no one had told her. Gerry reiterates to her students that such details are important to a mother.

Issues related to parenthood are also drawn into other courses as well. A math teacher, for example, developed a text on math applications in the home, which was written to be adaptable to regular math classes, to GED classes, and for use by students alone. In an effort to help prepare young mothers for the financial obligations of parenthood, the school also provided classes on seeking employment and further training.

Unlike educators in many other schools, teachers at New Futures see pregnancy and motherhood as a powerful motivator for student engagement. Students are encouraged to believe that they can be effective caregivers and providers. A girl who had been out of school for one-and-a-half years prior to entering New Futures was now intent on completing her GED. She had a one-year-old daughter and said she had returned to school because "my daughter will need lots of things. I need to make more money than in fast food."

For many students, parenthood brings with it a new maturity. New Futures enables these young women to link their concern for their children to an educational process aimed at empowering them to be good parents. The extrinsic value of educational effort and success is inescapable when presented in this way. So, too, is the intrinsic value of such involvement when the applicability of information taught in classes has so much bearing on one's immediate personal experience. Focusing on topics in depth and providing experiential settings in which lessons can be mastered help students at New Futures to develop the competencies they will need in the labor room and in their own homes after delivering their children.

In summary, the four exemplary schools demonstrate major departures from conventional education to respond to the needs of students at risk. These relatively small and autonomous organizations offer different programs and structures to groups of students who are not well-matched to traditional definitions of school. The programs emphasize different patterns of social relations than generally exist between students and staff in larger public schools. Many educators have suggested that these examples of curricular and instructional experimentation and social relations will enhance engagement not only for at-risk students, but for most others as well. As we argued in Chapter 1, the key is to find ways of affirming membership and designing authentic work. The ways in which these schools have created caring communities and opportunities to apply one's mind to problems of public and personal significance can serve as lessons to all schools. An important issue remains: Is it possible to replicate the policies and practices that produce membership and authentic work in these alternative schools so that conventional schools embedded in large bureaucratic systems can better engage students at risk? We confront this in the next section.

## DISTRICT PROGRAMS FOR AT-RISK YOUTH: THE ANNIE E. CASEY NEW FUTURES INITIATIVE

Transporting the structures of small successful alternatives to conventional schools with large enrollments of at-risk students appears difficult. Several problems surface immediately. Since the successful alternatives we studied were often newly created, unique organizations, they did not show us how to change existing schools on a large scale. They were typically the product of a small group of educational "entrepreneurs" who saw a need to serve disengaged students and were able to design their own unique response. These entrepreneurs generated consensus and unity because they were highly focused on targeting a particular group of students. They forged consensus not only on the goal of serving these youth, but also on the means of doing so.

Existing secondary schools with all their factions, traditions, and cultural baggage pose obstacles to educational entrepreneurs' gaining the opportunity and resources to create powerful, effective, school-wide alternatives. A typical comprehensive middle or high school has a diversity of interest groups in its different subject areas or departments, at least some of whom have competing notions about what public education should offer and demand of students. High school teachers, in particular, value a high degree of professional autonomy that is likely to impede the creation of school-wide changes that substantially alter curriculum, instruction, and social relations both among staff and between staff and students.

The problem is even more complex when taken beyond the school to a system such as a district or state. Changing individual schools from the bottom up is one thing, but how does a system stimulate change in many different schools simultaneously? Some of these alternatives were successful primarily because they were ignored by their central office. Systemic change calls for a coordinated effort among central office and staff from several buildings. The tendency of central offices is usually to insist on some degree of uniformity of policy and practice, which tends to stifle inventiveness and entrepreneurial spirit.

We studied this problem by examining a major national effort to help several communities restructure their educational, economic, political, and social service institutions to serve at-risk youth. In 1988 the Annie E. Casey Foundation launched the five-year New Futures Initiative in Dayton, Little Rock, Pittsburgh, and Savannah.

New Futures is a comprehensive community-based initiative aimed at improving the education and opportunities of disadvantaged youth. It contains a number of components, including coordination of social services, employment opportunities, and school restructuring, each developed through a collaborative organization representing youth-serving agencies and public interest groups. While New Futures extends beyond school reform, its efforts at changing school policies and practices affecting at-risk youth in conventional schools are especially informative.

Six middle schools were studied intensively in three of the cities over three years; two high schools were also studied during the same time in the fourth city. Marvin, whose experiences we described in Chapter 1, attended one of the middle schools. Based on a variety of data—observations, interviews, and quantitative measures of student outcomes—we have arrived at some preliminary conclusions about the impact of school restructuring activities in New Futures cities at the halfway point of the initiative. These preliminary conclusions have been considered in the cities with the intent of overcoming some of the problems encountered in trying to restructure schools.

In all, about 18 major educational interventions were developed under New Futures sponsorship in the four cities during the first half of the initiative. The primary interventions implemented in each school system are listed and described below.

## Dayton

In Dayton, two middle schools were selected to try a number of interventions. The proposal called for

1. Clustering of students and teachers
2. An advisory period called "home-based guidance"
3. Extended day activities
4. Incentives to reward student performance
5. "Beyond the Basics" curriculum and interdisciplinary units
6. Case managers for all students

Clustering was the centerpiece innovation in Dayton; it brought together core subject teachers (English, reading, math, social studies, and science) to share a common group of about 120 to 150 students. Cluster teachers have been given a common daily planning period during which they can address a variety of issues that range from difficulties with a particular student to jointly planned and taught lessons. In principle, clustering has provided an opportunity for students and teachers to participate in a learning community capable of providing a level of caring and support generally absent in large secondary schools.

To cultivate more supportive teacher–student interaction, a home-based guidance period was added to the daily schedule. The 16 to 20 students enrolled in each home-base were to receive counseling from teachers on a regular basis in an effort to overcome the inability of typical counseling staffs to provide frequent, personal contact with students.

To encourage student engagement in academic work, cluster teachers were to implement a variety of curricular reforms. Among these was a "Beyond the Basics" curriculum that stressed problem solving and the discovery of meaning, connections, and patterns as opposed to rote learning. To facilitate the development of this curriculum, each cluster was given the freedom to create interdisciplinary teaching units, vary instructional groups, and alter class schedules. Assistance for implementing these changes was to come from the central office in the form of funding and advice, while day-to-day teaching was to be supplemented by remedial teachers or aides within the cluster setting.

For the students, particularly those having academic difficulties, incentives have been offered. A fund of $15,000 was available to teachers in each pilot school to create student rewards for good attendance, academic improvement, and good behavior. The money was spent on items such as T-shirts, pizzas, and amusement park trips.

## Little Rock

In Little Rock, five junior high schools participated in the reform effort during the first three years. The proposal called for

1. Clustering in several grades based on four core subject teachers sharing about 120 students
2. In-school suspension (in year 2)
3. A pilot program using teachers as student advisors (TAP)
4. Interdisciplinary units
5. Case managers for some at-risk students

Like Dayton, Little Rock placed its greatest hopes on clustering. Unlike Dayton, clustering did not involve all grade levels or all pilot schools. Teaching staffs could vote on whether or not they wanted to cluster, and some chose not to do so. In one school, 7th and 8th Grade teachers clustered, while at another, it happened only in the 8th Grade. As in Dayton, the purpose of this structure was to create common times for teachers to discuss students, teaching, and curriculum. The proposal argued that closer teacher–student relations could be developed as a result of clustering, something especially beneficial for children at risk. Cluster teachers were expected to develop one or more interdisciplinary units during the year. These units were to study a common theme from the perspective of each discipline. For example, a unit on violence included reading a novel on the subject, discussing causes of violence (in social studies), and reading statistics on violent crimes (in math).

The in-school suspension (ISS) program was developed in response to disciplinary problems and the high rate of suspension in these schools. Students were assigned to the ISS self-contained classroom for "nonaggressive" disciplinary infractions, such as repeated tardiness to class. While in ISS, students were required to continue work on their regular assignments. This new program was intended to avoid the harsh consequences of out-of-school suspension, which often results in course failure and even retention because of missed academic work.

The Teacher Advisor Program (TAP) was established at two junior high schools where 16 teachers agreed to counsel about 190 students identified as those most at risk. Teachers meet with students regularly to serve as mentors and counselors regarding both school and nonschool topics.

## Pittsburgh

In Pittsburgh, eight schools, including elementary, middle, and high schools, were proposed sites for New Futures, but the major reform activities have occurred at two high schools. In addition to case management, educational interventions have taken two forms: (1) academies within the traditional high school, and (2) extended day or after-school activities.

The academy concept was adapted from a successful business and finance academy already operating in the city. At one high school, "health care technology" has been adopted as the curricular theme for about 40 10th Grade students. A contract between parents and students and the faculty has been developed to elicit commitments from students that they would attend and participate in class in exchange for a promise from teachers that students would graduate on time. Curriculum and instruction have emphasized cooperative learning and a "hands-on" approach to health care. Students have been bused for one class to a local technical school for the health care training.

At the other high school, about 90 incoming 9th graders not enrolled in several other special options have been targeted. Four core subject teachers with a common planning period have taught this group. This academy has no specific vocational theme, but teachers concentrate on providing a more personal school-within-a-school atmosphere. Students with high math scores have been placed in a college-bound program, and those with lower scores have been placed in the vocational program. The elimination of the "general" track in Pittsburgh has also been part of the general school restructuring proposal.

## Savannah

In Savannah, three middle schools served as pilots for a set of interventions that included

1. A STAY team in each school (counselor, social worker, nurse, and in-house suspension specialist)
2. An Individual Success Plan for each at-risk student
3. Comprehensive Competency Program (CCP) learning labs
4. Accelerated promotion policy for retained students
5. Modified academic curriculum for at-risk students
6. In-school suspension
7. Extended day activities
8. Case managers for all identified at-risk students

In conjunction with case managers, the STAY teams have written Individual Success Plans for all at-risk students, similar to the individual educational plan employed in special education programs. By involving case managers, the school social worker, and the nurse, the Individual Success Plans were meant to address students' home and social problems that interfere with school success. Home visits and conferences with parents have been included.

Maximizing students' academic success has been the goal of the "modified curriculum" and the Comprehensive Competency Program. The latter has been situated in a specially constructed laboratory setting in which students use programmed materials and computer-assisted instruction developed originally for Job Corps participants. Students scheduled into the CCP lab spend about three hours a day learning math, language arts, and an amalgam of "social functions" subjects. The modified curriculum was essentially a remedial program designed to teach basic skills in each of the core subjects.

To encourage student engagement in the modified curriculum and CCP labs, a new district policy allowed previously retained students to receive "accelerated promotion." Those who succeeded in raising their achievement on a standardized test to a higher grade level were promoted an additional grade at the end of a semester. For example, a twice retained 6th Grade student can skip 7th Grade by testing at that level in math and reading.

In response to the very high rate of out-of-school suspension, Savannah middle schools also implemented an in-school suspension program like the one in Little Rock.

In summary, the four districts undertook a variety of strategies, some of them quite similar. Intended to respond to the academic problems and to the social/personal needs of students, the strategies were implicitly designed to enhance engagement and in the long run produce more favorable outcomes for students.

Did these interventions result in greater student engagement in school? To answer this question we examined the extent to which schools were successful in (1) developing more supportive and positive social relations between students and teachers that resulted in greater school membership; and (2) bringing about changes in curriculum, instruction, and assessment practices that generated more authentic forms of academic work.

## MEMBERSHIP

Survey data indicated that nearly all children in New Futures schools believe that education is important, but fewer are certain that teachers are committed to their success. To build a sense of membership, particularly for typically marginalized groups, educators must demonstrate commitment to the success of all students regardless of their academic achievement, race, or social circumstances. The clear articulation and fair application of performance and behavioral expectations in conjunction with sustained support and encouragement can also increase the likelihood that students will have a positive school experience (Wehlage, Rutter, Smith, Lesko, & Fernandez, 1989).

Some positive impact on peer and student–teacher relations occurred as a result of New Futures educational interventions. Although few of the improvements in social relations have become school-wide in scope, interventions have provided some teachers with both the opportunity and permission to assume more personal and supportive roles with students. This has been especially true in the small Pittsburgh academies, CCP labs in Savannah, and clusters in Little Rock and Dayton. Each of these has placed teachers with smaller student groups that cultivated improved expectations and working relationships. These grouping practices have facilitated more care and support by teachers for students in academic trouble. Some teachers eventually came to speak of students as "our kids" and during common planning periods explored strategies for addressing students' problems. Unfortunately, teachers' discussions frequently resulted in recommendations to refer students elsewhere (e.g., to school counselors, psychologists, social workers, or other human services professionals) and thus did not become a catalyst for more fundamental changes in teachers' own practice.

Despite pockets of enhanced membership, as a whole teacher–student relations in most New Futures schools remain adversarial. Even though some teachers developed positive social relations with at-risk students, these practices have not been adopted by the majority of faculty. Instead, school staff are often preoccupied with maintaining control and discipline through punitive methods. This contributes to an environment characterized more by conflict and exclusion than by care and support. Even though alternatives to suspension, such as in-school suspension, have been introduced into a number of New Futures schools, these programs have not called into question either the use of disciplinary sanctions for fairly trivial offenses such as tardiness, gum chewing, or loose shirttails, nor have they led to an investigation of the underlying institutional causes of student misbehavior.

Adversarial relations between staff and students in the Savannah middle schools were identified very early as a major problem area, and proposals indicated a need for schools to revise their practices. Yet data on out-of-school suspensions have continued to reveal the persistence of the problem. For example, about one third of all 6th Graders in the Savannah system were suspended during the 1988–89 and 1989–90 school years. Slightly more than one half of all African-American male 6th Graders were suspended during each of these two school years. These data reflect a well-entrenched practice by school administrators of suspending students for a wide variety of offenses, including being tardy to class, "sassing" a teacher, and "not showing proper respect" to adults. A large number of the suspensions are for more than one day, resulting in many unexcused absences. This means that classwork cannot be made up, which, in turn, leads to lowered grades and even failure and retention in grade for some students.

Despite an explicit intention to reduce out-of-school suspensions through the use of ISS and the counseling assistance of the STAY teams, former punitive practices continued. During the second year (1989–90) of the initiative, one school suspended 215, or 66 percent, of its New Futures students. A second school was somewhat more successful, suspending 127, or 42 percent, of its targeted at-risk students. A third school, just beginning a small pilot New Futures program, suspended 60, or 74 percent, of its at-risk students during the year. Of course, suspending students is sometimes necessary and should remain one of the tools available to administrators, but the scale on which it is used in Savannah has a serious negative impact on the learning environment of the schools.

Within individual schools social relations also reflect inconsistencies easily interpreted as hypocrisy, which further undermine membership. In Dayton, for example, one of the pilot schools has painted in large letters on the most visible wall in the school office the following statement:

> We will work as a team in a trusting environment where every
> student will be treated with dignity, experience success, and
> have access to caring and supportive adults.

Despite these words, a proposal to tighten conditions in the in-school suspension room was brought before the faculty. The proposal, written by teachers, advocated that blinds in the ISS room be kept closed all day, that students not be allowed to eat lunch in the cafeteria, that the room be stripped of its computer and television monitor, and that students be prevented from contacting their friends between the first and last bells of the day. During the discussion of the proposal, a teacher protested that ISS was not intended to be punitive and that the recommendations verged on the inhumane. She said she would not allow her daughter to be placed in this kind of detention. Nevertheless, a majority of faculty felt that the purpose of ISS was to punish students and voted in favor of the proposal.

To foster students' attachment to the school, New Futures interventions did provide informal academic and personal counseling and other demonstrations of care and support by adults. In some schools, despite these new opportunities, teachers continued to resist a more extended role with students. Without forging a school-wide culture of adult support, as is found in some alternative schools, adults may not accept the responsibility for mentoring students.

It has become clear that simply creating new structures — such as STAY teams, clusters, and case management — has not been sufficient to bring about changes in social relations that also dominate the day-to-day life of schools. Teachers have continued to respond to misbehaving students in ways that undermine membership and the formally stated goals of new programs. Rather than finding ways to alter the conditions that lead to behavioral problems, many teachers and administrators respond by removing students from the school. As yet, no New Futures school have systematically examined how school experiences themselves produce student misbehavior.

## AUTHENTIC WORK

Curriculum characterized by "authentic work" emphasizes production of socially useful, personally meaningful, and aesthetically valuable knowledge. Curriculum should build on students' strengths and interests (Knapp & Shields, 1990; Levin, 1988) while recognizing that they are capable of exercising multiple forms of intelligence (Gardner, 1983).

As explained in Chapter 1, authentic work requires students to actively produce, rather than reproduce, knowledge. Authentic work involves students in solving "rich problems" that allow them to construct their own meanings and thereby give significance and coherence to abstract concepts (National Council of Teachers of Mathematics, 1989; Resnick, 1987a, 1987b). In contrast to the superficial coverage of many topics that tends to create shallow or false understanding, an authentic curriculum stresses in-depth knowledge and a role for teachers that is akin to coaching (Sizer, 1984).

The initial New Futures proposals promised to change teaching and learning in order to increase student interest, motivation, and achievement. Most of the proposed interventions, however, were not implemented, were implemented in only a cursory fashion, or were implemented and then abandoned. As a result, the bulk of classroom activities observed in most New Futures schools remained traditional. Teachers relied on worksheets, textbooks, and district guides, and were preoccupied with covering discrete facts and basic skills. That is, in New Futures schools, remediation and a slower, low-level curriculum are the normative response to underachieving students. Most schoolwork in New Futures schools can be described as repetitive drill and practice exercises and the accumulation of fragmented bits of information, apparently irrelevant to real-world problems and the kinds of thinking done by productive adults (cf. Newmann, 1988, 1991).

Authenticity comes partly from giving students concrete experiences similar to those they will encounter in the social, political, and economic organizations they will have to negotiate when they leave the classroom (Wehlage, Rutter, Smith, Lesko, & Fernandez, 1989). Such a curriculum not only reinforces the usefulness and applicability of knowledge, but also introduces poor, minority, or otherwise marginalized youth to institutions they might not otherwise encounter. A variety of community service, internship, apprenticeship, and college programs can provide the experiential basis for the application of mathematics, science, language arts, and social studies.

A curriculum characterized by authentic work requires more than altering instructional strategies, teaching to different learning styles, or developing new instructional materials — although all these might be necessary. The more fundamental barriers to authentic work in school are the beliefs in which the current model of curriculum is rooted. What is needed is a paradigm shift at all levels of the school system and the forging of a professional culture around a new conception of curriculum and instruction.

Typical of the teaching in many classrooms is the following scene from a 7th Grade social studies class in Little Rock:

> The teacher asks, "What are the varieties of products in Latin America?" Several students shout out answers. He lists them on the board. "Write these down. You'll need to know them for the test."
>
> Then he asks, "Why is the population growing?" A boy says, "Because they want to urbanize." "No!" he says and then proceeds to offer his own extended explanation. "Take that down, too, it may be on there." There is no discussion.
>
> They move on to labeling countries and capitals on mimeographed maps of Latin America. After finishing the labeling, the teacher repeats and reviews the process they just completed, this time on an overhead projection. A girl says, "El Salvador — isn't that where they're having a lot of trouble?" "Well, yes," the teacher replies, "it's very volatile, but we'll talk about that another time."
>
> After again reminding the class about the need to know the information for the test, he tells the students to spend the re-

maining 25 minutes of the period finding the answers to the questions at the end of the chapter. Meanwhile three boys pass around a comic book, another boy reads a sports magazine behind his book. In the back row, a boy is rendering a remarkable likeness of a 1957 Impala in his notebook, and there is an endless procession to the pencil sharpener.

Of course, not all classes were as uninspired and mindless as this one. We observed a few instances in which teachers attempted significant curricular innovations that had the potential for making school interesting and providing students with challenging, worthwhile content. In one case, a math teacher in Little Rock used a number of imaginative techniques to teach algebra to "regular"-track students who ordinarily would be taking a general math curriculum. The teacher tried to make her students mathematical thinkers and problem solvers, rather than stressing the memorization of mathematical procedures. The experiment was successful in that most of her "regular"-track students learned concepts and problem-solving skills associated with algebra.

Yet the next year, upon entering Algebra II, these students were at a disadvantage. They were not properly "prepared" because they had not covered the same curriculum as other students, which was the expectation of the Algebra II teachers. There was no institutional support for students who had taken an alternative route to learning mathematics. A teacher's innovations and success were canceled out because they were not part of a school-wide effort to improve the level of math achievement for "regular"-track students, most of whom were at risk.

The Health Academy in Pittsburgh has provided some engaging learning experiences for students. The health technologies class featured learning opportunities to build skills associated with different medical professions. For example, students had an opportunity to practice CPR and to use different medical equipment. Student response to this program has been positive, in part because of its use of experiential learning, but this was restricted to one course. Curriculum and instruction in core subjects such as social studies and English remained little changed from courses found elsewhere in the Pittsburgh school district.

In Savannah's CCP labs, many students with long histories of school failure found an instructional format that enabled them to succeed with highly structured programmed basic skill materials. The self-paced and supportive environment staffed by specially trained teachers produced clear learning gains in conventional content by low-achieving and failing students. Without the CCP labs, many of these students would have ended their educational careers in middle school.

But we must not neglect the content of CCP materials. The CCP labs have provided remedial education by drilling students in basic skills associated with reading, mathematics, and career awareness. They have not challenged students to engage in problem solving or higher-order thinking activities. This "successful" CCP intervention has provided low-achieving students with little more than a mechanical education in narrowly defined basic skills.

Overall, then, New Futures has not produced promising changes in the substantive content that students learn. It has stimulated almost no fundamental change in the primary intellectual activities that dominate students' lives in school. In these districts no policies or interventions have yet succeeded in moving educators, whether at the top of the school hierarchy or at the building level, beyond the patterns of curriculum and instruction that have characterized schools for decades. Most educators continue to rely on familiar objectives, methods, texts, and conceptions of testing and assessment that fail to offer opportunities for higher-order thinking and authentic work.

Our observations and conversations with educators suggested a number of reasons for the absence of fundamental curriculum reforms. The most important reason was that the school and district staff saw little need for fundamental changes in curriculum. Most educators in the New Futures schools believed that the difficulties faced by at-risk students originated within the students and their families, not in the school and its curriculum. At-risk students were seen almost exclusively as the product of homes and communities in social disarray.

Further, it was assumed by some teachers that each subject was defined by a clear sequence of topics, concepts, and skills that must be learned in the proper order. Teachers expressed the belief, for example, that students cannot perform more difficult "higher-order thinking tasks" in a subject until they have mastered prior "basic" knowledge and skill.

We found other impediments to broad changes in curriculum and instruction, but few have been addressed by the New Futures initiatives. In all of the districts, national norm-referenced tests, pupil performance objectives (PPOs), minimum performance tests (MPTs), or district-mandated examinations have been cited by teachers as reasons for stifled innovation. In Pittsburgh, each subject has a syllabus-driven exam originating in the central office for which teachers must prepare their students. Teachers in Little Rock said they had little choice but to focus on rote skills in subjects like mathematics and language arts because of the state's MPTs, which determine whether or not students can move on to high school.

A few teachers indicated a desire to develop more challenging curricula, but said they found little support from their district for the intensive and extensive professional development needed to reshape curriculum and instruction. With the exception of Pittsburgh, teachers pointed out that no sustained and coherent staff development programs were available to support the adoption of new instructional strategies. Although the Casey Foundation has funded a number of staff development activities, these have generally consisted of short introductions to discrete strategies such as cooperative learning or interdisciplinary instruction; no long-term guidance has been offered to teachers for restructuring the curriculum.

## COMPARISONS AND CONCLUSIONS

In this chapter, we explored two kinds of innovations designed to serve at-risk students: One was a set of small alternative schools, and the other was an effort at the district level to restructure existing schools. Generally, the small alternative schools were more successful than those that attempted restructuring. But even the alternatives had their limitations; social support for students that built school membership sometimes came at the expense of developing a valuable, substantive curriculum. A few succeeded in offering this kind of curriculum, but several were either still struggling or had failed to confront the problem. That there were clear examples of alternatives that created an exciting, more authentic and intellectually stimulating curriculum, such as at the Media Academy, was very encouraging. The high level of engagement at the Media Academy is a form of proof that it is possible to offer a program of experiences that stretches the intellectual capacity of those considered at risk of failure. In addition, several other alternative schools demonstrated the power of authentic student work to engage otherwise disengaged and lower-achieving adolescents.

On the other hand, the New Futures schools generally failed to generate either the degree of school membership or more authentic schoolwork that is needed to produce significantly more engaged students. The one possible exception to this was the small health technologies program in one Pittsburgh high school. This exception proved interesting in that it was a school-within-a-school similar in a number of respects to the alternatives. However, efforts to create school-wide reforms that involved most students and teachers were far less successful in each of the New Futures cities.

What can we learn from comparing these two general strategies? One interpretation is that the size of a school is an absolutely crucial variable to engagement. Small schools are more likely to have conditions that provide for engagement. Building school membership is more easily achieved in small organizations where frequent face-to-face contact permits adults to personalize their relations with students. Moreover, small organizations are more likely to reach consensus about educational goals along with the rules and roles that help achieve them. It may be that small school settings encourage people to act consistently and fairly toward each other as a result of this consensus. Clear, consistent rules and standards carried out in a face-to-face and fair manner are likely to be interpreted by students as evidence of care and commitment from adults. In contrast, the larger bureaucratic schools tended to retain their impersonal, inconsistent, and even chaotic character despite the efforts of some teachers to build a more personal, caring environment.

A second interpretation of the findings is that academic engagement by students grows largely out of the adults' own passion and expertise. Passion refers to educators' commitment to their students' success; expertise refers to educators' knowledge and skill in providing authentic work and challenging experiences. To harness that passion and expertise, however, it seems that schools need to create more entrepreneurial opportunities for staff. Beyond believing in and being excited about what they do with students, teachers probably need to express their commitment through opportunities to invent, implement, and sustain innovative curricula and programs, which in turn produce clear evidence of student growth and success.

The Media Academy is an example of such entrepreneurship. The staff, and particularly the lead teachers, have a vision of what young people can become if they master the skills and substance of the disciplines that are encompassed in the mass media. The vision is a powerful one for students and teachers; it places students in the role of constructing their own knowledge, not just learning what others have discovered, as they create media products that have personal and social value. For teachers, students' products were evidence of the development of fundamentally important skills in reasoning and expressing ideas, basic strengths that would serve a person in different ways as student, worker, and citizen. The work that students produced was satisfying evidence of student and teacher success; such concrete evidence may be as important to teachers as it is to students if the former are to sustain their commitment and effort.

In contrast to the alternatives, no core group of staff in the New Futures schools stepped forward with a vision that could generate consensus about how to draw alienated youth into the process of education. The lack of consensus meant that contradictory and counterproductive practices continued unabated in the schools. While some teachers found ways to personalize their relations with students, others acted in ways that only distanced themselves from these same students. These schools failed to shed their culture of failure that had accrued over the years. The result was that programs designed for at-risk students were too often unable to generate passion among practitioners because too many professionals did not believe that educating at-risk youth was possible.

The New Futures schools were unable to find ways of drawing upon educators' entrepreneurial spirit, as the alternatives did. Most of the New Futures school systems were not prepared to authorize entrepreneurship at either the individual teacher level or the building level. The very notion of an entrepreneurship that might stimulate truly unique variations of curriculum and school organization was jarring to bureaucratic systems that were more comfortable with uniformity of procedure and content. Whatever the variations between and within schools that occurred in the New Futures systems, they were conceived and implemented from the organizational top of the system.

Perhaps inventing new schools, especially small ones, is much easier than restructuring larger ones that already exist. Restructuring existing schools to serve at-risk students appears to be especially difficult. These schools tend to have a history of failure and a legacy of unproductive practices. Developing a vision that challenges this cultural baggage becomes a prerequisite if schools are to be successful in generating academic engagement in at-risk students. The process might begin by breaking such schools into much smaller units that allow for new identities. Part of the new identity can be created if educators within the smaller units are seen as entrepreneurs charged with finding better ways of responding to their clients. If student work provides both students and teachers with evidence of success and competence, then there will be inherent rewards to teaching and learning.

## NOTES

1. We base this estimate on frequently cited high school drop-out rates of about 25 percent, course failure rates in urban middle and high schools that often exceed 50 percent, and Hodgkinson's (1991) synthesis of data suggesting that about one third of preschool children are destined for school failure.

2. See, respectively, Shepard and Smith, 1989; Oakes, 1985; Epstein and Dauber, 1991.

## REFERENCES

Epstein, J. L., & Dauber, S. L. (1991). School programs and teacher practices of parent involvement in inner city elementary and middle schools. *Elementary School Journal, 91,* 289–301.

Foley, I. M., & McConnaughy, S. B. (1982). *Towards school improvement: Lessons from alternative high schools.* New York: Public Education Association.

Gardner, H. (1983). *Frames of mind: The theory of multiple intelligences.* New York: Basic Books.

Hodgkinson, H. (1991). Reform versus reality. *Phi Delta Kappan, 73*(1), 9–16.

Knapp, M. S., & Shields, P. M. (1990). Reconceiving academic instruction for the children of poverty. *Phi Delta Kappan, 72*(10), 753–758.

Levin, H. (1988). *Accelerated schools for at-risk students.* New Brunswick, NJ: Center for Policy Research in Education, Rutgers University.

National Council of Teachers of Mathematics. (1989). *Curriculum and evaluation standards for school mathematics.* Reston, VA: Author.

Newmann, F. M. (1988, January). Can depth replace coverage in the high school curriculum? *Phi Delta Kappan, 69*(5), 345–348.

Newmann, F. M. (1991). Linking restructuring to authentic student achievement. *Phi Delta Kappan, 72*(6), 458–463.

Oakes, J. (1985). *Keeping track: How schools structure inequality.* New Haven: Yale University Press.

Resnick, L. B. (1987a). *Education and learning to think.* Washington, DC: National Academy Press.

Resnick, L. B. (1987b). Constructing knowledge in school. In L. S. Liben (Ed.), *Development and learning: Conflict or congruence?* Hillsdale, NJ: Lawrence Erlbaum.

Schorr, L. (1988). *Within our reach: Breaking the cycle of disadvantage.* New York: Doubleday.

Shepard, L. A., & Smith, M. L. (Eds). (1989). *Flunking grades: Research and policies on retention.* Philadelphia: Falmer Press.

Sizer, T. R. (1984). *Horace's compromise: The dilemma of the American high school.* Boston: Houghton Mifflin.

Slavin, R. E., Madden, N., & Karweit, N. L. (1989). *Effective programs for students at risk.* Needham Heights, MA: Allyn & Bacon.

Wehlage, G. G., Rutter, R. A., Smith, G. A., Lesko, N. L., & Fernandez, R. R. (1989). *Reducing the risk: Schools as communities of support.* Philadelphia: Falmer Press.

# CHAPTER 5

# Cultivating Teacher Engagement: Breaking the Iron Law of Social Class

## Karen Seashore Louis and BetsAnn Smith

As indicated in Chapter 4, increasing numbers of students can be expected to be disengaged from schooling because they differ substantially from the white, upper-middle-class students that public secondary schools have been designed to serve. In increasing numbers of public schools students are raised in families with a range of cultural heritages and are deeply affected by low incomes and an absent parent. This demographic shift poses many problems in developing school membership and authentic work for these students. This chapter delves more deeply into implications of this demographic shift for teachers' own engagement with students.

Research literature suggests a strong association between the socioeconomic characteristics of students and teacher satisfaction and engagement with their work. It has been predicted that as the proportion of low-income families rises, it will be more difficult not only to engage students in academic study, but also to recruit and retain teachers who can teach them successfully. Why should the concern for student engagement be extended to engagement of teachers themselves?

Many reformers have attributed the problems of student learning to poorly prepared teachers, but evidence suggests that an equally if not more serious problem is an increasing level of teacher detachment and alienation from their work and students (Corcoran, Walker, & White, 1988; Metz, 1990; National Education Association, 1987). Portraits of unengaged teachers have appeared in the reform literature (see, for example, Powell, Farrar, & Cohen, 1985). In our own study we heard such teachers described as "bored teachers who just go through the textbook and aren't thinking," teachers nicknamed "Mrs. Ditto or Mr. Filmstrip," teachers who "taught one year for 30 years," and teachers "who barely know their students' names."

Because teachers' work and students' work are inextricably inter-twined, teacher alienation is a primary stumbling block to improving student engagement. From the student's point of view, teacher engagement is a prerequisite for student engagement ("Why work for a teacher who doesn't really care or make learning stimulating?"). From the teacher's point of view, student engagement is critical to teacher investment ("Why waste my time on students who don't try?"). In this sense, teacher engagement is a critical step in the process of creating schools that increase student learning opportunities and improve student achievement.[1]

This chapter explores the development and sustenance of teacher engagement in three innovative schools with large numbers of low-income students. First we explain in more detail the nature of teacher engagement and its relationship to student engagement and social class. We then give an overview of our study and four general factors that help explain levels of teacher engagement. We present findings on each of these factors and conclude with how the schools promoted different aspects of teacher engagement.

## TEACHER ENGAGEMENT, STUDENT ENGAGEMENT, AND STUDENTS' SOCIAL CLASS

Teacher and student engagement both involve a psychological invest-ment in doing good work, but teacher engagement has its own specific character. It is a teacher's psychological investment in and effort toward teaching the knowledge, skills, and crafts he or she wishes students to master. Engagement can be indicated by a variety of behaviors, such as planning and developing lessons and curriculum, and teaching through describing, explaining, helping, listening, reflecting, encouraging, and evaluating. And, just as student engagement involves more than ritualistic completion of assigned tasks, teacher engagement involves more than meeting the minimum outlines of assigned duties.

Four distinctive types of teacher engagement can be identified, two of which focus on general qualities of human relationships in the school, and two of which focus on specific goals of teaching and learning (Bryk & Driscoll, 1988; Firestone & Rosenblum, 1988; Newmann, Rutter, & Smith, 1989; Wehlage, Rutter, Smith, Lesko, & Fernandez, 1989).

1. *Engagement with the school as a social unit.* This form of engagement reflects a sense of community and personal caring among adults within the school and promotes integration between personal life and work life. We see this form of engagement among teachers who "wouldn't want to work at any other school," teachers who refer to peers and

students as friends and family, teachers who attend after-hours school events as often as they can, and teachers who are quick to rally together if faced with a troubling event.

2. *Engagement with students as unique whole individuals* rather than only as vessels to be filled with specific, predetermined bodies of knowledge. Teachers demonstrate this type of engagement when they lead classes in ways that acknowledge and respond to students' thoughts and knowledge, listen to students' ideas, involve themselves in students' personal as well as school lives, and in general make themselves available to students needing support or assistance. Many types of formal and informal coaching, sponsoring, mentoring, and counseling activities are additional examples of engagement with students.

3. *Engagement with academic achievement.* Curriculum writing and development, sharing with other teachers ideas and experiences about teaching as a craft, making creative use of class time, expressing high expectations for performance, providing useful feedback to students, and actively considering how students are assessed are all ways teachers can be engaged in their students' achievement.

4. *Engagement with one's subject* and the body of knowledge needed to carry out effective teaching. Particularly in secondary schools teachers need to keep current in their content fields and incorporate new subject-related ideas into their classrooms. Expressing one's personal passion for a subject, seeking ways to connect the subject to students' lives, being involved in professional organizations, and pursuing advanced degrees in one's field are examples of this form of engagement.

The four types of engagement are distinct, but distinct structures or activities are not necessarily required to sustain each dimension of engagement. For example, a staff development retreat focusing on cooperative learning can support both the development of a sense of community among adults and a focus on student achievement.

When they enter the profession, most teachers are engaged with their work on several of these dimensions. But over time, engagement is almost always affected by the presence and absence of various demands on teachers, including the demands teachers place on themselves and the demands of their students, their peers, their principal, and students' parents. While demands may be stressful, they can also energize: Students who ask for more and parents who involve themselves in the school create an environment of high expectations for teachers. In order for engagement to be sustained, however, teachers (like students) need positive reinforcers such as a sense of membership in the school and the opportunity to invest oneself in authentic work.

Some popular case studies have shown that even in the most unprom-

ising contexts — where demands on teachers are low and positive reinforcers limited — some forms of teacher engagement remain high among
some teachers (Freedman, 1990; Kidder, 1989). But teacher engagement
anchored in only a few of these dimensions will not necessarily serve
students well. A staff may be highly engaged with the social community
of adults in the school, but may neglect students and their achievement.
Or, they may become so obsessed with the achievement of some students
that they neglect others. While each form of engagement may be desirable, all need to be present for teaching to remain vital and effective for
all students.

As we shall see below, the patterns of demands and positive reinforcers often vary in schools of different socioeconomic climates in ways
that penalize teachers of lower-income students. Thus, redesign of school
organization so teachers working with disadvantaged children enjoy the
same opportunities for engagement as those who work with more advantaged children is as fundamental to improving education as is altering
curriculum.

The connection between teacher and student engagement and social
class is empirically demonstrated in recent qualitative studies and those
based on large-scale survey data.[2] Dworkin (1987), for example, reports
that teachers in schools with students from low socioeconomic backgrounds are more likely to be burned out and disengaged, while Purkey,
Rutter, and Newmann (1986–87) show that teachers in urban schools
(presumably with higher proportions of children from lower socioeconomic contexts) are less satisfied with their work.

Metz's (1990; Metz & Colleagues, 1988) study of eight "ordinary"
high schools, which preceded this study, is most pertinent to this chapter.
Metz used detailed descriptions of three of the schools to demonstrate the
thesis that the socioeconomic characteristics of the community affect not
only the characteristics of students, but also the behaviors of parents in
relation to teachers, the socioeconomic and educational characteristics of
teachers who are recruited to the schools, the behavior of the principal,
and staff expectations of the role that education will play in the lives of
children. We briefly summarize the schools studied by Metz.

## High SES Community

Cherry Glen, an affluent suburban school, had active parents who
intervened frequently when grades dropped and demanded much of
teachers. Most of the student population performed at or above national
norms, worked hard, and took school seriously. The principal hired "the
best" — largely middle-class teachers with advanced degrees from good
universities — and reinforced the value of hard work and ingenuity among

teachers. The image presented by Metz is almost like that of a law firm: hierarchical, but with a clear reward structure for the right kind of work. Teachers were involved in students' learning, albeit with a preference for higher-ability groups, where student engagement is much stronger. Challenging students, hard work, and creative teaching were all valued and promoted by policies that gave teachers autonomy in how they designed and conducted their classes.

## Middle SES Community

Pine Hill, an established blue-collar suburb, was markedly different. First, the community wanted to keep education costs low. Parents wanted their children to graduate, "but they were less concerned about the level of challenge they were exposed to, or the content of the curriculum" (Metz, 1990, p. 53). Teachers felt little pressure to create a stimulating classroom environment and often used over half of the classroom time for "homework" or relatively unsupervised solitary activities. Curriculum and instructional emphasis was on learning values, such as respect for authority, rather than content, which most believed to be uninteresting to adolescents. Teachers were largely working class in origin. Their lives outside school involved significant gender segregation, finding gratifications they did not receive from teaching, and a skepticism about the value of intellectual work. Skepticism about the value of knowledge and intellectual inquiry was high for many, such as this (biology) teacher.

> I think biology is probably one of the most useless courses in the world. What do you remember about biology! . . . Some teachers think that their subject matter is so godly important that if these kids don't get this idea that I'm trying to put across, they're not going to be better people . . . I know that if I would give the kids a test on what I taught six weeks ago, they'd all flunk it. (Metz, 1988, p. 10)

Although the principal supported the few teachers who had new ideas for courses or curriculum, he directed his main efforts at maintaining good relationships between the community and the school. Teachers who valued learning did their best to lead productive classes, but their engagement came from isolated personal commitments sustained with little support from those around them.

## Lower SES Community

Demands and value orientations within low-income schools can present contrasting pictures. Those who teach in lower-income areas are subjected to more problems of value conflict and ambiguity. In one of the schools studied by Metz, a largely African-American teaching staff worked with fervor to deliver a traditional college preparatory program, including calculus and physics, to low-performing students with tremendous educational and personal difficulties. Yet these standards did not elicit student engagement and achievement. Many students failed, and few would go to college. In another school, a predominantly white group of teachers, overwhelmed by a student body that they perceived to be declining in aptitude and interest, barely tried to deliver educational content above the most basic skills. Both of these responses were dysfunctional. In the first case, the teachers denied the irrelevance of the curriculum to the students' abilities and life circumstances, while in the second, teachers abandoned the goal of pushing students to do their best.

### The "Iron Law of Social Class"

The policy and research literature suggests three parts to what we call an "iron law of social class"; namely (1) the higher the socioeconomic status of the community, the higher the value placed on education; (2) the higher the value placed on education, the more the system will press teachers to perform; (3) the greater the pressure on teachers to deliver, the higher the performance of the students.

The policy implications of this line of argument are clear. Since low performance of students in lower socioeconomic communities is largely the fault of the community itself, the only way to change this is to pressure teachers to have "high levels of expectation" in contrast to the community (see also Hallinger & Murphy, 1986).

In traditionally organized schools where teachers' professional lives focus almost exclusively within their classrooms, it is not surprising that teachers who work with the most responsive and quickest students—predominantly those of the middle classes and the higher tracks—feel most rewarded, since both positive reinforcement and demands are high. The arguments of Metz (1988) and Cohen (1988) that teachers are dependent on their students for their professional satisfactions are empirically accurate. Yet the point may obscure how school organization can affect teacher engagement.

## AN ALTERNATIVE PERSPECTIVE: OVERVIEW OF THE STUDY

Our study began with a different perspective. We realized that it is not possible to change students' social origins. However, it may be possible to change the relationship between social class and teacher commitment and engagement by creating organizational conditions that make it easier for teachers to experience success with students. The main point of our research was to study this prospect, that is, to see how to release teachers from an unhealthy "ultimate dependency" on their students by increasing the alternative sources of satisfaction and fulfillment.[3] Thus, rather than viewing teacher engagement solely as a function of student engagement, we sought out the connections between teacher engagement and the organizational conditions of the school. In doing so we acknowledged that success with students is fundamental to teacher satisfaction. We thought it was also critical to acknowledge the range of professional and organizational conditions in schools that can provide additional sources of demands and reinforcements.

From 1987 to 1990, we conducted research in eight public, nonselective high schools actively involved in efforts to improve working conditions for teachers. We deliberately chose a diverse sample of community environments. One school was in a predominantly affluent community; three schools — one suburban, one rural, and one urban — were in mixed socioeconomic communities of middle-class status overall, and four served communities where over half of the student body came from disadvantaged homes, including students from poor, minority, and immigrant families. In these latter schools, between 55 and 65 percent of the students were considered disadvantaged by the principal.[4]

In each school, two members of the research staff spent five to six days observing classrooms, interviewing teachers individually and in groups, interviewing groups of students, "shadowing" the principal, and attending routine meetings and events, ranging from lunch to evening activities. The focus of both interviews and observations was to gather information about the impact of district and school organization on teachers' work lives (see Louis, Purkey, Rosenblum, Rossmiller, & Smith, 1991, for a more detailed discussion of methodologies).

## A Profile of the Schools and Their Communities

To illustrate how schools serving the disadvantaged can secure for their teachers working conditions similar to those of schools serving more advantaged students, we focus on three of the schools, referred to here by pseudonyms.[5] These three schools had the least affluent student bodies of all the eight schools in the study, based both on principal reports and our own observations. However, when we analyzed survey data on engagement with teaching, these schools reported levels of engagement for the average staff member that were as high as or higher than the more affluent schools. Specific survey measures of teacher engagement are shown in Figure 5.1.[6] Our point is not that these teachers prefer the professional

**Figure 5.1**
**Ten Survey Items Measuring Teacher Engagement**

I frequently take on extra tasks or responsibilities that I think will benefit the school.

I wouldn't want to work in any other school.

The reputation and performance of this school are important to me.

I try very hard to show my students that I care about them.

It's important for me to know something about my students' families.

I try to make myself accessible to students even if it means meeting with them before or after school, during my prep or free period, etc.

It is important that as teachers we try to ensure that all students master basic skills and subject-matter coursework.

I am always thinking about ways of improving my courses.

Interdisciplinary classes benefit teachers as well as students.

Given the opportunity, I would take additional college or university courses in the subject area I teach most often.

---

Standardized Item Alpha = .66. All items were measured on a six-point scale ranging from "strongly agree" to "strongly disagree." A total of 26 items were included in the survey battery, including measures of negative attitudes toward students, availability of resources needed for teaching, concerns about safety in the school, etc.

---

conditions of lower SES schools. In fact, teachers in lower SES schools had many complaints about working conditions and their students' behavior. Nevertheless, in these schools teachers brought more effort, energy, and hope to their teaching tasks than would be predicted by the "iron law."

*City Park Secondary School*

City Park is a small, innovative secondary school located in an impoverished section of a major northeastern city. Surrounded by a public housing project, stores, and other tenements, the community is one where poverty, crime, drugs, and violence touch lives on a daily basis. The school shares a large 1950s-era building with two other small schools—a common practice in the district, which allows parents and students to choose which school to attend. Although the immediate neighborhood is largely Hispanic, the school aims for a diverse enrollment and has largely succeeded:

Its student body is approximately 45 percent African-American, 35 percent Hispanic, and 20 percent white, with a broad range of academic ability.

Opened in 1984, the school is rooted in the progressive education tradition of John Dewey and Lillian Weber, and is structured around the following principles: minimization of bureaucracy; a humanistic, open environment characterized by equal respect for staff and students (students do not need passes to go to the bathroom and students and staff are both addressed by first name); no tracking; an integrated core curriculum planned and developed by teams of teachers; significant teacher team planning time; instructional/learning strategies oriented around "essential questions" and critical thinking; parent involvement; and an overall sense of family. City Park is a member of the Coalition of Essential Schools. The school enrolls around 600 students. The organization consists of three divisions (7–8, 9–10, and 11–12), which are further divided into houses of about 80 students. There are no traditional departments, but within each division there is a math-science team and a humanities team, each consisting of about five teachers. Teams meet weekly for two hours and are the primary unit for developing and coordinating curriculum, sharing ideas, and discussing what has and has not worked. Scheduling is nontraditional, with students and teachers meeting for two-hour blocks in cross-grade groups (e.g., 9–10). Students stay with the same teachers for two years. There is also a daily one-hour advisory period, where every teacher assumes guidance responsibility for the academic and personal growth of 12 to 15 students.

## Brigham Alternative High School

Like City Park, Brigham was designed to provide an alternative school experience to any student wishing to enroll. Established four years ago in a small southern city, the school sought to emphasize "open education" values, stressing a more interdisciplinary curriculum and student responsibility for learning. For several years Brigham was used as a "dumping ground" by other district schools, and it has continued to struggle to shed its image as a place where other schools send their most troubled and least successful students. Eighty percent of the student body is African-American, and, with the exception of the few students who are children of the school's teachers, most are from working-class or very poor families.

The school's evolving educational philosophy is based on commitment to experiential and cooperative learning, mixed-ability grouping, a humanistic curriculum, and a family-like environment. However, the ability of the school to implement its ideas fully is impeded by the requirement that it follow the rigid outcomes-based district curriculum and testing program, known as CBOK (Common Body of Knowledge), as well as a local culture that still strongly supports "paddling" as a form of student discipline.

The organization of the school has traditional components, with department heads, 50-minute periods, and age grouping. Teachers in some departments allocate teaching by grades, so that a small number of teachers are familiar with all the students in a grade, thus permitting easier monitoring of student performance and personal problems. The school also uses an advisory, which is expected to provide both guidance and opportunities for more personal interaction between students and teachers, and has several committees to deal with shared governance.

## Hillside High School

Hillside is located only a few miles from a medium-sized "border state" city, but it is in a hilly, rural setting that appears remarkably bucolic. Although the community is one of the oldest in the state, it never prospered and remains sparsely settled. Most residents used to work at one of several large industrial complexes close by, but layoffs and plant closings have created very high levels of unemployment. The educational level of the community is quite low, and the graduation rate has recently been only about 65 percent. Of those who graduate, only 30 percent have gone on to some form of postsecondary education. Three quarters of the student body are "local rednecks" — a term students and staff use freely; one quarter are African-Americans and are bussed in from the nearby city.

Unlike the two previously described schools, Hillside is a long established and large school (over 1,000 students) with a mostly traditional comprehensive curriculum delivered by 13 departments in a six-period day. Only five years ago Hillside was viewed as one of the worst schools in the district; now there is a waiting list of teachers who want to transfer in. For the past four years the school has been involved in major reform efforts stimulated by a local professional teacher academy's concern with teacher reform. More recently, the school has become involved with the Coalition of Essential Schools. Establishing ties with both the local academy and the Coalition has been approved by a staff vote and is strongly supported by the principal. The most critical change was the steering committee, which is composed of elected faculty members, the principal and assistant principal, a counselor, the athletic director, representatives from the district's teacher center, students, parents, and an elected member of the nonprofessional support staff. The open meetings of this committee are used to develop directions for program improvement at Hillside, and most of the work is carried out in subcommittees. The steering committee has introduced many new programs, such as a daily period that is used for teachers to work with students on specific problems or issues, multidisciplinary curriculum units, and a "9th-Grade bridge," which focuses on the development of an interdisciplinary curriculum and team teaching for a group of approximately one third of the incoming freshman class.

## A Framework for Analyzing Influences on Teacher Engagement

In studying how these schools promote teacher engagement, we considered each of the following four factors:[7]

1. *The community and district environment of the school.* A number of researchers have argued that life inside schools, particularly schools in larger districts, is continuously and often negatively affected by local politics and the district office (Farrar, 1988). Conversely, Louis (1989) notes that where district and community support is strong, the school "works better" and is more easily able to work on improvement issues; therefore, one might logically argue that teachers' sense of a "payoff" from making a commitment would be greater. As noted above, many hypothesize that the effects of community socioeconomic status are greater than all others — this chapter deals centrally with whether other factors are at least as important, if not more so.

2. *School culture, and particularly teacher culture.* Metz (1990) argues that school and teacher culture tend to conform to local community norms about education, which are socioeconomically based, and that where middle-class staffs teach in lower socioeconomic schools, it is especially difficult to generate both high expectations for achievement and sensitivity to students' social backgrounds. We were particularly curious to see whether school and teacher culture in these schools could break this "iron law" and reveal instead norms of high engagement and achievement.

3. *The leadership of the principal and others in the school.* Virtually every study of schools that function more effectively for students emphasizes the role of the principal and other leaders in matters such as setting a tone for what is expected, energizing staff, and creating an orderly environment (Brookover, Beady, Flood, Schweitzer, & Wisenbaker, 1979; Wilson & Corcoran, 1988). Louis and Miles (1990) have shown that certain forms of principal leadership and management are associated with improvement in working relations among teachers and gen-

eral climate. Leadership style would, therefore, also seem to have a major impact on teachers' willingness to engage.

4. *The alternative or unusual structures and activities in the school.* This study was initiated in a period when there was a growing assumption that schools could be altered to improve teachers' work. Reports such as those from the Holmes Group (1986) and the Carnegie Forum (1986) have argued that until the organization surrounding the classroom — and even the classroom and curriculum itself — is changed we can expect no improvements in our ability to attract and retain the best teachers. The implied problem is that current work is structured so as to be alienating rather than engaging. We wanted to learn about the extent to which innovative structures contributed to teacher engagement.

## HOW THREE SCHOOLS PROMOTE TEACHER ENGAGEMENT

We discuss findings in relation to each of the four factors just described.

### Community and District Context

Community and district contexts can be demanding environments for urban schools and schools that serve lower socioeconomic communities. But these three schools didn't simply react to their contexts; they attempted to mold and create them in a variety of ways.

#### Stressing Challenge and Respect for the Community

Metz (1990) argues that school norms tend to conform to local community norms about the value and purpose of education, some stressing challenge, others stressing compliance. City Park, Brigham, and Hillside have all departed from such mirroring by stressing their own norms about education's importance. Despite the fact that parent and community support for educational achievement has often been very weak, the schools seem to have reconciled two potentially conflicting norms. While being sensitive to community feelings and respecting parents, they also push students toward levels of success that may appear to exceed parents' own initial expectations.

By reaching out to parents, the schools established the norm that parents care about their children's education and deserve to be listened to. Each of the schools designed conference schedules and locations that were supportive of explicit and clear communication, even bringing in third-party social workers and counselors to help mediate differences and providing translators for parents who are not comfortable speaking in English. The schools also set high standards for parent involvement and knowledgeability. City Park required parents to visit the school and to discuss their child with an administrator or teacher before the child was admitted. They also required parents to come to the school for conferences if the child was not performing well. Similar requirements and relationships were sought by Brigham and Hillside. Also, all three schools involved parents in various school committees, including major governance committees at Hillside.

## Negotiating Positive or Minimal District Relations

More often than not, high schools serving low socioeconomic communities operate within large districts, while those serving more advantaged communities operate in much smaller, more supportive, and less regulatory districts. Our case studies suggest that schools serving disadvantaged students can support teacher engagement by seeking school relationships with the district office more like those in high socioeconomic communities, where high schools typically enjoy considerable autonomy. Nevertheless, the difficulties of achieving better school-to-district relationships should not be underestimated.

In Brigham, the district office and other schools were generally viewed as unsupportive and even hostile. Much of this attitude was traced to the school's beginning, where its "alternative" title was confused with the regional proliferation of "alternative schools" that were last-chance institutions for dropouts, disruptive students, or other children who failed to thrive in a normal school environment. As one teacher said,

> This school has had a lot of negative publicity that was unwarranted, and still today a lot of people will be surprised that if you work at Alternative that we [don't] work in a prison or something.

In addition to the negative image of the school among fellow educators and the community at large, Brigham teachers and administrators worked in a district setting universally perceived to be unfriendly to the goals of the school and to teachers in general.

> I don't feel that teachers are a respected force downtown, within the district.

> . . . We are so lucky that, almost by chance, we report to the
> Associate Superintendent for junior high schools. He is suppor-
> tive of what we do [and helps us to get around some of the rules
> governing the curriculum], but if we reported to anyone else we
> wouldn't have a chance to try anything that deviated from dis-
> trict policy.

To support their contentions, Brigham teachers pointed to their extremely
low salaries, the efforts of the district to develop a "teacher-proof curriculum" in which teachers had virtually no choice about what to teach or
when to teach it, and the lack of money for inservice or professional
activities. In addition, resources that many schools take for granted—such
as up-to-date audiovisual equipment—were not available, and the school's
discretionary budget was minute compared with other schools in our sample of eight.

Surprisingly, despite these conditions, most teachers reported that the
environment allowed them to come together and build an esprit de corps
that might not have otherwise existed. Many teachers said that their deter-
mination for success increased after a terrible first year during which they
were sent "the rejects" from other schools and shared the building with
another school whose staff was antagonistic.[8]

> I think [the faculty] were strong and I think they were commit-
> ted and I think they were very determined that this school was
> going to make it come hell or high water, no matter what. . . .

The ability of the school to build itself into a strong community was, in
part, a consequence of the fact that the principal was able to attract and
hire the staff that she wanted, rather than being "sent" teachers from
downtown.

The bureaucratic environment of City Park, despite its location in a
school system noted for its massive and insensitive central structure, was
in many ways more benign. The district in which the school is located
had demonstrated a decade of support for innovative, alternative pro-
gramming. In addition, because it was designated as an alternative school,
City Park had the prerogative to request flexibility in rules such as hiring
practices, class size, and curriculum issues. City Park also benefitted from
the national visibility of its principal. Considerable media publicity for
the school helped to buffer it from district interventions. Thus, although
teachers didn't look at the city school system as an advantage, the district
did not figure heavily in their perception of their work setting. In general,
teachers viewed the district and school system as a "black box" that the

principal dealt with effectively, and the community as a turbulent environment that posed many hazards for their students.

Finally, district leadership provided Hillside with a powerful catalyst for heightening teachers' morale and commitment. The district loosened its requirements on schools and allowed them more individual flexibility in determining their programs. For example, the district supported Hillside's request, made in order to establish the teacher-guided assistance program, for a schedule that was not in compliance with state mandates. Furthermore, teachers who worked on new projects were provided both professional and psychological sustenance from the nearby professional academy. During the week that our research team was at Hillside, a 9th Grade teaching team spent an entire day at the academy building to plan for several weeks of instruction. There, teachers had access to consultation, working space, and reference materials. In short, the academy provided both time and resources to create, develop, and implement new ideas.

*School Site Control*

What all three schools sought — and gained to some extent — was control over several key functions, including the ability (1) to develop an educational mission specific to their school, (2) to hire staff directly, (3) to develop their own curriculum and instruction plans, and (4) to design staff development opportunities accordingly. Having this sense of organizational control improved the sense of membership and ownership among the school staff. Teachers in all three of these schools emphasized how important it was for them to be part of a school that pursued a collective definition of goals and strategies. Released from predetermined conditions, they were freer to develop a school environment and program reflecting the educational values they were most committed to. By being allowed to conduct their own hiring, these schools could employ teachers who were committed to work with the school's vision rather than against it. All these benefits helped the schools promote teacher engagement in their schools as a whole, and in their students' personal and academic development.

## Teacher Culture

All three of the schools share norms that make teachers' work life different from that in conventional schools. We will limit the discussion here to norms that seem to have a significant positive impact on teacher engagement.

*A Strong Sense of Being in "a School with a Mission"*

Teachers in all three schools emphasized how important it was to them to be part of a school that had (or was striving for) a collective definition not only of its goals (high achievement) but also of its strategies for reaching them. A teacher at Brigham spoke for most of her colleagues when she said,

> I had previously taught at the elementary level and I taught reading on the junior high level. And I was attracted to this school because of the philosophy about reading not being just one discipline, but covering all the areas. . . . I was approached by a faculty member here who knew my philosophy on education, plus I had worked with the principal before. . . . We both had the same ideas about education.

In City Park, where the coherence of the pedagogical approach and the need to develop this approach through teamwork were most forcefully articulated, the need to subscribe to the sense of mission and to draw energy from it were often mentioned.

> People know that [the team approach] is . . . how we are going to work and they know why. If you want to work in this school, that is the bottom line. . . . I think [it] makes the job of teaching a creative experience, and creativity feeds on itself.

And at Hillside, where the faculty were still struggling with the precise nature of the "special quality" of the school, there was a strong sense of being engaged in a risky, but exciting, joint venture. As one physical education teacher said,

> My personal goals, as far as teaching, go along with this school. Now, not everybody would want to be here, not everybody would want to teach in [this community]. . . . I like the changes that have come about . . . I like it because we are experimenting. We don't know really where we're going. . . . And after 23 years of teaching, to have that freedom to do some things, and the fact that I do not work alone anymore, that I work with a group of people—it's made it so much easier.

Developing or being part of a collective vision of education necessitated commitment. As one City Park teacher put it, when asked if she would want to teach somewhere else, "There *is* nowhere else to teach." There was a "bottom line" — either the teachers subscribed to the vision and were part of the dominant group, or they did not and were viewed as "part of the minority, the small group that doesn't really see the point." While teachers can stay in the school and maintain a detachment from the collective commitment, teachers at Hillside and Brigham reported that it was hard on the more isolated teachers, some of whom "converted."

> One of the things that I have seen happen is that some of the people who were very negative about the whole deal at the beginning, three or four years ago, that I never thought would come on board and work on it, have finally come around and have started working on things because they felt like they've wanted to and they needed to.

In other words, a mission and vision create social pressures for teachers to make commitments to the school as a social unit and to the version of educational excellence that is embodied in the mission.

*An Emphasis on Closeness and Helping Among Staff Members*

At Brigham, this special quality was often described in terms of family imagery.

> Sure, this is what we stress here, this family group, this closeness. And I don't think we ought to grow (in size). . . . We are trying to be close to each other [as teachers], and know each other. . . .

In City Park and Hillside there was less use of the family imagery to refer to relationships among adults. However, there was much talk about trust.

> When I came here . . . I had to learn a lot. I got a tremendous amount of help. [The principal] helped me; [another teacher] with 14 years of experience became my best friend here. . . . I used to meet him every morning to talk about what we were going to do and how we were going to do it . . . and he would come observe my classes.

At Hillside, similar comments were heard, the most frequent being, "Everyone here is supportive."

*An Emphasis on Respect and Caring for Students*

The theme of respect and caring as significant aspects of teachers' work in restructured schools has been extensively developed elsewhere. The emphasis on caring for students, and the way in which it is inter-twined with teacher and student engagement, is probably best summarized by a teacher from City Park.

> Part of teaching is lending your ego for a kid to learn. . . . If you are only teaching a subject and not teaching kids — what you are talking about is communicating a subject. I am saying . . . that you may teach a subject well, but that you are only teach-ing it to the people who can pick it up exactly as you have pre-sented it. [But] if you are teaching the kids, you see where each kid is and what their next step is. You have to perceive all of the differences . . . you have to handle the resistance so that they may make steps for themselves. . . . *You have to do that, and that is an engaging process.*

In Hillside, students talked openly about teachers' caring.

> They're out to help you. They want you to learn. They will also sit down with you a lot of time, I mean work personally [with you]. It seems like they'll do it all the time, you know, to make sure you understand it.

At Brigham, caring was built into the school's vision, which emphasized the affirmation of individual worth. Brigham teachers saw this as a critical feature of the school, because it gave them a sense of self-worth as well.

> [This school] emphasizes self-worth. And if you can encourage, or you're successful in helping and enabling, a person to feel good about themselves and about what they are doing, then the opportunity for that person to be a successful person is enhanced significantly. And that's what we're doing here. We *are* doing that.

Caring is good for students, of course, but it is also good for teachers. Caring makes schools into ethical and moral environments, not just arenas for "getting the job done." Studies of beginning teachers indicate that the desire to be involved with a profession that has a moral character is a significant motivation. This is not simply altruism, but the teacher's need to be engaged with work that has significance broader than making a better widget.

## A Demand for Active Problem Solving Among Teachers

This theme arose repeatedly in the three schools. At City Park, one teacher commented about the way in which the problem-solving focus was reflected in student-teacher relationships.

> The assumption is that the kids are basically trying to do the best that they can, and that might not be so great at a given point in time, and you try to get everybody together and acknowledge that there's a problem, and rather than trying to blame some-one, you try to deal with what the problem is, what are the dif-ferent factors, and what can we do to change the situation. And that's the way problems are dealt with, even academically.

It should be noted that at all the schools, it was expected that teachers would involve themselves in maintaining constructive human relations, regardless of where they took place:

> I used to walk past two kids rolling around on the floor, having a fight. That wasn't my business, that was up to the security guards. That doesn't happen at City Park. Everything that hap-pens is everybody's business. After all, in your house, if your kids are acting crazy, your husband doesn't wait until you get home!

As a consequence of this strong focus on solving problems at their source, disciplinary problems were rare.

The problem-solving focus was also articulated in Hillside, where the emphasis was placed on the responsibility given to teachers to manage their own environment. As one new teacher explained,

> If you have an idea [you go to the principal] and usually, if you give her your idea she will say, "and how do you plan to put this idea into action?"

We observed another new teacher making the following remark to her colleagues in a meeting:

> You're all talking about what you want to accomplish at school. . . . At every other school I've ever been in they would

be complaining and whining and griping and saying how bad
the administration is. You all are figuring out what you're going
to do — that's good, and it's really different.

The essence of teachers' remarks was that at Hillside it was okay to complain about something, but only if you had ideas about how to fix it.

Problem solving was emphasized at Brigham, too, although teachers
also stressed that "if the district says no, then it's no." One teacher pointed
out that many of her colleagues "have been in traditional schools where
they feel that they're not going to be heard . . . so it's just a habit [they
have] of complaining to each other and not doing something about their
concerns." Still, relative to other schools in the district, Brigham teachers
saw themselves as being more active in looking for and solving problems.

My husband, who teaches in one of the other high schools . . .
he's surprised that [we] are allowed to make decisions that
stick . . . you know, about teacher time, teacher responsibility. . . .

I feel that in this school we have more say than in the other
schools, 80 percent more.

For teachers, the sense of being responsible for unearthing and solving
problems was the most powerful form of empowerment that they encountered. This sense of influence and responsibility made it difficult for most
to merely teach classes and grade papers without contributing in other
ways to the school and students.

### Peer Pressure to Work

Life in the three schools was more demanding than in most schools —
but worth it. As two Brigham teachers said,

The teachers [who] have left here and gone to other places in the
district . . . have said "Gosh, I miss it." They go to the room and
they work. And after school the bell rings, they hit the cars.

We have had meetings where we went through cooperative
learning until 5:30 . . . but at [school x], no one helped. . . .
And when I worked at [school y] . . . each teacher was out for
themselves.

City Park teachers talked about being exhausted, feeling that the work of
curriculum development and active teaching had no end. But no teacher

suggested that the effort made them want to leave. At Hillside, another teacher commented, "I do a lot more work and spend a lot more hours here, and I have to get along with a lot more people but I enjoy it more and so it is worth it."

Why is pressure to work more engaging? Because it is tied to a sense of doing work that addresses the vision of the school, and because it has visible payoff in the impacts on students — those that are often viewed as dull and uninterested in school. At Hillside, experienced teachers spoke with amazement about the differences in working with students now compared with previous years.

> The kids we have as juniors this year were 9th graders when [these changes] first started. They're better behaved, they're more interested, and they're more willing to learn to do the kinds of things that help them learn than kids have been before.

> My biggest ego booster this year has been several teachers who have come to me and said, "You know what? I've got some kids in my class that took your program last year and they are better prepared than the rest of the kids in the class." That has happened three or four times from three or four different teachers and that really makes me feel good. . . .

A lesson that we take away is that the demands that are put upon teachers by their peers increase engagement because they provide valuable professional feedback from peers. Instead of being isolated in a classroom, and depending only on students for feedback, teachers are able to work with colleagues in ways that make their best work visible. The downside is that their failures may also be visible, but other norms, especially teachers helping one another, cushion the potentially negative impact of more exposure.

## Teacher Engagement and School Leadership

Having indicated several features of school culture that promote teacher engagement, the challenge is to identify origins of this positive culture that might be deliberately influenced. Teacher culture at both Brigham and City Park was profoundly shaped by the fact that teachers were hired specifically to work in new schools with a particular mission and they had chosen to do so. This created a sense of being in a special place and of working with a special team. At Hillside, on the other hand, most teachers had worked there for more than a decade. Few experienced a sense of unique mission until recently, but in 1990 teacher engagement at Hillside was nearly as high as at Brigham and City Park.

The factor that all the schools had in common, however, was a leadership style that promotes engagement. The "leadership factor" was even more important than we expected. There was consensus that a school with an ineffective principal was unlikely to be exciting no matter how talented the staff — and schools became exciting quite rapidly after the arrival of a supportive principal. The role of the effective principal was described as one that enables staff to develop the culture described above, while taking responsibility for other actions as well. Five aspects of leadership seemed particularly salient in these schools.

### Buffering Teachers

Studies of conventional schools emphasize the role of the principal in buffering the teachers from unwanted outside interventions by parents (Rossmiller, 1988). In these three schools, however, we have already mentioned how the principals emphasize respectful relationships with their communities regardless of parents' social position or history of support for education. While parents and community were often invited in, two of the principals worked hard at buffering their staffs from the demands of district offices. At Brigham and City Park, located in district contexts that were not always supportive of the schools' differences and autonomy, the principals sought to protect their staffs from distracting external demands and requirements. They recognized teachers' limited energies and struggled to preserve them for students and teaching. Although this was only partially effective in Brigham, teachers recognized the effort that went into trying to create an alternative and more professional work life within a highly centralized and authoritarian district. Simply having a principal who *cared* so deeply about protecting teachers increased engagement for many.

### Spending Time on Daily Routines

Leadership in the three schools did not conform to the image of the efficient executive who participates only in the highest level of policy and leaves the daily work of the organization to others. Instead, these principals were visible and were available for spontaneous discussion or problem solving. They spent time with students and tried to be present at all school activities. They were in the lunchroom and around the halls, not to discipline, but to gather information. At City Park and Brigham the principals led student advisory groups. At Hillside we saw the principal personally praising individual students and teachers every day. This emphasis on the normal routines of school constantly reminded them of their own importance in the life of their school and students. Obviously, in a big school like Hillside, the principal cannot know everything. But even there faculty commented on her willingness to balance knowledge with empowerment.

> She keeps the staff together . . . she does facilitate what we want to do. There are so many things going on in this building that even she admits that she no longer can keep up with what's going on. But what's really neat about [our principal] is that she trusts our professionalism so much that . . . even if she's not aware of every small detail, it's okay.

### Delegating and Empowering

Promoting conditions that acknowledge the professional capabilities and judgments of teachers was another quality these principals shared. Principals who create healthy environments for teachers "make teachers invent solutions to problems — they aren't the only problem solver." The effective principal "can leave the building without things falling apart or hitting snags, and has staff empowered to respond to crises." At Hillside, the following comment was typical:

> She believes in shared decision making which is exactly what she says! If the faculty votes on something, she does everything she can, even if she disagrees with it, to put it through.

At City Park, the philosophical conviction was to empower the team rather than the individual teacher. Communal decisions prevailed (even when the administrators were not enthusiastic). It was up to the principal and other individuals in leadership roles to implement collective resolutions, with some autonomy and flexibility. Brigham was the slight exception here, since teachers were well aware that the principal's ability to support decisions made by faculty was limited by strong central control.

These leaders also recognized risk-taking as part of problem solving, and they encouraged teachers to take those risks. To stretch professionally, teachers must take risks in the classroom. For example, they promoted no single formula for maximizing student engagement. Classes that seek to make learning meaningful, appropriate, and fun require new ideas; an atmosphere of risk-taking allows teachers to try new approaches.

*Confronting Unengaged Teachers*

A clear and direct way of promoting teacher engagement is to require changes in teachers who do not invest themselves along the four dimensions outlined at the beginning of this chapter. Teachers are inspired to work hard by those around them, and over and over again the teachers in these schools stressed the positive impact of a principal's personal willingness to confront bad teaching. The schools provided a variety of supportive strategies to help less effective teachers improve, including mentor teachers, an environment that invited teachers to visit one another's classes and help one another, and staff development opportunities. For example, Brigham's principal worked with several teachers who had difficulty changing to a teaching style that minimized lecturing and teacher-centered instruction. This ultimately encouraged one teacher to leave, but for others it created a process that enabled them to make significant improvements. At City Park, some teachers experienced anxiety about their success with the advisories, but the assistant principal put a great deal of energy into sharing his knowledge about and experiences with dealing with students more personally. Still, if it was clear that a teacher was unable to develop supportive relationships with students, he or she did not return the next year.

*Providing Leadership About Values*

Teachers agreed that the principal set the tone for developing a vision and a clear value orientation for the school. It is important for the principal to understand and reflect the best in community ethical standards and values, and to "make clear what is valued — don't keep faculty guessing about what is important." Principals' articulation of strong values was most visible in Brigham and City Park, where each principal also founded the school based on a particular educational philosophy. In both cases, that philosophy emphasized the dimensions of engagement we discussed and was premised on eliminating teacher isolation through creating opportunities for collaborative work. In large and well-established Hillside, the principal's influence on values was more subtle, but still acknowledged by all teachers, particularly with regard to increasing parent involvement, focusing on interdisciplinary curriculum development, and caring for students.

## Teacher Engagement and School Organization

These principals encouraged engagement in additional ways by helping to initiate organizational changes that reinforced (or revived) the staff's commitments to teaching. Organizational changes attended not simply to instructional issues. Instead, a variety of teachers' needs figured heavily in administrative priorities.

### Creating Structures to Promote Teacher Decision Making

The principals of these schools went beyond informal, open-door discussions and problem solving. They also built formal decision-making structures. Although teachers valued informal opportunities to give opinions or make suggestions, formal decision-making bodies were important symbols of their professional status in the school. At Brigham a teacher commented,

> We have the opportunity to influence things that are going on,
> such as electing the assistant principal. We have the opportunity
> to come up with meaningful plans and implement them.

At City Park the faculty saw the entire school structure as being designed for empowerment.

> We are a decision-making school. We work as a whole school,
> we work . . . within our team and . . . within our classrooms
> where even kids are allowed to make some decisions about how
> things are to be done.

At Hillside, the steering-group structure worked well for teachers because it was tied to the kinds of curriculum renewal that were at the heart of their interests. Thus, it was the teacher-designed task forces that won their real commitment of energy. Brigham teachers were empowered by a formal Shared Governance Committee with authority to hire administrators and teachers and set policy. In a district that gave the school limited autonomy, they also valued the informal "Working It Out" committee, which worked to solve smaller problems before they escalated — creating, in the process, a sense that they controlled the school.

### Creating Structures to Promote Collaboration

In all three schools, teachers attributed high levels of engagement to organizational structures that permitted them to spend more time with each other. This not only strengthened personal bonds, but also infused new enthusiasm about instruction. City Park's schedule provided teams with a weekly two-hour meeting in which they developed curriculum, teaching strategies, and student assignments. The schedule reflected the value the school placed on teachers' own engagement with their academic program.

> In my other school, what I was good at, I stayed good at. What I wasn't good at, I never improved at. . . . I taught a self-contained class, and believe me, self-contained really means self-contained. . . . I really could have been in the building all by myself. There were never times when you could get together and discuss issues with other teachers, and if your class was quiet, you were left alone.

At Hillside collaboration usually revolved around task force work. In Brigham, due to lack of resources and the school's inability to change district schedules, collaboration was more informal and typically involved smaller numbers of teachers, except for the school's strong staff development work with cooperative learning. Nevertheless, it was expected that teachers would stay after school for collaborative development work.

The reduction in isolation was apparent in all settings. A Brigham teacher said,

> I have found . . . professional collegiality presented here that my husband does not benefit from even though he's been at his school for 20 years. . . . I mean, I have teachers on their off period come by and sit in my classroom who are not even in the English department. . . . I don't know of that ever happening [elsewhere] because in the other schools your room is your domain. . . . "You don't enter my room without my permission" type of thing. . . .

A Hillside staff member pointed to the collaboration–engagement link.

> We work together on so many things (because of the steering committee). And one of the things that has opened up is that if I want to do something within math, there are teachers here that I know I can go to and they will help me teach that in my classroom.

In City Park, the principal's work was based on a philosophy of the need for collaboration, tying it to both teacher engagement and student engagement.

You must remove teachers from isolation and make learning exciting. To make learning exciting for students, you must make learning exciting for teachers, because when learning is exciting for both teachers and students, kids can't get lost.

## Creating Structures to Promote Professional Development

Collegiality boosts engagement in part because it increases interpersonal knowledge and the "family" feeling. More important, however, is when collegiality is tied directly to the development of professional competence. At Brigham, where the district controlled staff development days and the school had few resources of its own, the opportunities seemed, on the surface, meager. However, for most of the teachers, simply teaching at Brigham was a learning experience. With few exceptions teachers had not engaged in "open education" or used cooperative learning, and they were called upon, as a group, to learn to do things differently. As they began to work together on this task, they also realized that they needed more collective reflection on these instructional issues.

It's been sort of a grope in the dark. But the last year or so we have had cooperative learning workshops. When we got the magnet school grant we were able to bring people in to the workshop with us. . . . But we do need to set up some type of program where we bring teachers together, where we have them visit other classrooms right at the beginning of the year and do some things over the summer.

At Hillside, with its enormous resources and new enthusiasm for change, each day was viewed as an occasion to learn from others.

There is tremendous opportunity to develop your skills and knowledge [in part] because of the collegiality that is so very prevalent. I mean, if you want to do it, there are people in this building that will do it with you. If you just want to sit back and be an observer, they'll let you come in and observe.

Another remarked that

Probably the nicest thing about being here at this school is the opportunity to use and/or develop skills and knowledge. And we do a lot of inservice giving. I mean, a lot of our faculty members give inservices to others.

Both Hillside and City Park viewed their school-wide retreats as critical structures for both individual and collective development. Yet, in none of the schools were the days officially dedicated to staff development as important as the provision of more ad hoc or semi-planned development opportunities. The importance of continuing experimentation and skill development to engagement was best summarized by a teacher from City Park.

> We're not always doing the same thing. There's always something new to be thinking about. . . . It encourages you to think about issues, to grapple with important questions.

### Creating Structures to Improve Curriculum

At the beginning of this chapter we briefly described some unengaged teachers and how, in ordinary schools, teachers can spend their energies on curricula of questionable benefit to their students. In one case teachers taught a traditional college preparatory curriculum to students who lacked basic skills; in another teachers were so frustrated by declining student engagement that they often taught nothing but basic skills.

Our study suggests that allowing and supporting teachers to write curricula specifically for the students they work with can increase many forms of engagement. Autonomy over curriculum was a feature in City Park and Hillside; Brigham has only recently been released from rigid district controls. Even at Brigham, however, teachers spoke of how they "worked hard to make [the curriculum] ours." For example, a group of history and English teachers found that they could make district-assigned curricula more exciting for themselves and their students by merging the two departments into an interdisciplinary whole.

In most cases, teachers developed curricula, units, lesson plans, and instructional designs in teams. Curriculum development and discussion of instruction were the central purpose of City Park's weekly team meetings. At Hillside, both department and cross-department curriculum development teams were common. We have already described how collaborative group experiences benefit teachers. Beyond that, curriculum writing involved teachers in thinking about and discussing fundamental issues about the structure of knowledge and its relation to learning. They calculated what level of knowledge and what kind of instruction were best for the specific students they taught. That process engaged teachers with their students, with the academic program of the school, with the craft of teaching, and with the subject they taught.

## CONCLUSIONS

At City Park a teacher told us of a visit to her class by a Shakespearean actor: "This guy . . . transformed my class in a way I could never have done. I was overawed by how good he was with my kids. . . . He had one of my kids standing on her head!" Perhaps all of us dream of schools full of such people, but the prospect of transforming schools through exceptional charisma is unrealistic. Such people are rare. As this teacher said, "You would run out of them pretty quickly!" And even the most talented teachers can burn out if they are dependent for support only on their individual personal resources.

It is also a mistake to allow teachers to depend only on students as a source of external support and feedback. Doing so puts thousands of teachers in frustrating and lonely work environments, with dim prospects for high teacher engagement. At City Park, Brigham, and Hillside we saw teachers who energetically invest in the personal and academic progress of their students, even though most will not go to college. A variety of collegial, administrative, and structural supports help them remain engaged. Taking these examples seriously, we can think about how to change other schools to encourage teacher engagement.

Teachers' *engagement with the school as a social unit or community* is intensified most profoundly when there is a *collective* sense of vision or purpose about education and the specific students they serve. The importance of individual purpose and motivation should not be underestimated, but the schools suggest that a supportive culture within the school can compensate significantly for the lower demands from community and parents that occurred in City Park, Brigham, and Hillside. Knowledgeable leaders play a pivotal role in establishing such a vision, but a range of planning and decision-making opportunities can quickly involve staff in doing the same. Autonomy from district mandates and supportive district relations can facilitate developing vision, but may not be essential. At Brigham, staff often saw their district as a hindrance, but received enough support from each other and their principal to sustain the aspirations they held about how best to serve their students. The range of diversity within a student body also affected how schools put together their guiding principles and values. At City Park and Brigham, it was important to unify the whole school program around specific beliefs and practices about students and teaching. At Hillside, where the student body (and the staff) was much more diverse, teachers benefitted by being encouraged to develop a slightly more diverse set of programs and structures so the varying needs of students could be served.

*Engagement with student achievement* is also nourished by opportunities for teachers to collaborate both on school-wide decisions and on curriculum and instruction. Too often, collaborative activities attend only to the marginal necessities of school life, such as paperwork, purchasing, or staff parties. At the three schools, teachers participated as a whole staff and in smaller groups in decisions regarding the fundamental issues of the school: the qualities of individuals to be hired as teachers, the abilities and needs of the students, the nature of teacher–student relationships, the content of the curriculum and the methods of instruction, and the setting or abolishing of policies. Professional dialogue over these tasks builds ownership and empowerment of the classroom in ways that "zoning of decisions" (Johnson, 1990) — in which teachers make individual decisions about how they teach, but defer to administrators about policy matters — does not. Collaboration also contributes to teachers' engagement with achievement because it provides opportunities for teachers to support and give feedback, which they may not always get from their students. Finally, opportunities to develop curricula and instructional plans specifically for the students they serve allow teachers to assess an appropriate level of challenge for their students, increasing the likelihood of student engagement in the work.

*Engagement with students as whole individuals* is expedited by structures that allow teachers to interact with students more informally and in smaller groups. Advisories that emphasized a special bond between each student and at least one adult in the building were a feature of each of these case study schools. At City Park, the block schedule reduced the number of students with whom teachers worked with to around 60, thus further supporting more personalized interaction. Hillside sought a similar dynamic for some of its students through its own block programs. In addition to structures, we also found a general ethic of care for students. This cultural norm acknowledged the links between students' emotional well-being and their readiness to learn, and emphasized respect and concern for students' lives as a whole.

*Engagement with subject matter* took a somewhat different twist in the three schools, as compared with more typical high schools. The adage that "elementary teachers teach students, high school teachers teach subjects" would not reflect the priorities of these schools. Many teachers stayed current with developments in their field through participation in local and national associations, yet it was clear that their engagement with their specific subject was often subordinated to an interest in providing a more interdisciplinary curriculum. Teachers also tried to keep their focus on what worked best for their particular students, even if that meant abandoning a personal passion to lecture on a favorite topic. Some teachers, for example, concluded that students learned more by analyzing a historical event in small groups than by having a teacher explain a major theory. There is little doubt that making these changes required teachers to give up some of their personal attachments to subject matter: One teacher called it "lending your ego." But the improved opportunities to see students learning made the trade-offs worthwhile.

The relationship between teacher engagement and organizational leadership, culture, and structure is not simple. But the organizational reforms accomplished by these schools demonstrate that schools serving disadvantaged students can sustain levels of teacher engagement comparable to those in schools with more favorable socioeconomic circumstances. We acknowledge that the success of these three schools is not easy to reproduce, and it depends in part on securing autonomy from district mandates and on the skills and extraordinary energies of the schools' talented administrators and teachers. But we did find that schools serving disadvantaged children can make changes that positively affect teacher engagement. Although communities did not pressure these schools to perform, high demands for teacher performance and engagement were generated from within the schools. The schools we studied successfully freed teachers from an involuntary dependence on students by providing a richer array of feedback and rewards, but they also empowered teachers to make voluntary investments in their personal success with students. Teachers in these schools gave themselves freely to the task of instruction and student achievement — but had resources to turn to if classroom success was not immediate or as profound as they hoped. This is, perhaps, the foundation that any restructured school must build in order to break the "iron law of social class."

## NOTES

1. This proposition has received strong support in recent analyses. For example, Bryk and Thum (1989) showed that schools in which teachers exhibit higher levels of engagement and commitment were less likely to have high rates of student absenteeism and dropouts. Wehlage, Rutter, Smith, Lesko, and Fernandez (1989) provided case studies of programs staffed by engaged teachers who were successful in retaining and improving the achievement of students who are at risk. The "effective schools" research also suggests strong relationships between schoolwide teacher engagement with students and student achievement (Brookover, Beady, Flood, Schweitzer, & Wisenbaker, 1979; Wilson & Corcoran, 1988).

2. For qualitative studies, see Firestone and Rosenblum (1988) and Metz (1990). Quantitative analyses include Brookover, Beady, Flood, Schweitzer, and Wisenbaker (1979); Bryk, Lee, and Smith (1990); Dworkin (1987); and Purkey,

Rutter, and Newmann (1986–87). See Hurn (1985) for a review of earlier empirical literature.

3. This is hardly a novel idea in the literature on organizational management. In his 1938 classic, *The Functions of the Executive*, Chester Barnard counseled top administrators to avoid simplistic ideas about the importance of wages as a motivator and to be aware of the need to create conditions that maximized other incentives, such as the desire for meaningful work, the importance of valued social relationships on the job, and the need for participation. Yet, in education these ideas have rarely been applied to teachers' work and the problems of educational performance.

4. In giving estimates, principals were asked to take into consideration not only the usual indicators of eligibility for free lunch or other services, but also other information such as home visits, awareness of parents' employment status, and so forth. Most of the principals maintained that the official statistics underestimated poverty among the students, because many families, particularly immigrants, were unwilling to divulge relevant information.

5. Case accounts were completed in all three schools. City Park Secondary School was prepared by Sheila Rosenblum and BetsAnn Smith. Brigham High School was prepared by Stewart Purkey and Karen Seashore Louis. Hillside High School was prepared by Dick Rossmiller and Sheila Rosenblum.

6. Elsewhere (Louis, 1991), we explain procedures for estimating levels of teacher engagement in schools.

7. See Louis and Smith (1990) for more details on the framework.

8. This is almost a classic case of the sociological observation that groups under attack from the outside often show higher levels of internal solidarity. However, as we will go on to point out, simply being attacked is not enough — leadership, cultural cohesiveness, and other structural supports are necessary.

## REFERENCES

Brookover, W. B., Beady, C., Flood, P., Schweitzer, J., & Wisenbaker, J. (1979). *School social systems and student achievement: Schools can make a difference.* New York: Praeger.

Bryk, A. S., & Driscoll, M. E. (1988). *The high school as community: Contextual influences and consequences for students and teachers.* Madison: National Center on Effective Secondary Schools, University of Wisconsin.

Bryk, A. S., Lee, V. E., & Smith, J. B. (1990). High school organization and its effects on teachers and students: An interpretive summary of the research. In W. H. Clune & J. F. Witte (Eds.), *Choice and control in American education: Vol. 1. The theory of choice and control in American education* (pp. 135–226). Philadelphia: Falmer Press.

Bryk, A. S., & Thum, Y. M. (1989). *The effects of high school organization on dropping out: An exploratory investigation.* New Brunswick: Center for Policy Research in Education, Rutgers, State University of New Jersey.

Carnegie Forum on Education and the Economy. (1986). *A nation prepared: Teachers for the 21st century.* New York: Carnegie Forum.

Cohen, D. K. (1988). *Teaching practice: Plus ça change . . .* (No. 88-3). East Lansing, MI: National Center for Research on Teacher Education, Michigan State University.

Corcoran, T. B., Walker, L. J., & White, J. L. (1988). *Working in urban schools.* Washington, DC: Institute for Educational Leadership.

Dworkin, A. (1987). *Teacher burnout in the public schools.* Albany: SUNY Press.

Farrar, E. (1988). *Environmental contexts and the implementation of teacher and school-based reforms: Competing interests.* Paper presented at the annual meeting of the American Educational Research Association, New Orleans.

Firestone, W., & Rosenblum, S. (1988). The alienation and commitment of students and teachers in urban high schools: A conceptual framework. *Educational Evaluation and Policy Quarterly, 10,* 285–300.

Freedman, S. (1990). *Small victories: The real world of a teacher, her students, and their school.* New York: Harper & Row.

Hallinger, P., & Murphy, J. F. (1986). The social context of effective schools. *American Journal of Education, 3,* 328–355.

Holmes Group. (1986). *Tomorrow's teachers.* East Lansing, MI: Author.

Hurn, C. (1985). *The limits and possibilities of schooling.* Boston: Allyn & Bacon.

Johnson, S. M. (1990). Teachers, power and school change. In W. H. Clune & J. F. Witte (Eds.), *Choice and control in American education: Vol. 2. The practice of choice, decentralization and school restructuring* (pp. 343–370). Philadelphia: Falmer Press.

Kidder, T. (1989). *Among school children.* Boston: Houghton Mifflin.

Louis, K. S. (1989). School district policy for school improvement. In M. Holmes, K. Lriyheoof, & D. Musella (Eds.), *Educational policy for effective schools* (pp. 145–167). New York: Teachers College Press.

Louis, K. S. (1991, April). *The effects of teacher quality of worklife in secondary schools on engagement and sense of efficacy.* Paper presented at the annual meeting of the American Educational Research Association, Chicago, IL.

Louis, K. S., & Miles, M. B. (1990). *Improving the urban high school: What works and why.* New York: Teachers College Press.

Louis, K. S., Purkey, S., Rosenblum, S., Rossmiller, R., & Smith, B. A. (1991, March). *Alternative school structures and the quality of teachers' work lives.* In National Center on Effective Secondary Schools Final Report (pp. 61–69). Madison, WI: National Center on Effective Secondary Schools.

Louis, K. S., & Smith, B. A. (1990). Teacher working conditions. In P. Reyes (Ed.), *Teachers and their workplace: Commitment, performance and productivity* (pp. 23–47). Newbury Park, CA: Sage.

Metz, M. H. (1988). *Teachers' ultimate dependence on their students: Implications for teachers' response to student bodies of differing social class.* Paper presented at the annual meeting of the American Educational Research Association, New Orleans.

Metz, M. H. (1990). How social class differences shape the context of teachers' work. In M. McLaughlin & J. Talbert (Eds.), *The secondary school as a workplace* (pp. 40–107). New York: Teachers College Press.

Metz, M. H., & Colleagues. (1988). *Final report. Field study on teachers' engagement project on the effects of the school as a workplace on teachers' engagement — Phase one National Center on Effective Secondary Schools.* Madison, WI: National Center on Effective Secondary Schools.

National Education Association. (1987). *Status of the American public school teacher: 1985–86.* West Haven, CT: NEA Professional Library.

Newmann, F. M., Rutter, R. A., & Smith, M. S. (1989, October). Organizational factors that affect school sense of efficacy, community, and expectations. *Sociology of Education, 62,* 221–238.

Purkey, S. C., Rutter, R. A., & Newmann, F. M. (1986–87). United States high school improvement programs: A profile from the high school and beyond supplemental survey. *Metropolitan Education, 3,* 59–91.

Powell, A. G., Farrar, E., & Cohen, D. K. (1985). *The shopping mall high school: Winners and losers in the educational marketplace.* Boston: Houghton Mifflin.

Rossmiller, R. A. (1988, November). *Project on the effects of the school as workplace on teachers' engagement: Field study on principals' management of schools to affect teacher engagement* (Final Report). Madison: National Center on Effective Secondary Schools, University of Wisconsin.

Wehlage, G. G., Rutter, R. A., Smith, G. A., Lesko, N. L., & Fernandez, R. R. (1989). *Reducing the risk: Schools as communities of support.* Philadelphia: Falmer Press.

Wilson, B., & Corcoran, T. (1988). *Successful secondary schools: Visions of excellence in American public schools.* Philadelphia: Falmer Press.

# CHAPTER 6

# Putting School in Perspective: The Influence of Family, Peers, Extracurricular Participation, and Part-Time Work on Academic Engagement

## Susie D. Lamborn, B. Bradford Brown, Nina S. Mounts, and Laurence Steinberg

There is more to adolescence than schooling, and noninstructional influences can play an important role in academic engagement. Parents who actively participate in school activities and who support learning as an end in itself instill in adolescents an intrinsic interest in education and a willingness to persist at academic endeavors. Studying with a group of friends for an important exam provides a socially meaningful structure to support the discipline required to learn complex materials. Publishing a weekly column in the school newspaper involves personal responsibilities and satisfactions that bring lessons of English class to life. Meeting deadlines with an energetic boss who provides enriching work experiences highlights the connection between current school achievement and future career possibilities, a connection that is not readily apparent to many young people.

Of course, each of these areas of influence can also have negative effects on school performance. Teachers and other professionals who work with adolescents often feel powerless to promote academic excellence when experiences in the family, peer groups, extracurricular activities, and work obligations seem to undermine academic engagement. By understanding how each of these domains influences adolescents' involvement in school, educators will be better prepared to react to and, in some ways, to shape or make use of outside influences to promote student engagement and achievement.

We begin by introducing two engaged students, referred to throughout the chapter. After describing the design of the study, we report separately on the impact of families, peers, extracurricular participation, and employment.

## TWO ENGAGED STUDENTS

### Julius at Metro South

Julius, a sophomore at Metro South, a large urban high school with a diverse student body, explains what he likes about school: "Some classes I kind of get a thrill out of, you know, a challenge. I don't like 2 plus 2 classes and 'See John' and stuff like that. The hard stuff really gets me, I don't know, that's just the way I am."

With a 2.8 grade-point average, Julius is satisfied with his school performance. He explains, "I usually spend at least two hours on homework a night, including studying for tests and stuff. That's a lot more than I used to do; I used to just do my homework and just go out [with friends] and not care if I got it right or wrong." Julius plans to attend college and become an architect. He anticipates completing six years of education past high school to accomplish this goal.

Julius lives with his mother, her new husband, and his brother. He elaborates, "He's [my brother] younger. I'm the oldest one and then I have my father and his new wife, and they have two new kids, both younger . . . they're just about five blocks away." He describes a warm positive relationship with both parents, although he sees his father less frequently because of work. Without reservation, he quickly responds that he can count on them 100 percent, even though they bicker over day-to-day problems, "like I'll be home late or I'll forget to do something. . . . It'll get on her nerves if she's in a bad mood . . . but nothing big, 10 minutes of hassling at the most."

When asked if anything got in his way of doing better at school, he is quick to respond, "Probably my need to be with my friends, that's why I do my homework so quick. I come home, just scribble my homework, and just go out . . . most of them, the ones I hang around with at school, all live no more than two blocks away, so it's really easy [to go out together]."

### Kevin at Rolling Prairie

In a pastoral environment remote from the urban sprawl surrounding Metro South, Kevin is a sophomore at a high school nestled in a small community surrounded by farmland. A straight-A student, Kevin describes his favorite part of school life: "Taking a lot of courses to be challenged. I don't mind going to school. I like participating and involvement in a couple of clubs. I like both. The challenge of courses as far as being able to expand, and get a good feeling like you've done well. And as far as participation, I like to be known as someone who is always active."

Like Julius, Kevin attributes his academic success to hard work. "Well, I spent a lot of time on homework. I'd go home and even though I was in three sports a year I'd come home and do it and go to sports, then come home and do some more. I spent a lot of time on my homework, concentrating on my studies. I paid a lot of attention in class and tried to get a handle on the material." Although he has not defined a specific career, he knows that he will get a college degree in science or medicine.

Kevin resides with his mother and father and two younger brothers. He describes his relationship with them as open and warm. "My parents are one of the first people to pat me on the back if I do something good. And they care about what I do. . . . I think we get along good because I can talk about things openly with my parents . . . about drugs, sex, and things like that. And if I have a question about anything my parents would be the first to answer these." As in most families with teenagers, even Kevin's predominantly positive relationship with his parents is not conflict-free. "My mom's always on me about my room, for cleaning my room. It's always dirty. I used to always tell my mom I don't have time. They don't really get mad, they just kind of give you the eye and tell you to try harder because you're not doing as well as you should. If I screw up or something they're very supportive."

When asked whether anything makes it difficult to do well in school, Kevin commented, "Sometimes you see people coming home and they'd always be telling me how much fun they had and you shouldn't study. You wonder what the purpose is. You wonder why I'm trying so hard all the time when other people can just sit back and have fun in high school, and I'm trying really hard. I guess in the long run it all pays off, so. . . ."

Julius and Kevin have a lot in common, even though they come from different environments, one urban and the other rural. They both thrive in academically challenging situations; they invest effort in doing well in school; they describe positive family and peer relationships; they have defined a direction for their future. At the same time, there are differences in what they say about their families, peers, participation in extracurricular activities, and part-time work. For Kevin, influences from these four areas consistently direct him toward academic involvement. For Julius, however, these areas outside school have a mixed impact on his school performance, sometimes pulling him away from his studies.

## OVERVIEW OF THE STUDY

Previous research has studied noninstructional influences on school performance and academic aspirations but has had very little to say about how family, peers, extracurricular participation, and employment affect student engagement — the psychological investment in learning that takes place at school (see Steinberg, Brown, Cider, Kaczmarek, & Lazzaro, 1988 for a review). Instead the focus has been on the role of community and societal influences as primary contributors to *disengagement* from academic learning (Csikszentmihalyi & Larson, 1984; Cusick, 1973; Fordham & Ogbu, 1986; Wehlage, Rutter, Smith, Lesko, & Fernandez, 1989; Willis, 1977).

This study focuses on student engagement. Students from nine public, four-year high schools in Wisconsin and California described how they were influenced academically by four key arenas of adolescent life: family, peers, extracurricular participation, and part-time work. The schools they attended varied dramatically in size (from 400 to 2,400 students), socio-economic characteristics, ethnic composition (from 40 percent to 98 percent Anglo), and location (rural, suburban, innercity). In each school, self-report surveys were administered to the entire student body. We also invited a sample of students and their parents to discuss selected issues in more detail in individual interviews. General findings from the survey data were enriched by the students' own comments on their lives.

The survey measured engagement by asking students about their levels of effort, concentration, and attention in the four main subject areas of English, math, social studies, and science. Data were also collected on other forms of academic involvement: time spent on homework, academic expectations, and school misconduct. School achievement was measured by grade-point average (GPA).

Overall, students reported that they were engaged fairly often in classroom instruction. In general, girls were more engaged than boys, students from middle-class homes reported higher engagement than those from working-class homes, and 12th graders tended to be more engaged than 9th graders. Of the four major ethnic groups, Asian-Americans reported the highest engagement while non-Hispanic white students reported the lowest. Hispanic-American and African-American students fell between these two groups in their level of engagement.

How does student engagement relate to the other aspects of academic involvement? Students who were more engaged had somewhat higher grades ($r = .27$), spent more time on homework ($r = .32$), and had higher educational aspirations ($r = .21$) than their less engaged peers. Engagement in academic learning was also positively associated with lower frequencies of school deviance, such as cutting class, cheating on exams, and skipping school ($r = -.35$). None of these relations was dramatic, but the picture was consistent: Engagement is associated with higher academic performance, lower frequencies of school deviance, and higher educational aspirations.

## FAMILY INFLUENCES ON ENGAGEMENT

One of the first places a child acquires an interest in learning and the belief that education is important is in the home. As might be expected, parents can nurture student engagement by emphasizing the value of learning and by becoming involved in the student's school activities. But, consistent with other studies, we also found that a certain general style of parenting, "authoritative" parenting, is beneficial.

### Authoritative Parenting

Mrs. Hanson comments on her relationship with her adolescent children.

> They have *many* more privileges than other kids, but yet they have to be in at a certain time. They can only go out so many times a week. They know that if they tell me they are going to A and they change their minds and go to B, they call and tell me.

> I feel we're close. It's difficult to know a teenager. He talks to me about a lot of things. He's not embarrassed to tell me a dirty joke and explain it when I don't understand. I feel that he can talk to me about a lot of different things. . . . They feel they can discuss everything with me whether I understand or not. My kids don't have an off button. They were talking before they were born and they haven't stopped yet.

> We don't have a democracy in our house. However, I feel that I'm a benevolent despot, if you will. So I take a lot of input in what's going on and make some decisions and explain why I made the decision. . . . Sometimes if he can show me that his point is a better one and why . . . my mind can definitely be changed. . . . I don't feel that my kids feel put upon or that they don't have privileges that other kids have.

Mrs. Hanson wields a lot of authority in the household and feels comfortable in this role. She has clear expectations for her children and discusses them openly with the children. There are rules and guidelines to be followed and specific repercussions when they are broken. She knows where her children are and whom they are with.

At the same time she is aware of her son's interests and school activities. They talk openly and regularly. He often seeks her out to share daily events and experiences. Although the parents have the final say on family decisions, they explain why they make decisions, accept input from the children, and are flexible when they encounter a reasonable counterargument.

This mother is typical of the authoritative parent in that she combines high levels of warmth with high levels of demandingness. Authoritative parents also grant psychological autonomy through joint decision making with their adolescent (Baumrind, 1991; Steinberg, Elmen, & Mounts, 1989; Steinberg, Mounts, Lamborn, & Dornbusch, 1991).

Authoritative parenting is associated with numerous facets of social and academic competence (Baumrind, 1978; Baumrind, 1991; Maccoby & Martin, 1983). Originally, authoritative parenting was studied in white middle-class families with young children. More recent studies illustrate how adolescents respond to authoritative parenting in ways that are consistent with the responses of younger children. Authoritatively raised youth consistently outperform their peers from authoritarian (low on warmth but high on demandingness) and permissive families (high on warmth but low on demandingness) on various measures of competence. Conversely, various problem behaviors, such as delinquency, drug and alcohol abuse, and conformity to antisocial peer pressure, are lower among authoritatively reared youth (Dornbusch et al., 1985; Dornbusch, Ritter, Leiderman, Roberts, & Fraleigh, 1987; Lamborn, Mounts, Steinberg, & Dornbusch, 1991; Steinberg, Elmen, & Mounts, 1989).

In our study, only 16 percent of the students described their parents as having these qualities. But as shown in Table 6.1, students from authoritative families were more engaged in school, had higher educational expectations, received higher grades, spent more time on homework, and were less likely to become involved in school misconduct than students from nonauthoritative homes.[1]

Authoritative parenting has been criticized as a middle-class phenomenon that is not a reasonable alternative for minority, poorer, or nonintact families. Authoritative parenting is somewhat more common in white, intact, middle-class families, the sample on which the construct was originally tested and developed. And the positive influences of authoritative parenting on adolescent development are more visible in these types of families. Nevertheless, the positive impact of authoritative parenting crosses ethnic and social class boundaries (Clark, 1983; Dornbusch, Ritter, Leiderman, Roberts, & Fraleigh, 1987; Steinberg, Mounts, Lamborn, &

**Table 6.1**
**Group Differences on Academic Behaviors for Students According to Parenting Style and Parental Involvement in Education**

|  | Academic Engagement | GPA | Homework Time | Educational Expectations | School Deviance |
|---|---|---|---|---|---|
| **Parenting Style:** |  |  |  |  |  |
| Authoritative | 3.59 | 3.08 | 4.05 | 5.00 | 2.22 |
| Nonauthoritative | 3.41 | 2.79 | 3.72 | 4.69 | 2.40 |
| **School Involvement:** |  |  |  |  |  |
| High | 3.45 | 2.95 | 3.95 | 4.93 | 2.36 |
| Low | 3.27 | 2.70 | 3.58 | 4.52 | 2.38 |

NOTE:     Units of measurement are described in Note 1.

Dornbusch, 1991). Across a broad array of social environments, adolescents reared in an authoritative manner excel socially and academically.

## Parental Involvement in Schooling

While almost all parents feel that it is important for their children to receive a good education, they vary in the degree to which they support this commitment through specific actions aimed toward the children's education. Mrs. Bradshaw describes her involvement.

> They have to do their best. If they come home with C's and D's, I want to know why. I ask if they have homework assignments and if they say yes, then they usually come right home and get it done. There's no problem with that. That was instilled in them very early.

> They always come to me at night and we sit for a while and talk about things that went on in class.

> He has understood that we tell him to take as much of these academic classes in high school so you will have more time to apply yourself. . . . Starting in 7th Grade, that's when we started talking about college and what he's going to need so it will be easier when he gets there.

> I go to gymnastic meets. I have an active interest in his extracurricular activities. He's in video club. He tells me all the technical details and problems.

Like Mrs. Bradshaw, parents can become involved by helping with homework when asked, going to school programs, watching their adolescents in sports or activities, knowing how well they are doing in school, and helping to choose courses. Consistent with other studies showing that parental involvement in schooling improves academic achievement (Baker & Stevenson, 1986; Epstein, in press; Stevenson & Baker, 1987), we found that students whose parents are highly involved in schooling, compared with students whose parents are only modestly involved, have higher scores on all the positive academic outcomes (school misconduct is unrelated to parental involvement). The positive effects of parental involvement are stronger among middle-class than working-class students.

Julius and Kevin both describe strong family relationships. According to Julius, "Well, for some reasons like major problems, like drinking or sex or something, I'll go to my dad, but for just going out and hanging out, I talk to my mom cause she lives with me and that's kind of like, I don't know, it's really not that important so we'll decide on curfew together for that night and I'll tell her what I'm doing, where I'm going, who I'll be with." This comment indicates a warm open relationship but also one in which the parents have set clear limits. The impression is of a relatively flexible family in which the student participates in family decision making although the parents maintain final control.

Julius's and Kevin's descriptions of their relations with their parents fit the authoritative pattern. However, their families differ dramatically on parental involvement in school. According to Julius, "My mom doesn't worry if I was in school the whole day or if I was skipping or something, but she usually comes to conferences and she doesn't check up on homework 'cause she usually knows that I'm doing it and she just usually, as far as she'll go is conference, that's about it." Compare this modest level of involvement with the high involvement of Kevin's parents.

> I say my parents are almost completely involved. They're very
> concerned about how well I'm doing, what I'm involved with.
> And before I'm about to try something else new they're always
> questioning what's this gonna involve, what effect will it have
> on you. And I looked to them first thing when I decided to
> choose my courses. I look to them for help. And they say do
> what you want but you want to challenge yourself to be the best.

Kevin and Julius both report high engagement in school, but Kevin has superior grades. According to our survey results, a contributing factor to Kevin's superior academic performance is the combined positive influence of having authoritative parents who are also highly involved in his schooling. For most of the dimensions of school performance (grade-point average, homework time, and educational expectations), parenting style and parental involvement had additive, positive effects. That is, the students with the most positive outcomes were, like Kevin, from authoritative homes with high parental involvement. Outcomes were least positive for students in nonauthoritative families that were not involved in their children's schooling.

However, for student engagement, the association between authoritative parenting and parental school involvement was different. Engagement was relatively high in authoritative families regardless of the level of parental involvement in schooling. In contrast, for students from nonauthoritative families, engagement was higher when parental involvement was high.

In sum, the general child-rearing practice of authoritative parenting and the more specifically education-oriented dimension of parental involvement in schooling were positively related to academic engagement as well as other academic outcomes. Parental involvement tended to be the stronger of the two predictors of academic outcomes.

## PEER INFLUENCES ON ACADEMIC ENGAGEMENT

They call me a mix of everything. I'm a partyer, I love to joke around, you know, I love to get laughs. I get good grades, so they'll call me a semi-nerd. Then they'll call me semi-toughie — they generally view Hispanics as tough gangster fighters. And because I'm a mix of everything, I get along with everybody else. So, I hang around the shy people who don't have any friends. I hang around with popular people who have so many friends they don't have to count them. I'll hang around with moderate people. I hang around with trash or skateboarders. I hang around with people who supposedly have connections with gangs. I'll hang around mirrors. I'll hang around with basically anybody. So, I have connections with everybody. It's a motley crew. (Marcos, Metro South)

Peers play a central role in the social lives of adolescents. Over the years, adolescents spend increasing amounts of time with peers in activities that are unsupervised by adults (Csikszentmihalyi & Larson, 1984). Teenagers are particularly susceptible to the influence of their peers during middle adolescence (Berndt, 1979). As individuals move from childhood into adolescence they move into a more complex and differentiated social system in which peers are partitioned into a set of peer groups, or "crowds," that vary considerably in normative values, orientations, and behaviors (Brown, 1990). Peer influences are filtered through adolescents' membership in one of these crowds (Brown & Clasen, 1986; Mosbach & Leventhal, 1988), and becoming involved with a crowd is one of the major social mandates of early adolescence (Brown, Eicher, & Petrie, 1986; Newman & Newman, 1976).

Crowds are the large groups of students, familiar to most of us, that define the broad social organization of most high schools: jocks, preppies, druggies, brains, and so forth. Crowds are groups of individuals, larger than cliques, who share the same stereotypical behavior patterns. Membership in a crowd is established more by one's reputation than by specific behaviors, and the crowd structure of high schools makes it difficult to discard the reputation one garners from membership in a particular

group. Since membership is determined or denied as much by peer agreement as by a student's voluntary choice, it is difficult for students to leave
a crowd or gain entry into another one.

We examined relations between adolescent crowd membership and
academic outcomes for five major crowds that exist in most high schools:
brains, jocks/populars, averages, loners/nerds, and druggies. Adolescents
who were identified by classmates as leading members of the major crowds
in their school were interviewed and asked to share their perceptions of
classmates' crowd membership. Peer nominations of crowd membership
were integrated with other information collected from self-report surveys.[2]

The crowds differed in their academic behaviors and values in ways
that we had anticipated, based on previous studies and on students' general descriptions of crowds. Mean scores for each crowd are presented in
Table 6.2. As expected, brains were the most academically oriented.

> One of my friends and I have a competition going on to see who
> can get the best grades. . . . Last year we had one report due
> and I would have blown it off, but we put a $5.00 bet on it so I
> tried to do really good on it. Because of that there's real competi-
> tion, like every time we get our papers back we stick them in
> each other's faces. (Aaron, Metro South)

> I've probably been in the same group so everyone kind of expects
> me to get good grades and stuff. I guess that's how it's affected
> me. (Sharon, Ambassador Hills)

> See, my friends, they like to go out and have a good time but at
> the same time they also value education, and so really, although
> they don't tell me these things, they silently kind of influence me
> to do the best I can academically. . . . They frequently talk to
> me and ease the pressure a bit . . . big test or something, talk at
> the lunch table, lighten things up a little bit. (Ian, Rolling
> Prairie)

At the other extreme, druggies were the least invested in school. Students who identified themselves as members of the druggie crowd had this
to say about their peer group.

> You don't get straight A's. After school you go out and have fun
> instead of staying home and reading a book or something.
> Around here it's considered druggies but it's not really druggies
> because I don't do drugs. Yeah, we smoke. But I guess most of
> them do drugs. (Cindy, Rolling Prairie)

**Table 6.2**
**Group Differences on Academic Behaviors According to Peer Crowd Membership**

| Crowd | Academic Engagement | GPA | Homework Time | Educational Expectations | School Deviance |
|---|---|---|---|---|---|
| Brain | 3.46 | 3.85 | 4.12 | 5.41 | 2.75 |
| Jock/Popular | 3.36 | 2.92 | 3.76 | 5.02 | 3.48 |
| Average | 3.34 | 2.93 | 3.73 | 4.71 | 3.34 |
| Loners/nerds | 3.48 | 2.77 | 3.70 | 4.47 | 3.36 |
| Druggie | 2.75 | 2.02 | 2.84 | 3.66 | 3.46 |

NOTE: Units of measurement are described in Note 1.

They just don't care. They get D's and F's. It's like homework, throw it in your locker and forget about it. My advice to freshmen, don't be like us and fail. (Stan, Ambassador Hills)

The averages, loners/nerds, and jocks/populars fell between these two extremes. Surprisingly, the jocks/populars were not very different from the other two groups: the loners/nerds and averages. Given the prestige of the jocks/populars, we expected them to most closely resemble the brains.

In general, regardless of crowd membership, the more time spent with peers, the lower were the academic outcomes. Adolescents who spend more time partying and hanging out with peers are less engaged in their schoolwork. More time partying with friends was also associated with more frequent school misconduct. Druggies spent more time hanging out and partying with their friends than adolescents in the other crowds, and this tendency accounted for some of their impoverished school performance relative to students in other crowds. The association between time spent with friends and poorer grades was apparent when we asked students if anything interfered with their school performance.

Your friends like out of school, you know, friends on the street, some keep you from doing homework. . . . Like if your friends invite you somewhere and you got homework, you still go and don't do your homework sometimes. Just walk around, go to the movies, go to the mall, shop, stuff like that. (Anthony, Metro South)

I think it was the people I was hanging out with. Because I was never in school. I was always skipping out you know. And just my attitude about things. Going out for breakfast every morning instead of going to class. And I don't know. It wasn't anything, just as long as we weren't in school, we were having a good time. (Kim, Rolling Prairie)

They like to go to parties and stuff and they used to call me up and I just go with them. And I'll leave stuff behind that I should do. Well, during school they're kind of crazy, they go in the halls and act crazy. They yell and stuff and I'm usually with them. I'm not yelling or anything, but all of them get in trouble for something that one person did. (David, Metro South)

A dramatic exception to this profile of negative peer influences occurred among the brains. For students in the brain crowd, time with peers was associated with several aspects of positive school performance. Time spent hanging out with friends was related to higher engagement and grade-point averages. For brains, part of the time hanging out with friends included such academic activities as helping each other with homework and studying. Even adolescents in the brain crowd who spent more time *partying* with their friends were more engaged in their classwork and had higher academic aspirations. When asked how their friends influenced them, students belonging to the brain crowd frequently mentioned studying together and completing assignments before socializing.

> It makes me try harder to keep up with them. Sometimes we get together and have a study session together. They help each other on problems. At someone's house, whenever we want, like once a week. (Amy, Ambassador Hills)

What do Julius and Kevin have to say about their peers? Julius belongs to the average crowd, a group of students defined by their moderate standing along numerous dimensions. They do well in school but do not excel. They party and socialize in moderation and frequently participate in sports but are not as serious as the jocks. Julius mentions that he and his friends study together occasionally. At the same time, he explains the pressure to skip class within his group of friends: " . . . there are a few that skip a lot, don't do their homework. They're smart kids, they just don't use their heads, they're more or less good. . . . Number one, I'm not sly enough to go skipping away from school 'cause somebody's going to find out and I'll just get in trouble for it, so I usually, I myself stay in school." Later, he comments on his struggles not to conform.

> Well, sometimes when the ones that want to leave ask me to leave, then I have to say no and I always feel bad because I don't want them to think I'm not cool or whatever. . . . See, mostly for me [school] is social, I do my work and I do it well, but when it comes time to being social, I am heavily social, that's the way I have to be, I could not be myself, I am very insecure.

On the other hand, Kevin belongs to the popular-nice group. Within his peer network, academic study is a high-priority enterprise. Rather than viewing socializing and academics as competing demands, Kevin and his friends have been more successful at integrating academics into their social life.

> If we decide to do something together on a Tuesday or Wednesday night and we know that we have schoolwork, we'll say hold

on, we have work to do. We always put that first. I think school
is very important. And we're real supportive of each other. So as
far as encouraging each other, we do that a lot. Since they're in a
lot of my classes we feel almost like a family. . . . Competition
for one thing, because we all do pretty good. So we ask each
other what we got on some test. It just adds an element of challenge.

Both students describe positive relationships with their peers. However, Julius's friends have a mixed influence on him, pulling him both
toward and away from his studies, while Kevin's friends have a consistent
effect of investing in school studies.

To summarize, adolescent crowd membership was associated with
differences in academic outcomes, although we do not know the extent to
which these academic outcome differences predated crowd membership.
Especially for adolescents in the druggie crowd, time spent partying and
hanging out with friends predicts the lower levels of academic achievement that distinguishes this crowd from the others. It has sometimes been
assumed by researchers, practitioners, and the public that peers have an
overall negative effect on adolescents' academic achievement (e.g., Coleman, 1961), but in fact peer influences are quite variable (Clasen &
Brown, 1985; Steinberg, Brown, Cider, Kaczmarek, & Lazzaro, 1988).
In this study, time spent with peers had uniformly negative outcomes in
the druggie crowd and primarily positive ones for the brains, whose
friends provide a network that supports academic endeavors.

## ENGAGEMENT AND EXTRACURRICULAR PARTICIPATION

In wrestling you have to keep trying at something, you can't give
up. It helps you mentally to get ready for stuff. But it takes time
away from studying and stuff like that. (Phil, Ambassador Hills)

It is difficult to predict the effects of extracurricular participation on
engagement and academic achievement. On the one hand, extracurricular
activities could support academic accomplishment in a number of ways.
They might give students a sense of bonding to the school that indirectly
increases their commitment to academics. The close contact with teachers
who serve as coaches or advisors also could help forge relationships that
create more positive academic orientations among participants ("I don't
want to let the coach down by doing poorly in her class"). Extracurricular
participation may expose students to more academically oriented peer

groups who encourage engagement and achievement (Clasen & Brown, 1985). Finally, certain activities—the debate team or academic clubs, for example—develop skills and knowledge that build directly on learning strategies and subject matter that students are asked to master in classes.

On the other hand, extracurricular activities offer alternative avenues for the development of competence, discussed in Chapter 1 as the universal foundation for engagement in learning. Gaining competence in extracurricular pursuits may obviate the need to work hard on academic material. A student who develops a reputation as a great actor may feel little need to excel in the classroom. Furthermore, the time demands and performance pressures associated with some extracurricular activities may leave participants too preoccupied or too fatigued to concentrate on their schoolwork.

We have an incomplete picture of the broad range of extracurricular activities that exist in most high schools because, until recently, researchers focused almost exclusively on sports participation, primarily among boys in their senior year (Steinberg, Brown, Cider, Kaczmarek, & Lazzaro, 1988). Most researchers report that extracurricular participants do better in school than nonparticipants, but most of the difference seems to be a function of academic talent and motivation that predate participation (Holland & Andre, 1987). That is, students who go out for activities tend to be more academically prepared and motivated than those who do not. Researchers have not determined whether students' academic progress in school is affected by some activities more than others or by the number or diversity of activities in which students participate.

Julius and Kevin are both involved in extracurricular activities. Julius is a member of the baseball team and the architecture club. Kevin participates in a broader range of activities. "I'm involved in boys' volleyball, basketball, and track. And I'm also involved in clubs—the Key Club, I just joined the Alpha Theta, which is the math club. You have to have a 3.25. And then I'm also in student council." Nearly two thirds of the students in the study were involved in one or more extracurricular activities. Most, like Julius, participated in only one or two activities, but 10 percent, like Kevin, reported involvement in five or more activities during the year. Gender differences were negligible, but participation rates climbed modestly across grade levels and differed substantially among the nine schools in our study. On average, participants devoted approximately 7.5 hours per week to extracurricular activities, although 5 percent logged as many as 20 hours a week or more.

As expected, extracurricular participants fared well academically. Compared with nonparticipants, they had higher grade-point averages (by over one fourth of a grade point) and spent more time on homework (about an hour more per week). They expected to go farther in school and had slightly higher levels of school engagement. Mean scores for each of these factors are shown in Table 6.3. As Kevin says, "You learn to budget your time a little better, which makes you more efficient at studying . . . it helps you deal with people and just to be involved and using good sense. It's good to be doing something in school other than being just involved in academics."

The advantage, however, seemed to be more pronounced for students in leadership activities and clubs or interest groups than those out for sports or performing activities. In fact, sports participants actually had higher levels of school deviance than nonparticipants.

The more activities students were involved in, the better their scores were on our positive outcome measures (except for school deviance). Furthermore, students involved in two or more different types of activities did better than the "specialists" who went out for just one type of activity. In fact, academic effort and achievement tended to increase as hours spent on extracurricular activities increased.[3]

Ultimately, the effects of extracurricular participation probably depend on the environment that students encounter in the activities. Do coaches, advisors, and peers emphasize the need to achieve in the classroom as well as in the activity, or do they value students strictly on the basis of their accomplishments in the activity? Does the activity offer opportunities to apply classroom knowledge, or do the time and energy demands of the activity distract students from their studies?

For each student's favorite activity, we collected information on four specific processes that would seem to influence academic engagement and achievement.

*Advisor's support* examined how often the adult advisor would allow the student to miss practice in order to study, how often the advisor spoke to the student about college, and whether the advisor cared more about how the student did in school classes than in the activity. The degree to which the activity advisor encouraged or discouraged achievement had little effect on levels of achievement and education values.

*Peers' support* inquired about the frequency of receiving advice about classes from fellow participants, whether these peers cared more about studying than partying, and whether the other participants planned to go to college. Peer support, highest among students involved in leadership activities and lowest for those participating in a glory sport, was associated with students' level of engagement, grade-point average, and time devoted to homework. Karen, a member of the student council at Ambassador Hills, says about her fellow council members, "They're pretty smart and they do pretty good in school. Yeah, it helps. 'Cause you want to kind of get good grades like them."

*Personal resources* refers to how much participation contributed to

Table 6.3
Group Differences Among Extracurricular Participants and Nonparticipants on Academic Behaviors

| | Academic Engagement | GPA | Homework Time | Educational Expectations | School Deviance |
|---|---|---|---|---|---|
| | Mean | Mean | Mean | Mean | Mean |
| Participants | 3.50 | 3.00 | 4.31 | 5.04 | 2.36 |
| Nonparticipants | 3.41 | 2.72 | 3.40 | 4.66 | 2.38 |
| Participants in Different Activities | | | | | |
| Favorite Activity: | | | | | |
| Glory sports | 3.48 | 2.95 | 4.21 | 3.10 | 2.47 |
| Other sports | 3.52 | 3.10 | 4.43 | 3.23 | 2.39 |
| Leadership activities | 3.59 | 3.28 | 4.73 | 3.30 | 2.35 |
| Clubs and interest groups | 3.56 | 3.26 | 4.97 | 3.32 | 2.24 |
| Performing activities | 3.44 | 3.07 | 4.32 | 3.18 | 2.29 |

NOTE:     Units of measurement are described in Note 1.

planning homework time better or contributed to the development of confidence about doing well in school. Students who felt their favorite activity enhanced personal resources were substantially more engaged in school, spent more time on homework, and participated in deviant activities less often. One sophomore explained that after exercising in sports, he felt much more relaxed about studying. Another student told us that some of the techniques of concentration and close observation he learned in tennis were helpful in developing more precision with language skills.

Finally, the degree of *distraction* indicated how much participation undermined achievement by making students too tired to study or too nervous or excited to concentrate in class. Students who felt distracted from schoolwork by their favorite activity reported modestly lower levels of engagement and substantially more school deviance. Distraction was least common for students in leadership activities and most common for those in a glory sport.

> I'm in basketball and it hurts my schoolwork. We have practice every single day from 3:00 to 5:15. You get out at 5:15, run almost the whole time and then you get home you be so tired you want to go to sleep, but you still have around six or seven classes of homework to do. (Melanie, Metro South)

To summarize, participants in extracurricular activities were more engaged in school, put more effort into their studies, got better grades, and expected to go farther in school than nonparticipants — even after accounting for differences between participants and nonparticipants in background factors. Levels of engagement and achievement varied according to the type of extracurricular activity, however. Generally, students who concentrated on glory sports did less well on academic outcomes than those involved in clubs or leadership activities. In part, these differences could be traced to experiences in the different activities — how much the demands of the activity distracted them from studying, how much the activity bolstered personal resources (time management skills, confidence in their ability to do well academically, etc.), and whether coparticipants encouraged or discouraged academic pursuits.

## SCHOOL ENGAGEMENT AND STUDENT EMPLOYMENT

During the last decade, researchers, educators, and policy makers interested in adolescent development have directed increasing attention to the widespread employment of high school students during the school year (see Charner & Fraser, 1987, for a review). Uncommon in this country prior to 1950, and still rare in other industrialized countries, student employment in the United States grew steadily between 1950 and 1980 and has remained at a high level during the last 10 years. According to recent estimates, for example, between one half and two thirds of all high school juniors hold jobs in the formal part-time labor force at any specific time during the school year, and the vast majority of students will have had some school-year work experience prior to graduation (Greenberger & Steinberg, 1986). For many students, participation in the labor force is time-consuming: According to one national survey, over half of all employed high school seniors and nearly one fourth of all employed sophomores work more than 20 hours per week (Lewin-Epstein, 1981).

The emerging consensus among researchers is that negative effects of employment are linked to how much, not whether, a student works (e.g., Bachman, Bare, & Frankie, 1986; Damico, 1984; Mortimer & Finch, 1986; Schill, McCartin, & Meyer, 1985; Wirtz, Rohrbeck, Charner, & Fraser, 1987). Studies that examine weekly hours of employment generally find an important drop in school performance at around 20 hours per week. Some students talked about this.

> [Does having a job help or hurt your schoolwork?] It hurts greatly. . . . You have to work to get the money, the more you work the more you get, so I try to work as much as I can without killing my schoolwork totally, but sometimes it just doesn't work out that way. . . . I work at a fast food restaurant and I clean up tables, wash dishes, make the food. I work 3–4 school nights, 15–20 hours, then I work every weekend, which is another 13 hours. (Rob, Ambassador Hills)

> I liked [working as a cashier] a lot. But when you get home at night you're tired and you don't want to do homework when you get home. (Camille, Metro South)

> Like if I had to work at night, I didn't get anything done 'cause I worked from 4:30 to 10:30, sometimes past midnight. [So that got in your way?] Yeah and I was sleeping during class. (Michelle, Rolling Prairie)

Studies that focus solely on differences in school performance, without examining other aspects of youngsters' involvement in school, may underestimate the impact of working on schooling, because there are constraints on the range of youngsters' grades and on the amount of time they are expected to devote to homework (Greenberger & Steinberg, 1986). For example, because the national average for time spent on homework is less than four hours per week (Greenberger & Steinberg, 1986), it is unlikely that employment, in whatever amount, will markedly diminish youngsters' already very modest involvement in homework. Similarly, because teachers adjust grading practices and class requirements, and pupils select easier courses in order to accommodate job demands (McNeil, 1984), the ultimate impact of employment on school performance may be attenuated. Studies that examine more affective and attitudinal components of schooling—how engaged students are in their education—may uncover stronger effects of extensive employment than studies of school performance alone. Anecdotal evidence from teachers (e.g., Kotlowitz, 1986) and ethnographies of high schools (e.g., Powell, Farrar, & Cohen, 1985) suggest that extensive commitment to a part-time job takes a toll on students' investment in school in ways that may not be evident when only "objective" indicators are studied.

In our study, longer hours of work during the school year were clearly associated with diminished school performance and lowered school engagement. Students who worked more hours each week earned lower grades, spent less time on homework, paid attention in class less often, exerted less effort in school, were less involved in extracurricular activities, and reported higher levels of mind-wandering in class, more school misconduct, and more frequent class-cutting.

It has been suggested that the negative association between work hours and school performance is due not to the fact that working interferes with achievement, but to the fact that students who choose to work longer hours are initially those students most disaffected with school. Some survey items assessed students' general positive or negative orientations toward school. When school orientation was statistically controlled, the association between work hours and academic outcomes remained the same. The lower performance and engagement of students who work a lot cannot, therefore, be attributed to initial alienation from school.

When asked about part-time work, Kevin responds, "My mom and dad said during summer they wouldn't mind me having a job. But during school they want me to concentrate on my studies and stuff rather than having a job." Julius, who does have a job, describes his work situation.

> I'm a utility clerk at Pick-N-Save and I basically push the carts in
> and out of the parking lot and I'll sweep or mop or whatever,
> that's mostly what I do. I work approximately two days during
> the week and then I work Saturday and Sunday for six hours so
> that's about 25 hours a week.

In response to an inquiry about how the job affected his schoolwork, Julius said, "It hurt because I had to work at 5:00 so I didn't have any time to concentrate on my homework and get it done right 'cause I'd have to leave by 4:30 to drive to work."

In contrast to students who worked about as much as Julius did (20 hours or more), students whose work hours were more moderate (10 hours or less) had grade-point averages about one third of a letter grade higher, spent approximately one third more time each week on homework, and cut class about 25 percent less often. It may be suggested that older students are better able to combine heavy work responsibilities with serious academic investment. We found, however, that effects of working on school performance or engagement were similar for older students and younger students (and for middle-class and working-class students).

Taken together, these findings suggest that students' involvement in paid work outside school may affect their performance and engagement in school in at least three important ways. First, working long hours is associated with lower grades and less time spent on homework. Second, working takes its toll on student engagement in the classroom, with students who work longer hours reporting more mind-wandering and exerting less effort in school. Finally, student workers compensate for their job commitments through cheating, copying assignments, and cutting classes when convenient. As has been speculated elsewhere (Greenberger & Steinberg, 1986; McNeil, 1984), these behaviors may permit student workers to reduce the deleterious effects of working on their school grades.

These results, like those from earlier studies, suggest that debates over the employment of high school students should focus on the number of hours students work. Generally our analyses did not reveal clear hour thresholds beyond which the correlates of employment became dramatically more negative. The most prudent interpretation of these data, therefore, is simply that the potential risks of employment during the school year increase with increasing time commitment to a job.

## IMPLICATIONS

In this study we tried to put school in perspective by studying the impact on engagement and school achievement of students' noninstructional experiences. Realizing that we did not examine the complex cultural settings in which youth develop, or their experiences with other potentially significant influences (media; social service agencies; political, ethnic, and religious groups; extended family and other adults), we now consider what the study suggests for how to enhance student engagement and school achievement. In what ways might schools themselves exert constructive influences on parenting, peer relations, extracurricular participation, and part-time work? What are the implications for parents, employers, or youth-serving agencies beyond school?

We found that effective parenting for school success includes monitoring children's activities and setting limits, showing affection openly and becoming involved in their lives, and allowing students to state their own point of view and to share in family decisions. This combination of demandingness, warmth, and granting psychological autonomy enhances the development of competence in adolescence. Monitoring without warmth, or affection without limit setting, is much less effective. Parents can also improve school achievement and engagement by attending school activities and helping with homework and choice of classes. The combination of authoritative parenting and involvement in schooling maximizes the chances of improving adolescent engagement and achievement.

These parenting practices are easier to achieve in emotionally and economically stable family environments in which at least two adults share the responsibilities of caretaking. Increasingly, however, American families deviate from this description. Furthermore, increasing numbers of families in the United States identify with social and cultural roots that vary from white middle-class norms. The challenge is to encourage parenting practices that facilitate achievement while respecting cultural diversity. Educators may be especially successful in trying to raise the level of parental involvement in schooling. Most parents want their children to succeed in school. When they refrain from active participation, schools need to reach out.[4]

Turning to peer influences, we presented two main findings: Crowd membership is associated with school outcomes, and regardless of crowd membership excessive partying hurts engagement and achievement. Crowd structures and individual membership are difficult to change. Because cliques are frequently embedded within crowds, and friendships tend to be embedded within cliques, a transition from one crowd to another often entails a major disruption in the adolescent's social world. Academically and socially at-risk students like the druggies or loners face many obstacles in joining a different crowd, even when they are willing to make the move. Entry to a crowd more in the mainstream of school life demands not only the student's desire to belong, but also possession of the qualifications (e.g., nice clothes, good looks, athletic prowess, intellect) required for acceptance by its members. These students may face strong and unyielding perceptions that they belong in their original crowd. Rather than risking potential rejection by attempting to join another crowd, students may decide it is less stressful to stay put. If adults become familiar with norms in the different crowds, they can assist in crowd transitions by empathizing with the student's difficulties, and by encouraging the development of skills and participation in activities that are prerequisites for entry into the new crowd.

Across all crowds, time spent partying with friends was associated with higher levels of deviant behavior in school, such as cheating on exams, skipping classes, and so forth. Students may need help scheduling their socializing so that it does not interfere with either study time or rest. Adults' efforts to limit students' partying time can conflict, of course, with students' desire to be more autonomous and to take responsibility for their own actions. Our findings indicate, however, that showing concern for and awareness of students' activities, and setting reasonable limits within a context of support, will pay off.

Our findings support the common belief that extracurricular activities bolster teenagers' academic interests and performance. But academic benefits of participation are not equivalent in all types of extracurricular activities. Much depends on the extent to which the specific activity supports rather than distracts from academic pursuits. In some activities, long practice hours and high performance expectations can make students too tired or too nervous to concentrate on classwork. Many clubs, interest groups, and leadership activities, for example, offer environments more supportive of classwork than glory sports do.

If academic engagement and achievement are to be high priorities, these findings suggest the need for incentives for participation in the more supportive activities. But rather than relying on disciplinary and screening policies such as "no pass–no play" rules, educators would do well to attempt to reshape the peer norms and distracting demands and pressures common in glory sports.

The common image of the advisor or coach serving as a mentor who reaffirms the importance of school achievement was not borne out in this study. Why? Perhaps coaches fail to establish close relationships with most participants. Perhaps they get too caught up in the performance demands of the activity (the need to maintain a winning record at all costs). Perhaps the fact that many extracurricular advisors or coaches these days are community volunteers rather than school staff members weakens their role as academic mentors. Further study is needed to clarify these questions.

Our findings contradict the popular assumption that working during adolescence is beneficial to young people's development. In all ethnic and socioeconomic groups, working long hours is detrimental. Long work hours are associated with lower grades, less time on homework, and diminished engagement. At the same time, students who work more are more likely to cheat, copy assignments, and skip classes. This study, like earlier ones, suggests that debates over the employment of high school students should focus specifically on the consequences of long work hours.

Parents, educational practitioners, and policy makers should consider limiting teenagers' employment to a maximum of 20 hours a week during the school year.

The monitoring of student employment can be carried out by parents, schools, government agencies, employers, or preferably a combination of all four (Steinberg, 1990). In states in which parental or school permission is necessary for a student to obtain a work permit, limits may be imposed on an individual student's work hours by adults who are in a position to monitor the youngster's school performance, such as parents or guidance counselors. States in which prevailing child labor laws permit extensive school-year employment should reexamine such policies and consider restricting student employment to fewer than 20 hours weekly during the academic calendar. And major employers of teenagers need to recognize that overworking students, despite the short-term advantages to the employer, may have negative long-term consequences for the development of a competent adult labor force, since too much time at work may detract from students' engagement in school.

It is important for teachers to enhance student engagement and achievement by attending to the issues of membership and authentic work in instructional activities. By examining influences of noninstructional experiences, we have shown that teachers need help from others. Parents can make major contributions by becoming involved in school activities, by helping students face negative peer pressures, by encouraging participation in extracurricular activities that support academic work, and by setting limits on work hours. Schools can reach out to parents, can improve ways in which extracurricular activity supports academic engagement, and can work with public agencies and private employers to limit student work hours.

## NOTES

We would like to express our gratitude to Don Albright, Ted Carlsen, Bob Jasna, Priscilla Kuehn, Diane Kocs, Steve McNeal, and dear Mary Truitt for their tremendous support during the data collection for this study. We also are indebted to the many students, faculty, and staff of the participating high schools for time and energy contributed to this study.

1. GPA was derived from an eight-point scale including response categories of "Mostly A's" (4), "About half A's and half B's" (3.5), "Mostly B's" (3), "About half B's and C's" (2.5), "Mostly C's" (2), "About half C's and D's" (1.5), "Mostly D's" (1), "Mostly below D's" (.5). Students also had the option of choosing "I am not sure." This information formed a scale similar to that used in many high

schools in which a 4.0 represents straight A's. Homework time per week was based on a six-point scale ranging from "None" (1), "About 15 minutes" (2), "About 30 minutes" (3), "About an hour" (4), "About 2 or 3 hours" (5), "About 4 hours or more" (6). School deviance items included the four response categories of "Never" (1), "Once or twice" (2), "Several times" (3), "Often" (4). For educational expectations students chose one of six options: "Leave school as soon as possible" (1), "Finish some high school" (2), "Get some vocational or college training" (3), "Finish a two-year community college degree" (4), "Finish college with a four-year college degree" (5), "Finish college and take further training (medical, law, graduate school, etc.)" (6).

2. Although girls and boys were nearly evenly distributed among the jock/populars, there were large differences in gender in each of the other crowds. Girls were overrepresented in both the brain and average crowds (60 and 62 percent), while the druggie and loners/nerds were disproportionately composed of boys (58 and 68 percent).

Adolescents are more likely to be perceived as part of some crowd in the 10th or 11th Grades. Subsequently, there is a slight drop for 12th graders in the proportion of students assigned to each crowd. The small proportion of adolescents assigned to each crowd in the freshman year is due, in part, to the large number of new peers that adolescents come into contact with when beginning high school. They may know only a few people well enough to determine crowd membership. In contrast, sophomores and juniors are familiar with many more of their classmates, resulting in a higher proportion of crowd assignments. The drop in proportion of crowd assignments during the senior year is not surprising as adolescents begin to form heterosexual couples (Dunphey, 1963) and to assert individuality in ways that frequently take them away from participation in crowd activities (Brown, Eicher, & Petrie, 1986).

3. Grades seemed to suffer for students who devoted 20 hours or more per week to these activities, but few students logged this many hours in extracurricular activity.

4. Our study did not focus on specific school strategies most successful for enhancing parental involvement. For more information on this, see Chrispeels, Boruta, and Daugherty (1988), Epstein and Herrick (1991a, 1991b), and *Phi Delta Kappan* (1991).

# REFERENCES

Bachman, J. G., Bare, D. E., & Frankie, E. I. (1986). *Correlates of employment among high school seniors* (Monitoring the Future Occasional Paper No. 20). Ann Arbor, MI: Institute for Social Research.

Baker, D., & Stevenson, D. (1986). Mothers' strategies for children's achievement: Managing the transition to high school. *Sociology of Education, 59,* 156–166.

Baumrind, D. (1978). Parental disciplinary patterns and social competence in children. *Youth and Society, 9,* 239–276.

Baumrind, D. (1991). Parenting styles and adolescent development. In R. Lerner, A. C. Petersen, & J. Brooks-Gunn (Eds.), *The encyclopedia of adolescence* (pp. 746–758). New York: Garland.

Berndt, T. (1979). Developmental changes in conformity to peers and parents. *Developmental Psychology, 15,* 606–616.

Brown, B. B. (1990). Peer groups and peer cultures. In S. Feldman & G. Elliot (Eds.), *At the threshold: The developing adolescent* (pp. 171–196). Cambridge, MA: Harvard University Press.

Brown, B. B., & Clasen, D. R. (1986). *Developmental changes in adolescents' conceptions of peer groups.* Paper presented at the biennial meeting of the Society for Research in Adolescence, Madison, WI.

Brown, B. B., Eicher, S. A., & Petrie, S. (1986). The importance of peer group ("crowd") affiliation in adolescence. *Journal of Adolescence, 9,* 73–96.

Charner, I., & Fraser, B. (1987). *Youth and work.* Washington, DC: William T. Grant Foundation Commission on Work, Family, and Citizenship.

Chrispeels, J., Boruta, M., & Daugherty, M. (1988). *Communicating with parents.* San Diego, CA: San Diego County Office of Education.

Clark, R. (1983). *Family life and school achievement: Why poor black children succeed or fail.* Chicago: University of Chicago Press.

Clasen, D. R., & Brown, B. B. (1985). The multidimensionality of peer pressure in adolescence. *Journal of Youth and Adolescence, 14,* 451–468.

Coleman, J. S. (1961). *The adolescent society.* New York: Free Press.

Csikszentmihalyi, M., & Larson, R. (1984). *Being adolescent: Conflict and growth in the teenage years.* New York: Basic Books.

Cusick, P. A. (1973). *Inside high school; the students' world.* New York: Holt, Rinehart & Winston.

Damico, R. (1984). Does working in high school impair academic progress? *Sociology of Education, 57,* 157–164.

Dornbusch, S. M., Carlsmith, J. M., Bushwall, P. L., Ritter, P. L., Leiderman, H., Hastorf, A. H., & Gross, R. T. (1985). Single parents, extended households, and the control of adolescents. *Child Development, 56,* 326–341.

Dornbusch, S. M., Ritter, P. L., Leiderman, P., Roberts, D., & Fraleigh, M. (1987). The relation of parenting style to adolescent school performance. *Child Development, 58,* 1244–1257.

Dunphey, D. (1963). The social structure of urban adolescent peer groups. *Sociometry, 26,* 230–246.

Epstein, J. L. (in press). Effects of parent involvement on change in student achievement in reading and math. In S. Silvern (Ed.), *Literacy through family, community, and school interaction.* Greenwich, CT: JAI.

Epstein, J. L., & Herrick, S. C. (1991a). *Implementation and effects of summer home learning packets in middle grade students.* Baltimore: Johns Hopkins University.

Epstein, J. L., & Herrick, S. C. (1991b). *Implementing school and family partner-*

*ship in the middle grades* (CDS Report No. 20). Baltimore: Johns Hopkins University.

Fordham, S., & Ogbu, J. U. (1986). Black students' school success: Coping with the burden of "acting white." *Urban Review, 18,* 176–206.

Greenberger, E., & Steinberg, L. (1986). *When teenagers work: The psychological and social costs of adolescent employment.* New York: Basic Books.

Holland, A., & Andre, T. (1987). Participation in extracurricular activities in secondary school. What is known, what needs to be known? *Review of Educational Research, 57,* 437–466.

Kotlowitz, A. (1986, May 27). The fruits of teen labor: Bad grades, profligacy and a jaded view of working? *The Wall Street Journal,* p. 29.

Lamborn, S., Mounts, N., Steinberg, L., & Dornbusch, S. (1991). Patterns of competence and adjustment among adolescents from authoritative, authoritarian, indulgent, and neglectful families. *Child Development, 62*(5), 1049–1065.

Lewin-Epstein, N. (1981). *Youth employment during high school.* Washington, DC: National Center for Education Statistics.

Maccoby, E., & Martin, J. (1983). Socialization in the context of the family: Parent–child interaction. In E. M. Hetherington (Ed.), *Handbook of child psychology: Vol. 4. Socialization, personality, and social development* (pp. 1–101). New York: Wiley.

McNeil, L. (1984). *Lowering expectations: The impact of student employment on classroom knowledge.* Madison: Wisconsin Center for Educational Research, University of Wisconsin–Madison.

Mortimer, J. T., & Finch, M. D. (1986). The effects of part-time work on adolescents' self-concept and achievement. In K. Borman & J. Reisman (Eds.), *Becoming a Worker* (pp. 66–89). Norwood, NJ: Ablex.

Mosbach, P., & Leventhal, H. (1988). Peer group identification and smoking: Implications for intervention. *The Journal of Abnormal Psychology, 97,* 238–245.

Newman, P. R., & Newman, B. M. (1976). Early adolescence and its conflict: Group identity versus alienation. *Adolescence, 11,* 261–274.

*Phi Delta Kappan.* (1991). 72(5). [Several articles on parental involvement].

Powell, A. G., Farrar, E., & Cohen, D. K. (1985). *The shopping mall high school: Winners and losers in the educational marketplace.* Boston: Houghton Mifflin.

Schill, W., McCartin, R., & Meyer, K. (1985). Youth employment: Its relationship to academic and family variables. *Journal of Vocational Behavior, 26,* 155–163.

Steinberg, L. (1990, October). Invited testimony before the National Commission on Children, Minneapolis–St. Paul.

Steinberg, L., Brown, B. B., Cider, M., Kaczmarek, N., & Lazzaro, C. (1988). *Noninstructional influences on high school student achievement: Contributions of parents, peers, extracurricular activities, and part-time work.* National Center for Effective Secondary Schools, Madison, WI.

Steinberg, L., Elmen, J. D., & Mounts, N. S. (1989). Authoritative parenting, psychosocial maturity, and academic success among adolescents. *Child Development, 60,* 1424–1436.

Steinberg, L., Mounts, N., Lamborn, S., & Dornbusch, S. (1991). Authoritative parenting and adolescent adjustment across varied ecological niches. *Journal of Research on Adolescence, 1*(1), 19–36.

Stevenson, D. L., & Baker, D. P. (1987). The family–school relation and the child's school performance. *Child Development, 58,* 1348–1357.

Wehlage, G. G., Rutter, R. A., Smith, G. A., Lesko, N. L., & Fernandez, R. R. (1989). *Reducing the risk: Schools as communities of support.* Philadelphia: Falmer Press.

Willis, P. (1977). *Learning to labor.* Lexington, MA: D.C. Heath.

Wirtz, P., Rohrbeck, C., Charner, I., & Fraser, B. (1987). *Intense employment while in high school: Are teachers, guidance counselors, and parents misguiding academically-oriented adolescents?* Washington, DC: George Washington University Graduate Institute for Policy Education and Research.

CHAPTER 7

# Conclusion

## Fred M. Newmann

What have we learned about how to enhance student engagement and achievement in American secondary schools? I will first integrate the findings of separate projects into an interpretive framework, then illustrate some of the findings through events in a single school, and finally consider the implications of this perspective for improving secondary schools in the future.

## STUDENT ENGAGEMENT AND ACHIEVEMENT IN SECONDARY SCHOOLS: AN INTERPRETIVE SUMMARY

The studies reported on diverse aspects of school life, and the research findings can be synthesized into four topics: school culture, curriculum/instruction, organizational structures, and change processes. The bulk of our research concentrated on conditions of engagement and achievement in individual schools, not on how to change conditions throughout a district or state.

### School Culture

Secondary school students' engagement and achievement are affected profoundly by experiences that cannot be identified simply by listing what is prescribed in the formal curriculum, what students do in their classes, and what is tested. Instead, the effects of any specific school activity are best understood as cultural phenomena; that is, as outcomes that evolve through complex webs of institutionally sanctioned meanings, values, and incentives or disincentives for particular kinds of behavior. Educators tend to agree that students are influenced by a variety of conditions in their lives, but debate continues on which parts of school culture have the most

182

impact on engagement and achievement and which can be most easily influenced through deliberate action by school professionals, policy makers, or parents.

From the students' point of view, a basic cultural requirement for engagement is sense of school membership. We learned from the more successful schools that achieving this quality requires that schools communicate clear, noncontradictory purposes as the goals of education; that they treat students fairly; that they offer reliable personal support to help students undertake the hard and risky work of school; that they communicate high expectations and demonstrate accountability for the success of all students; and that these responsibilities be discharged in a climate of care that shows respect for all, regardless of the level of individuals' performance.

These different dimensions of membership may imply the need for attention to distinct norms, behaviors, policies, and practices, but it is important not to lose sight of the underlying principle of *inclusion* as the basis of membership. This means listening to students, trying to comprehend their own meanings, and responding in ways that incorporate their perspectives, concerns, and interests—many of which originate from and concentrate on experiences beyond the formal tasks of classroom instruction.

The membership principle has multiple implications for school practice. These can include curriculum revision to study cultural groups previously omitted from history courses; having teachers consider how to elicit ideas from students that might help the *teachers* understand a work of literature; teaching teachers how to give students rigorous criticism in ways that maximize students' sense of competence and success; establishing mentor or advisory programs that ensure each student long-term support from a single adult; sponsoring student recognition programs that reward students for participation and success in diverse activities; building systems of governance that give students a more meaningful voice in matters of policy and rule enforcement; and developing alternatives to ability grouping to enhance membership for low-achieving students.

Building a culture of inclusion also requires initiatives to affect students' noninstructional experiences. These can include programs to increase parents' sense of membership by encouraging their involvement in school activities and by assisting them with parenting styles that support student engagement; policies to increase participation of marginal student groups ("outcasts," "druggies," "loners") in extracurricular activities; programs to help athletic activities reinforce norms for academic achievement; counseling and support groups to help students resist peer pressure destructive to academic engagement and to help them change crowd membership; rules, incentives, and advising to put reasonable limits on the time students spend in part-time work and partying so they can give more attention to school.

It is not enough to examine school culture from the student's point of view. Since teachers are the most important people in schools for boosting student engagement and achievement, a critical task for school culture is to nurture teachers' commitment and competence to teach all students. Syntheses of research attest to the benefits of a communal culture for both students and teachers (Bryk & Driscoll, 1988; Bryk, Lee, & Smith, 1990). Consistent with and extending this finding, our studies found that successful schools were characterized by collegial faculty culture. Teachers in these schools showed consensus on the school's mission, with high expectations for all students; collegial help that focused on professional issues; respect and caring for students; demands among teachers for active problem solving, experimentation, and entrepreneurship to develop new programs; and peer pressure among teachers to work hard for students and the school. Thus, just as a culture of school membership builds student engagement, so does a culture of collegial professionalism nurture the will and skill of teachers to teach effectively.

How can the norms of student membership and collegial professionalism be developed in secondary schools? Conclusions on organizational structures and the process of change described below offer some guidelines, but first I will consider how the core of schooling—what is taught and how it is taught — affects student engagement and achievement.

## Curriculum and Instruction

Rather than specifying content and methods appropriate for subjects of study, the Center's research sought criteria for the design of curriculum and instruction that would increase student engagement and achievement in all subjects. To maximize the power of this inquiry, we examined qualities of work both in and out of school that tend to generate human interest and investment in doing one's best. We explained the importance of designing instructional tasks that provide, to the extent possible, extrinsic rewards, intrinsic interest, sense of ownership, connection to the "real world," and fun.

These criteria reflect several other recommendations for the reform of curriculum and instruction. For example, recommendations for higher-order thinking emphasize students as active interpreters who reason about the meaning of information, rather than simply as reproducers of knowledge fragments. This recognizes the importance of student ownership of the content. The principle of "depth over coverage" is also consistent with

our criteria: Studying topics in depth offers the opportunity to see relationships and is, therefore, likely to be intrinsically more interesting than
racing through expository material to cover a wide variety of unconnected
topics. Our studies indicated that students were more engaged when they
were expected to be active interpreters of knowledge, rather than docile
recipients, and when they were involved in in-depth study rather than
superficial coverage of information. All of this is consistent with a major
body of research that shows that students learn not by passively absorbing
information, but instead by constructing and reconstructing meanings —
by trying to make sense of information thrown at them (Resnick, 1987). If
there is no opportunity to make sense of it, the knowledge that is "taught"
will not be learned.

Unfortunately, authentic instruction rarely occurs. In a study of 9th
Grade literature instruction, less than a third of the teachers' questions
built on what students had to say, and less than a quarter of a minute per
class was devoted to discussion that involved free exchange of information
lasting longer than 30 seconds. In a study of social studies in Grades 9–12,
less than a quarter of the lessons clearly emphasized depth, less than a
third showed students giving reasons and explanations, and in only 15
percent of the lessons did teachers carefully consider the reasons and explanations that students gave. This was particularly disturbing, because Keating's (1988) synthesis of research on adolescents' ability to engage in critical thinking refuted the opinion we heard from many teachers that
adolescents are incapable of complex, abstract thought. This research review, plus the many instances we observed where students of all socioeconomic groups were being challenged to think, convinces us that high
school expectations for students using their minds are far too low.

We found that well-intentioned efforts to build a culture of school
membership could lead to unanticipated *negative* results for curriculum.
In their effort to reach out to low-achieving students and to incorporate
student interests in the curriculum, many teachers have virtually abandoned the teaching of complex content in the main subjects of mathematics, science, English, and social studies. To feel included, students need
support, success, caring, and incorporation of their ideas into academic
study. But students' prior experiences and viewpoints must not be confused
with the formal knowledge that educators are obligated to provide. The
point is not to build curriculum on student personal experience instead of
disciplined knowledge, but to show how disciplined knowledge can empower students by expanding and offering new tools with which to interpret personal experience.[1]

It is possible that we have arrived at a critical moment in thinking
about curriculum and instruction. On the one hand, we have learned

from research on student cognition and student engagement that students' perspectives must be taken more seriously in the design of curriculum and in the practice of teaching. This tends to suggest a student-centered approach. We have also learned that students are more capable of complex thought than previously assumed, but that they are rarely challenged to understand academic content in depth. So, on the other hand, we find many voices urging curriculum reform in the direction of challenging, subject-centered content.[2] These raised expectations for student understanding of disciplined knowledge suggest the need for more rigorous, subject-centered standards.

What are the alternatives to instruction through expository texts, teacher lectures, and the recitations typically demanded in worksheets and class discussions? The "new pedagogy" would restructure traditional classrooms by connecting students to computers and electronic media, by emphasizing cooperative small-group work and individually paced study, and by replacing worksheets with projects. The problem is that these new techniques and processes do not define what should be taught or the degree of depth desired. Nor do they communicate a sense of what outstanding teachers do or how they talk with students about the subjects of study in these new circumstances.

We have seen numerous examples of teachers and students engaged in the "new" pedagogy: interesting, hands-on science projects; students working cooperatively to solve applied mathematics problems; intense debates where students analyze historical episodes to clarify their reasoning on persisting public issues; creative writing that uses literature to illuminate a personal experience. These provide glimpses of an alternative curriculum model. But the isolated examples have not yet been synthesized into total school programs. Only a few teachers, students, and parents have experienced them. Educational literature describes them briefly, but has not shown in compelling detail how such teaching, over a sustained period of time, actually provides students with the information, the intellectual skills, and the dispositions they need to understand and to use insights from the major subjects of mathematics, science, history, and literature. In short, this emergent vision of education has not been developed in enough detail nor has it been experienced even occasionally by enough people to compete with traditional forms and to inspire the reconstruction of curriculum and instruction.

To successfully integrate the challenging-content and student-centered perspectives, we need new substantive rationales for particular secondary school subjects. Years ago progressive educational philosophy offered a foundation for the development of an alternative model of education. Since then, however, academic discussions, revisions of instructional materials, and case studies of successful teachers have not paid enough attention to (1) defining the kind of content appropriate for education in a modern, multicultural society with vast disparities in the social capital its students bring to school, and (2) showing how teachers, by drawing on student experiences, can use challenging content to engage students in deeper levels of understanding. A number of projects are beginning to work on this problem (e.g., the Coalition of Essential Schools, the Paideia Project, and Project 2061), but none have produced replicable models of classroom discourse clear and strong enough to replace the coverage principle, expository text, teacher lecturing, and student reproduction of transmitted knowledge as the currency of curriculum and instruction. Projects that have focused on building more authentic curriculum have encountered a number of organizational obstacles that indicate the need for new organizational structures in secondary schools.

## Organizational Structure

Our examination of organizational structure focused mainly on the lives of students and teachers within individual schools, and less on the schools' relationships to external bodies such as districts, states, or national reform initiatives mounted by different organizations. Our theory of student engagement and empirical results indicates the need for change in the common organizational structure of comprehensive secondary schools, but also that organizational changes alone offer no guarantees of enhanced student engagement and achievement. I first consider the kinds of changes suggested and then some findings indicating that organizational changes alone offer no panacea.

### Types of Structural Change Within Schools

What features in the typical organizational structure of secondary schools should be changed and why? The criteria of school membership, for example, suggest the need for more focused instructional missions for the school, channels for student input into rule making and enforcement, learning communities within schools that provide more sustained contact with staff who function in advisory as well as instructional roles, and minimizing the stratification of students into ability groups. All of these can be facilitated in smaller schools.

We found that students at risk benefit particularly from programs based on a "family" model in which a small group of teachers (about four) take collective responsibility for planning and delivering education in the main subjects to a group of students (about 100) that stays together for at least a two-year period. The main strengths in the family model are its potential for developing stronger bonds of student trust, higher teacher expectations for students, teachers feeling more accountable for student performance, and teachers providing one another with the technical assistance and emotional support required for success with these students.

Criteria for authentic schoolwork suggest the desirability of more flexibility in the scheduling of instruction to allow for both much shorter and much longer instructional periods than the typical 50 minutes; reduced time in large-group instruction and increased time in small-group and individual study; making greater use of peers, libraries, and computers; formal and informal procedures for increasing student influence over the planning, execution, and evaluation of schoolwork; easier access to learning resources beyond the school (e.g., through use of telephones and community-based learning experiences); new arrangements and incentives that facilitate the display of student work to the public at large and feedback on its quality from audiences other than a single teacher (e.g., peers, the public, and outside authorities); and reduction in teachers' total student load to allow more personalization. We saw examples in which each of these organizational innovations, in concert with other important factors (especially improved curriculum and teaching), was associated with high levels of student engagement and achievement.

Criteria for a culture of collegial professionalism beckon for such organizational changes as increased opportunities for ongoing professional development (in contrast to four half-days per year); school-wide faculty committees to influence decisions on curriculum, staff development, budget, hiring, student affairs, and other aspects of school policy; incentives that reward teachers for experimentation and program development; teachers working in teams; and increased common time for teachers to plan and evaluate their work. Consistent with other literature, we found schools where such organizational features contributed to teachers' high level of commitment and technical competence. But, as discussed next, none of these structures alone produced the kind of student membership, authentic curriculum, or collegial professionalism required to boost student engagement and achievement.

### Limitations of New Structures

Changes in organizational structure are unlikely to enhance student engagement and achievement unless structural changes are deliberately linked to efforts to improve the substance of educational missions, cultural norms, curriculum, and teaching. Students working with faculty tutors or in small groups, for example, can be exposed to either boring or exciting material. Even dramatic reductions in class size (e.g., from about 25 to 10) will have little effect unless they are accompanied by changes in teaching (Bennett, 1987). Our study of social studies departments indicated that restructuring assisted in the promotion of higher-order thinking, but that the more intense programmatic emphasis we found in select conventional schools allowed these schools to perform better than restructured ones. Our study of teachers' work lives in restructured schools concluded that collegial professional culture depended as much or more on the quality of leadership as on the presence of new organizational structures.

Research on ability grouping provides a further illustration of the indeterminate effects of specific structures. There seems to be consensus that overall the use of homogeneous ability grouping in secondary schools does not raise average achievement levels in the student population (Slavin, 1990). The main issue is whether high-achieving students gain and low-achieving students lose as a result of homogeneous grouping, and if so what instructional processes account for this. The instructional quality of low-ability classes tends to be inferior to that of high-ability classes, and students tracked into several low-ability classes throughout secondary school encounter a cumulative regimen of fewer academic courses and less academic content, leading to reduced levels of engagement and achievement (Gamoran, 1987; Oakes, 1985). This suggests either that major efforts must be devoted to improving instruction in low-ability classes or that these should be replaced with heterogeneously grouped classes. On the other hand, we recognize the difficulties teachers face with heterogeneous classes, particularly the problem of providing sufficient challenge to high-achieving students in these classes.

All of this indicates the need for reconsidering the way students are grouped, so as to reduce the problems of large-group instruction and to rely more on small, cooperative learning groups and individual study. New grouping patterns might avoid some of the problems of whole-class ability grouping, but the new patterns alone offer no guarantee of at once raising the achievement level of all and reducing the disparity between the most and least successful students.

Changes in organizational structure offer much potential, and in some cases seem logically necessary, for boosting student engagement and achievement. But no single organizational structure *alone* (e.g., school-site council, heterogeneous grouping, teacher mentors, longer school day, team teaching) is likely either to advance or to impair valued outcomes. It all depends on how the innovations are used. The effects of organizational innovation are influenced largely by the values, beliefs, and technical capacity that individuals bring to their work. Educators' instructional goals; their knowledge of subjects; their patterns of interaction; their commitments to excellence, equity, or the development of children; and their receptiveness to innovation constitute the "content" that ultimately determines what impact schools have on students. Yet new structures, by providing opportunities, limits, incentives, and sanctions, can themselves help stimulate changes in educational vision and school culture. We have seen, for example, that frequent scheduling of small classes devoted to discussion, or scheduling of instructional periods that last two hours, have led teachers to reexamine their assumptions about the main educational mission and how to achieve it with today's students. Later I will say more about the balance between structure and content in school change.

## Change Processes

How can secondary schools be changed to realize those aspects of school culture, curriculum, and organizational structure that boost student engagement and achievement? Our theoretical and empirical research did not concentrate on the process of changing schools, but our studies of higher-order thinking, programs for students at risk, and the quality of teachers' work life familiarized us with diverse change efforts in more than 30 middle and 60 high schools. For the most part these innovations were initiated and sustained primarily within single schools, but we also observed efforts by districts to mandate and support school change across several schools at once. Research in these schools, along with the broader literature on school change, lead to conclusions on the importance of a school's social context, the nature of effective leadership within schools, the role of change agents external to the school, and problems in planning and managing systemic change.[3]

### Social Context

Secondary schools are complex environments that pose enormous obstacles to fundamental change. There are common obstacles across schools, but the social context of each school has a powerful impact on how these can be attacked. Three aspects of the social context of comprehensive public secondary schools in the United States make change particularly problematic.

The first is diversity. Schools serve student constituencies with widely diverse needs and expectations, and there is profound disagreement on the essential goals of education. The plurality of needs and goals arises from major differences in students' economic resources and in their ethnic and cultural backgrounds, from long-standing and unresolved philosophical argument over the proper ends of socialization and education of children, and from the increased demands for knowledge and skills in a technologically advanced, multicultural, democratic society. The diversity leads to a complex agenda of multiple goals for all children and for separate programs for particular constituencies. Such a context makes it difficult to develop and implement common solutions to problems in school culture, curriculum, and organization. This issue will be discussed further under "Choices for the Future."

The second is satisfaction. In spite of evidence that millions of adolescents are poorly served by secondary schools, that thousands of teachers are burned out, and that politicians and corporate leaders are dissatisfied with school performance, most students, teachers, and parents continue to believe their own schools are working well enough. In the 1991 Gallup poll, 73 percent of the parents graded their oldest child's school as A or B, 42 percent of all adults gave A's or B's to the schools in their community, and only 15 percent of all adults rated their community's schools as D or failing (Elam, Rose, & Gallup, 1991). When most of the people touched by the nation's 20,000 secondary schools feel reasonably well served, it is hard to muster commitment for fundamental change.

The third is systemic constraint. Even school staff who would like to change their schools in major ways face a host of obstacles thrown up by different parts of the social system. District, state, and federal jurisdictions impose regulations on schools and subject them to vagaries of leadership. Schools' dependence on colleges, universities, and the economic and regulatory structures of the teaching profession limits the quality of teachers they can hire. Relying for instructional materials on a centralized, market-oriented publishing industry restricts the availability of engaging texts. The quality of students' education prior to secondary school and the entrance requirements for higher education also influence the nature of secondary school instruction. Finally, the system of social support for children offered by families, private social networks, and community agencies magnifies the range of problems schools face in engaging students.

Efforts to change what happens in a single classroom (e.g., increasing teacher questions that build on students' knowledge), to spread a single innovation to several classes (e.g., cooperative learning), or to fundamentally change a school's organizational structure (e.g., eliminating ability grouping) must face the problems of diversity, satisfaction, and systemic constraint within the special historical and social context of the school.[4]

*Leadership Within the School*

As we observed changes in school culture, curriculum, and organization, we found, as have others, that leadership within the school seemed critical both in the initiation and maintenance of innovation. Consistent with research on secondary school leadership (Peterson, 1989), we found significant leadership emerged not only from the school principal. In many cases department chairs and teachers took the most visible initiatives to establish a sense of mission and to develop new curricula, programs, and school policy. Often principals acted largely as facilitators and supporters to these other leaders. Since effective school change depends on school leadership beyond the principal, a major function of effective administrative leadership is to nurture it in others — a point recognized in the literature, but not prominently emphasized in common images of the effective school principal.

Effective leaders differed in many ways, but all seemed to strike a delicate balance between directive decisions and guidance, on the one hand, and the support/empowerment of staff on the other. These leaders (principals, department chairs, and teachers) helped to establish visions, to argue for some priorities over others, and to become highly involved in program details and in the daily lives of students and teachers. But they also delegated considerable authority, provided financial and moral support, buffered staff from hostile forces, and stayed out of the way when teachers exercised constructive initiative.

These qualities of leadership, exercised with sensitivity to the school's social context, suggest an evolutionary notion of school change (Louis & Miles, 1990). According to this notion, productive school change does not proceed on a tight linear path from a detailed plan to implementation to evaluation of success in terms of original intentions. Instead, specific objectives and approaches to implementation evolve in a less predictable fashion as participants respond to unexpected challenges in the school's social context. Accepting an evolutionary concept of change has significant implications for the way leaders behave and the way school participants react to explicit school change efforts. This notion suggests, for example, that the precise consequences of proposed changes can never be fully anticipated, that criteria for evaluation of success or failure may themselves need to be modified in the process, and that changes originally intended may never be implemented in a stable, final form. School change itself is considered an endless dialectic rather than a journey with a beginning and an end. This is not to suggest that effective leaders lack direction and simply "go with the flow," remaining open to all alternatives and directions. On the contrary, they help to develop organizational commitment to goals and missions that guide the course of evolution down certain paths.

## Change Agents External to the School

The systemic constraints of individual schools described earlier portrayed an almost endless maze of obstacles. But different parts of the system might also be viewed more positively as a set of potential resources to help schools increase student engagement and achievement. School districts, states, universities, and publishers could and ought to be helpful in stimulating school improvement. Other agents external to the school also try to play constructive roles, such as teacher unions, other professional organizations, foundations, businesses, federally sponsored research centers and educational laboratories, and reform-oriented projects and consortia supported by these sources (e.g., Coalition of Essential Schools, Project 2061, National Council of Teachers of Mathematics, and National Network for Educational Renewal). External change agents represent diverse goals and strategies. They wield varying degrees of influence over what actually happens with students in schools.

The most successful change efforts we saw in individual schools did rely in some way on stimulation, ideas, and support from people, projects, or agencies beyond the school. Like Louis and Miles (1990), we found that the most successful of these were sought out by the school or provided assistance tailored to the school's situation. We are convinced of the need for outside stimulation and support to fulfill the kinds of changes suggested in our conceptions of school membership and authentic work. Ultimately the staff in individual schools must own their innovations, but current structures within schools that prescribe teachers' and students' work and that influence professional development are unable by themselves to stimulate and sustain significant change in school culture, curriculum, or organization. Just as schools depend on external agents to maintain the status quo, so also do schools need pressure and support from external agencies to change.

We have not, however, discovered a productive way of harnessing and linking the resources that many external agents might use to support individual school change. Consistent with other literature (e.g., David, Purkey, & White, 1989), we found that local districts can help to stimulate significant school-level change. But more often we found either that the great bulk of district and state policy was irrelevant to school-level efforts to enhance student engagement and achievement or that top-down mandates and regulations undermined school efforts.

Much work needs to be done to devise approaches that maximize benefits from external change agents. It will be important to maintain a balance between putting direct, explicit pressure on schools to change in some specific directions while at the same time offering the kind of support and autonomy that empower them to chart their own courses. We have seen examples of district-initiated reforms that fail to take root in schools or in teachers' minds because people at the school have insufficient opportunity to reexamine their practice and to reach their own conclusions about the need for and the most appropriate strategies toward improvement. While some articulation of higher standards is necessary, top-down imposition of new curricula, new assessment procedures, or new organizational forms alone can exacerbate the difficulties that teachers have engaging students. Striking a proper balance between institutional pressure and support from external change agents will be a major challenge of district, state, and federal efforts to restructure schools.

## THOMAS JEFFERSON HIGH SCHOOL:
## A STORY IN BUILDING STUDENT ENGAGEMENT

The findings from diverse studies in the Secondary Center can be illustrated through events in a school. Here we show students in a variety of engaging learning activities and how the school made changes to produce them. The description of Thomas Jefferson represents a composite of events and processes observed in actual secondary schools, including those with large proportions of students at risk. We have observed no school that actually integrates all of the scenes, but believe that the story of Thomas Jefferson offers a realistic vision for any school to work toward.[5]

Most of the students at Thomas Jefferson come from minority groups and from economically disadvantaged homes. They live in an urban area beset with problems of unemployment, crime, and family disruption. Many students have been retained in earlier grades, and a number have records of misbehavior and truancy. When entering the school as 9th graders, most read below grade level and test below the 50th percentile in mathematics achievement. Despite what some might see as a discouraging situation, the atmosphere at Thomas Jefferson is upbeat. Staff are generally positive about teaching, and in contrast to the bored, reluctant learners that occupy the seats in many secondary school classrooms, most students here display an air of interest and even excitement about their academic work.

### Curriculum and Instruction

In the science and technology laboratory, students from an interdisciplinary science-mathematics class work in groups to program a computer that is capable of controlling a small robot. Their challenge is to create a program that controls the robot's movement to do several mechanical tasks such as sharpening a pencil and opening and closing a door. While each group must successfully learn to program the robot, the class will enter its best collective project in the state's science fair later in the year.

In another wing of the same lab, a group of students conducts a series of experiments with small-scale bridges constructed of balsa wood. The students are trying to apply principles of engineering, physics, and mathematics learned earlier, as they prepare for a contest with several other schools to determine who can build the strongest bridge.

Across the hall in the school's humanities office, a mixed group of freshmen through seniors prepares for the publication of the school newspaper using desk-top publishing equipment. The work is part of the English curriculum in which each course requires an "applied" experience. Several younger students are huddled around the hardware as an experienced senior teaches them about various operations in the printing process. In one corner of the room, the teacher and student editor discuss with two students revisions of an article they wrote after interviewing a local writer about issues of violence and racism. They are trying to decide what revisions need to be made in the article before it can be published in the school paper. In another corner, advertising sales representatives are holding a meeting prior to calling on local businesses. Nearby, a small group of photographers are sharing tips on action photography, such as sporting events.

In the classroom next door, students from a social studies class are completing their social research project on the homeless. They are rehearsing a skit that they wrote to be performed and recorded in the school's television production studio. Later, with guidance from both the social studies and drama teachers, they will edit the video to be played on the city's public cable channel. Other students from the class chose to present their findings through written articles. The teacher helps them check the statistical tables and offers suggestions for rewriting the papers as articles suitable for the "guest column" in the city's newspaper to which some students want to contribute.

In another wing, seniors in the community involvement class meet in their weekly seminar. The class satisfies the 12th Grade social studies requirement. Monday through Thursday students spend at least two hours per day in volunteer community service outside the school. On Fridays students and the teacher meet in a two-hour seminar to reflect on their experiences. Students keep a daily journal and write an essay once a week that links some social science concept or theory with their activities that week.

Across the hall, occasional cries from infants announce the location of the school's special program for teenage mothers or mothers-to-be. The community has a high pregnancy rate among teenagers, and Thomas Jefferson provides girls with extra support intended to help them complete high school and also become good mothers. Pregnant students help tend others' babies and toddlers in one of three nurseries. The on-site child care facility provides child care for mothers with no other child care options and also serves as a "lab" for expectant mothers. In classes they learn about their own developing fetus and the stages of development in infants. Information about exercise, nutrition, labor, and delivery is shared within an environment where love for children and concern for their well-being are evident.

Toward the back of the building, students in the technical studies program spend most of their class hours designing, constructing, and repairing things. They solve special practical problems related to auto mechanics, woodworking, machine shop, drafting, and electrical studies. Half the final exam for each course in the program is a conventional written test, but students must also demonstrate their ability to use their technical knowledge with hands-on performance. For instance, the written test in electrical studies covers, among other things, Ohm's law and theories of parallel circuitry. In demonstrations, students are required to create an electrical device based on a wiring diagram. In a recent exam they constructed an alarm unit to warn drivers that their headlights remain on after the ignition has been turned off.

From nearby practice rooms clustered around a rehearsal room come strains of music from strings, brass, piano, diverse electronic instruments, and voices. Students are encouraged by the school to use a free study period to practice. In the rehearsal room, the school orchestra is rehearsing for the spring orchestra tour. Some students are competing to be selected as the orchestra soloists. Three small bands are working to polish their sets in order to gain entry in the upcoming festival that includes rock, jazz, and folk. The competitions will be judged by music faculty from a local college and professional musicians in the area.

Outside the building students from a biology class walk back and forth systematically through the tall, uncut weeds and grass behind the athletic field. Each has been given a long, oversize wool sock to wear over one shoe. The sock accumulates a variety of seeds that will become the raw material for study and experimentation in their biology class during the coming weeks.

## School Change

A few years ago, these scenes did not exist. Instead, teachers and administrators spent most of their day trying to control students and cajole them into studying topics and texts that seemed to provoke resistance rather than engagement. How did the school become what most agree is a stimulating place for both students and teachers?

There were many starting points for this transformation, and in retrospect it is difficult to say which came first. Some would say it was the superintendent's revelation of the high failure and retention rates in the district's secondary schools. He, along with the school board, argued that these were unacceptable outcomes and that new resources needed to be directed at the secondary schools. The superintendent publicly promised to begin creating exemplary places of learning for adolescents and invited teachers to join him in this task. His challenge stirred excitement and controversy, and it became a signal that authorized educational entrepreneurship in a number of schools. In fact, at Jefferson many of the staff had for some time been unhappy with the results of their teaching. In response, the principal had already sponsored a series of faculty discussions around issues of school improvement and these had prepared some staff for the challenge in the superintendent's message. With enthusiasm, a handful of teachers began to openly question old assumptions about the way school was organized, what was taught, and how students and teachers related to each other. One especially spirited discussion focused on the well-entrenched practice of tracking students into low- , middle- , and high-ability groups. Research on the effects of tracking and the prospects of accelerating the learning of those who were labeled as low achievers was brought into the discussion. Eventually the pros and cons of tracking permeated dialogue in the school, and the issue was brought before the faculty for a policy decision. Despite some initial dissent, consensus was reached that tracking would be eliminated in all subjects at the school.

Prompted in part by the superintendent's publication of rather shocking data about the low achievement, failure, and retention rates in the system, a group of parents and teachers began to study these problems at Jefferson. Determined to change what most agreed was an unacceptable situation, this group became known as the "school improvement" committee. It tapped into district funds for staff development, began discussing a set of readings on school improvement, and sponsored visits by teachers to schools in other districts that had been described as "excellent" and "effective." As one teacher recalls, the difference between this and previous committees to improve school was the depth and substance of the issues discussed.

In the past we always identified superficial things to change, like using the latest teaching technique, but we didn't consider changes in what we taught, what we asked kids to learn, or what we expected them to be able to *do*. When teachers began to see that we needed to make some fundamental changes in these areas, like focusing on student performance as our teaching goal, things got real exciting.

Membership on the school improvement committee began to grow, and the committee eventually split into subcommittees. The most aggressive of these was a group of science and mathematics teachers who were convinced that student interest and achievement in their subjects could be substantially improved. Ideas developed from visits to other schools and from their readings eventually led to a decision to create a science and technology laboratory that could provide a focus for almost all science and much mathematics coursework. The lab would provide a place and special equipment for an applied, hands-on approach to curriculum, but this also required a complete restructuring of the science and mathematics curriculum.

The lab got its biggest boost when the subcommittee was successful in getting a grant from a local foundation to remodel a large classroom and buy some state-of-the-art equipment the school system said it was unable to afford. Several professionals from the community who worked in scientific areas had been brought onto the subcommittee to provide guidance about the knowledge required by contemporary technology. This group of citizens has since become permanent advisors. In addition, they are active in helping raise small amounts of money, identifying surplus science and technology equipment in local businesses that can be donated to the lab, providing occasional assistance with special projects, and opening their own businesses and labs for use by teachers and students. Several employees of these businesses have volunteered as mentors to work with students especially interested in pursuing careers involving science. One member of the advisory group is now working with the local university to develop a summer "college for kids" focused on attracting minority youth into science fields.

The science and technology lab immediately became a highly visible and successful feature of the school, and soon the language arts and social studies teachers at Jefferson were developing their own variation. After extensive joint discussions and planning, teachers from these two subjects created an interdisciplinary program of study that utilizes media technology. However, securing the hardware required by the new curriculum proved difficult. A subcommittee consisting of teachers, the principal, and one of the language arts specialists from the central office eventually was successful in persuading the district to provide funding for the necessary equipment. As a result, the school now has three media labs — a desk-top publishing center, and radio and television studios.

New curricula and supporting hardware are not the only new features at Jefferson. The school day was lengthened and scheduling was reorganized to create teams of math/science and English/social studies teachers with common teaching and planning periods. These changes came about only after lengthy, and sometimes heated, discussions by the staff. Some teachers raised objections to required teaming and a longer work day without a corresponding increase in pay. Eventually, however, consensus was reached that the new curriculum was important, and that it required increased structured time and new teaming arrangements, and in an expression of collegial and professional commitment, the teachers' union and staff agreed to support the changes.

In addition, restructuring of staff roles has provided a high level of social support for students who come from homes under stress because of unemployment, poverty, divorce, and drug and alcohol abuse. Additional counseling staff was obtained through an experimental state program that helps counselors develop skills in home assessment and a knowledge of social services in the community that can assist families in difficulty. Counselors now must spend a portion of the time linking students and families to social services. Another change in role makes each staff member, including the principal, a student advisor. Three mornings a week adults meet with their "advisees" to provide academic and personal guidance. Contact with the home about each student's academic and personal progress is required at least once a month.

Another major innovation is the Student Responsibility Committee, made up of students and staff, which deals with disciplinary and school climate problems. This committee has real governing authority, and among the things it has accomplished are creating alternatives to out-of-school suspension, a student conflict resolution team, and a community service program. The latter provides student volunteers to aid the elderly and handicapped. The principal credits these initiatives by the Student Responsibility Committee for creating a much improved school climate, discipline, and a sense of pride in the school. As evidence, he cites data showing a 90 percent reduction in out-of-school suspensions over the last three years.

In discussing life at Jefferson with teachers, one finds that the school is a good place to teach, partly because of the excitement the new curriculum has created. Teachers generally believe that teaching is more satisfying because students are more successful. Teaching is also satisfying because of teachers' commitment to a curriculum they have constructed. Also contributing to staff satisfaction is the school's shared governance system that gives staff real decision-making power.

Despite this optimistic picture, there are still problems that remain to be solved. A few teachers resent the loss of autonomy that resulted from the new organization and curriculum. Also, the governance system continues to take substantial time and requires teachers to perform a role for which they have little preparation. For example, each week the Principal's

Cabinet, composed of teacher representatives, meets to take up a wide range of governance issues such as spending money to develop new courses, hiring teacher aides, and modifying class schedules. While these are important issues to teachers, some claim that the governance process contributes to a burnout problem. The work load from serving on the Principal's Cabinet, the Student Responsibility Committee, and other committees is exacerbated by the fact that some faculty participate minimally, which creates a burden on those who are active. Ultimately, these are problems that will require more resources to provide staff with additional noninstructional time. Finally, a more serious problem is finding a way to strengthen and sustain the additional resources the staff has already generated from social services, the business community, and the university. Despite these problems, most teachers and administrators say they could never go back to the "bad old days" when teachers were ignored and felt alienated from administrative directives and decisions.

## CHOICES FOR THE FUTURE

What are the implications of Thomas Jefferson and the summary of findings for improving secondary schools in the future? No single model or set of alternatives will work in every community. Thus, rather than offering a formula for success, it makes more sense to clarify some critical choices that need to be faced. After listening to teachers, administrators, parents, students, and policy makers, and studying research on education, we find confusion, lack of understanding, and reluctance to confront several critical issues. There is a tendency to view education largely as a technical enterprise and to underestimate its moral and political content. There is confusion on goals, especially on how to resolve differences between progressive and traditional conceptions of education, and on the extent to which schools should promote common curriculum for all. Almost no attention is given to the relationship between organizational structure and educational content. There is ambivalence about the priority to place on large-scale systemic reform versus changing one school at a time. And there is profound neglect of the problem of building social capital so that students can benefit from schooling. In making choices about the future, each of these issues must be carefully considered.

### Education as a Moral and Political Enterprise

The solutions to educational problems will not be found simply through research that discovers how to teach reading or mathematics, how to lead a school, how to run a community service program, or how to assess students. Behind each of these apparently straightforward questions lie significant moral and political choices. Education is a moral activity, because it prescribes, either explicitly or implicitly, what people ought to do, what they ought to think, and even what they ought to feel. There is no escape from the controversies entailed in taking on this responsibility. The familiar injunction that education can and should *avoid* moral prescriptions — by teaching tolerance and respect for diversity and by teaching critical inquiry rather than one right way of thinking — offers little refuge. These "protections" themselves are, of course, also prescriptions for certain kinds of behavior, thought, and affect. They define at least in part what it means to be a good person and to live a good life. This is not to say that all educational activity necessarily indoctrinates, narrows one's options, or limits freedom. But even the choice to maximize freedom and choice is, of course, a prescription for valued behavior.

Education is political in the sense that it allocates scarce resources and power. What resources are invested in affluent versus poor students, English-speaking versus limited-English-proficiency students, gifted and talented versus disabled students? Whose cultural heritage is emphasized in the curriculum? What kinds of adult work are honored through the curriculum and what kinds are neglected or devalued? Which citizens have more and less opportunity to influence the conduct of schooling? Beyond the allocation of scarce resources, education is political in another sense; namely, for schools to function they must earn the support of particular constituencies. What schools do to earn community support may not always be consistent with offering students the best education possible. Some questions about how to teach or how to organize schools may seem to call for technical knowledge independent of politics, but often they must be answered with great deference to the kinds of power relations that school participants need to support.

The connection between moral and political aspects of education is illustrated in judgments about educational equity. The effective schools movement began as an effort to narrow the gap in reading and math achievement between low-income minority children and the more affluent middle class. National test results indicate that considerable progress has been made in narrowing the achievement gap in basic skills between minority and white students. Average results, however, obscure the fact that in thousands of secondary schools enormous disparities remain between students at risk due to low income, limited English proficiency, or lack of family support and those whose advantaged positions in the social-economic mainstream bring them much higher levels of school success. Disparities abound between these two groups in the quality of instruction offered and in the achievement of both basic skills and more complex understanding of important subjects. What investment should be made to reduce these disparities is a moral issue, but how the issue will actually be decided depends not simply on moral argument and scientific evidence about the costs and benefits of alternative positions. The actual resolution will depend heavily on existing power relations in the political environment.

An awareness of the moral and political bases of educational decision making should temper the extent to which we expect technical knowledge alone to resolve four issues likely to become increasingly troublesome; namely, education goals, structure versus content, reforming separate schools versus the whole system, and the connection between schooling and social capital.

## Goals

We have spoken a good deal about the importance of consensus on clear goals, and have argued that goals such as membership and authentic academic work are likely to enhance engagement and achievement. At the same time, there is substantial disagreement in the society on what to teach and the extent to which there should be one set of goals for all students.

### Traditional and Progressive Educational Visions

Disagreement over educational goals is due in part to long-standing issues in educational philosophy that are unlikely to be resolved soon, even with societal agreement that schools should be improved, that students should come to school ready to learn, or that all students should have more science and mathematics. The most publicized debates highlight issues such as the importance given to science versus humanities, vocational versus college prep curriculum, or programs for gifted vs. at-risk students. A less publicized, less articulated, but more fundamental tension often centers around a set of apparently competing choices between traditional and progressive visions of education. In all curriculum areas, these visions harbor conflicting assumptions about the nature of knowledge and its use in education. Some of the assumptions that have major implications for curriculum and teaching are summarized below.[6]

### Traditional

1. Knowledge as conclusive and objective
2. Education for surveys of knowledge and basic skills
3. Absorption of knowledge for future use

4. Knowledge grounded in formal disciplines external to the learner
5. Education for verbal and mathematical competence

*Progressive*

1. Knowledge as tentative and socially constructed
2. Education for in-depth understanding and critical thinking
3. Using knowledge in order to learn
4. Knowledge grounded in interaction between student experiences and formal disciplined knowledge
5. Education for multiple intelligences

This is not to suggest that people take clear, categorical positions on these issues or that it is always necessary to choose between stark alternatives. What makes the issues so persistent is that each side contains enough truth that it cannot be completely dismissed. Disagreement of this sort will never be conclusively resolved on one side or the other. Instead, opposing sides will continue as horns of persisting dilemmas for thoughtful educators.[7]

The historical record shows that school reform movements have pushed in both traditional and progressive directions, but that traditional visions have consistently dominated.[8] Progressive visions have been tolerated only occasionally as alternatives for special groups of students. The overall conclusion of this book, however, supported by material in most of the chapters, is that to enhance student engagement and achievement, far more weight should be given to the progressive side than is typically found in secondary schools. Scenes at Thomas Jefferson High School illustrated what this might look like.

## Differentiation and Commonality in Curriculum

In spite of recent movement toward national education goals and increased large-scale testing, implying increased uniformity in curriculum, several forces push toward differentiation, both of student experiences within schools and of schools from one another. The forces that drive differentiation are cultural, vocational, pedagogical, and political.

Rapidly increasing numbers of racially and ethnically diverse students and of students without English as a first language have raised, and will continue to raise, questions about what should be taught in common and what educational content should be different to respond to needs of unique cultural groups.

There are increasing pressures to design education so that students are placed into different career tracks. Even with agreement that the work force needs more advanced competencies in thinking and problem solving and more education beyond secondary school, clear divisions in academic preparation exist between students aiming for elite liberal arts institutions, state universities, community colleges, and technical schools. Oregon has adopted a system that accentuates such differentiation after 10th Grade.

Research and experience in teaching continue to highlight individual differences in student motivation and learning style, accentuated even further by dramatic differences in students' cultural backgrounds and home environments. In the face of these differences, teachers are increasingly reluctant to shape all students into one mold.

One way of handling human diversity and disagreement over educational ends or means is to allow individuals, schools, communities, and states to choose their own paths, rather than requiring uniformity. Resistance to formal centralized control of curriculum in the United States has bolstered a tradition of local control. Individual schools, districts, states, and parents united through neighborhood or common interests have exercised unique influences over school curriculum, which leads to further differentiation in the nation as a whole.

Significant tension exists between the differentiation of schooling due to cultural diversity, vocational specialization, individual differences, and local political control, and the desire for standard, more uniform outcomes across a large number of schools. The case for more uniform standards is based largely in arguments for equity for all students regardless of social background and residential location, for more efficient assessment of results, and for increasing student achievement on a state or national scale.

Discussion of education goals within a school or a unit containing more than one school (district, state, nation) is likely, therefore, to involve difficulties not only on the substance of education to pursue (e.g., along traditional or progressive lines), but also in deciding which goals should be common to all students (schools) and which should be different.

### Structure Versus Content

Recent alarm over the condition of public education, expressed most visibly by political and corporate leaders, has focused attention on structural issues. Enormous energy and resources have recently been invested in debates over and attempts to implement a variety of changes in the organization of schools. The more visible proposals are summarized below.

- Parents should choose their children's schools, and schools should compete for funding based on student enrollment.
- Individual schools should have autonomy from district and state regulations in basic decisions on curriculum, hiring, and budget.
- Teachers and parents should share decision-making authority with administrators in local school governance.
- Schools should be held accountable for student performance by districts, states, and parents.
- Tracking and ability grouping should be abolished and replaced by heterogeneous grouping.
- Schools should operate year-round.
- Community social services should be coordinated with school programs.
- There should be national certification of teachers and ladders of professional advancement within the teaching profession.
- There should be more opportunity for teachers to plan and work together in school.
- Students should spend more time in small-group and individual study, and less in large-group instruction.
- Students should advance in school not according to grades attended and credits earned, but according to demonstrated proficiency.

Literature on educational restructuring is remarkably silent on the question of why or how particular organizational structures such as these are likely to improve student achievement. The assumed, but rarely well-argued, connections between organizational structure and specific student outcomes can usually be reduced to two types of claims. New structures will presumably either increase the *commitment* (motivation) of adults to teach and students to learn, or they will increase the *competence* (technical capacity) of adults to offer a more effective learning environment.

The reasoning can be illustrated in arguments for school-based management and shared decision making. If teachers and administrators are given more autonomy, discretion, and control in conducting the work, they will feel a greater sense of ownership of and responsibility for its quality. This sense of control leads to more pride in success and more personal culpability for failure, both of which inspire greater commitment to do a good job.

Increased control allows educators to use their professional knowledge and experience to the fullest. Rather than having to rely on technical direction from authorities far removed from the scene, the teacher is free to teach only according to approaches that his or her best judgment says will work. Access to and application of technical know-how are thus made more efficient. In this sense, local empowerment can be expected to enhance teachers' competence.

Enhancing school-level teacher control seems likely to promote commitment and competence, but this alone offers no guarantees. Will the teachers be sufficiently committed to low-achieving students? Will they know enough about mathematics to teach it well? Will they have access to new knowledge on assessment? Will they be committed to traditional or progressive visions of education? Will ideological and personality conflict within the group of teachers prevent their developing consensus and learning from one another? Whether any given organizational arrangement actually leads to improved student engagement or learning depends largely on the content of commitment and the content of competence exercised.

A variety of structural changes may seem reasonable, but the challenge is to determine how to maximize the probability that apparently more sensible structural arrangements will actually be filled with valid educational content that engages students. In short, "where's the beef," or what kind of "beef" should fill the new structures? What particular kinds of commitments and what particular kinds of competencies should new structures promote?

A comprehensive look at the kinds of commitments and competence needed in restructured schools would consider administrators, parents, publishers, test-makers, and others. I focus here on teachers, because they have the most direct opportunities to influence students. The three themes discussed next represent, in my view, the most important substantive goals for teachers that new structures should serve.

## Theme 1: Depth of Understanding and Authentic Learning

The content of school restructuring can conceivably lead in either direction, but the more well-developed proposals aim more toward the progressive vision. To infuse restructuring with powerful content calls for building teacher commitment to an educational vision that emphasizes depth of understanding and authentic learning, rather than only transmission and reproduction of declarative knowledge. This emphasis on the progressive vision does not deny, as many erroneously believe, the importance of teaching basic information, concepts, and skills. The point is to move beyond the "basics," recognizing that unless such knowledge is applied to questions more complex than those of quiz shows or crossword puzzles, it will rarely be useful to individuals or society. To execute this commitment, teachers will need lots of help. The earlier discussion about the synthesis between student-centered and challenging content approaches to curriculum suggested some of the issues that must be faced in helping teachers with this theme.

## Theme 2: Success for All Students

The escalating diversity of the student population and the growing numbers of students at risk have dramatized failures of the current social and educational system. Dominant structures of schooling can respond to students who come to school eager to learn, competent in speaking English, and from home environments that provide food, health care, intellectual stimulation, emotional stability, and the belief that working hard in school will lead to economic success and full-fledged membership in white, middle-class society. But teachers face increasing numbers of students who don't fit this mold. Instead, poverty, poor health, emotional turmoil, limited proficiency in English, increased responsibilities for family care, cultural norms that differ from the white middle class, and histories of failure in school make it very difficult for children to invest themselves in conventional forms of schoolwork. These students pose major challenges for teachers, especially those from white, middle-class backgrounds. When students don't seem to learn within the conventional structure of schools, teachers begin to lower their expectations. As children experience failure, they lower expectations for themselves. This creates a self-fulfilling downward spiral for both students and staff.

As discussed later, some of the problems of students at risk will ultimately be solved only through massive societal efforts to rebuild social capital. But schools cannot and need not wait. Research has already shown that teachers with high expectations can successfully teach culturally diverse students and at-risk students (see Brice Heath & Magnolia, 1991; Brookover, Beady, Flood, Schweitzer, & Wisenbaker, 1979; Edmonds, 1979; Madden, Slavin, Karweit, Dolan, & Wasik, 1991; Slavin, Karweit, & Madden, 1989; Stedman, 1985; U.S. Department of Education, 1987; Wehlage, Rutter, Smith, Lesko, & Fernandez, 1989). The problem is how to help all teachers become more effective with these students. White, middle-class teachers, for example, will need to gain new understanding of students' diverse cultural and social backgrounds. They will need opportunities to get to know these students better through working relationships that nurture the kind of personal bonding and trust on which mutual commitment to teach and to learn must be built. They will need to develop understanding of important competencies that these students possess but may not be able to express through conventional school routines. As teachers participate in such new organizational structures as teams, school councils, or student advisory groups, critical attention must be given to this second arena for powerful content: building commitment and competence to teach all students, especially those from culturally diverse backgrounds and with histories of school failure.

### Theme 3: New Roles for Teachers

Themes 1 and 2 suggest that teachers may need to function in new roles that depart substantially from the familiar role of pedagogue within a self-contained class, teaching many students simultaneously in a large group. Restructuring projects suggest a variety of new roles for teachers, including instructional coach, instructional or curriculum team member, facilitator of new programs, student advisor, and participant in organizational decision making. These roles extend the responsibilities of teaching enormously and call for a host of commitments and competencies.

Will teachers commit themselves to new responsibilities? Will they function competently in the new roles? There is no reason to assume that simply placing teachers in the new roles of coach, organizational decision maker, or even team member with other teachers will necessarily build teacher commitment or proficiency to perform the role well. Most teachers have had little experience and no formal training in these roles. And, as indicated earlier, the knowledge base on how to be effective in some of these roles is weak. As with other innovations, new roles can become overplayed as ends in themselves without critical examination of their necessity and relevance to improved instruction. There may be an important trade-off, for example, between helping teachers become better decision makers on governance issues versus helping them learn how to respond more constructively to student writing. This third theme calls for close analysis of the new roles needed, along with reinforcement for and education in the roles that new structures require.[9]

These three areas of teacher commitment and competence offer an agenda of content to be infused into new organizational structures through the selection of staff, the building of organizational missions, and the conduct of professional development activity.

The merits of this particular agenda, of course, will be debated. The debate will take us back to consideration of fundamental goals and the moral and political issues that lie at the heart of much educational controversy. The point here is not to claim that research has resolved the controversies, but to show that deciding to change the structures of schooling will not necessarily enhance student engagement and achievement. Decisions about the particular directions of commitment and particular forms of competence to promote in both teachers and students are equally, if not more, important.

To implement their progressive educational vision, staff at Thomas Jefferson relied on specific organizational structures and also on substantive commitments and competencies of faculty. Efforts at school reform can focus too much on either structure or content. Schools will be more effective if organizational structure and content reinforce one another.

## School-by-School and Systemic Reform

To improve education, choices must be made not only about goals and the emphasis given to structure and content, but also about the underlying reform strategies. For the most part, our research took a bottom-up perspective, trying to understand the process of student engagement and achievement within individual secondary schools, in contrast to studying how the broader system might be changed for the benefit of many schools at once. My comments on social context, leadership, and external change agents focused on how schools might be changed, essentially one at a time. This approach to research was consistent with several studies on school change that document the unique nature of schools and the difficulties of top-down strategies for changing them.

Thomas Jefferson High School offered an illustration of the process of individual school improvement, and other research has shown how it is possible to improve secondary schools one by one (see Grant, 1988; Lipsitz, 1984; Louis & Miles, 1990; Metz, 1986). At the same time, it is important to consider educational improvement as a collective social responsibility. This requires thinking about systemic reform: What programs and policies might make it possible to change many schools within a district, a state, or the nation? Recent national concern for systemic change is illustrated by the U.S. Department of Education's issuing of "National Goals for Education" in 1990 and the plan "America 2000" in 1991. Many initiatives have been proposed and some implemented by commissions and agencies. They include new systems of district, state, and national assessment to hold schools more accountable for student outcomes; new curriculum standards (for teachers, schools, and publishers of instructional materials) that emphasize thinking and in-depth study; reform of preservice training and of staff development of teachers and administrators; new career and reward structures for teachers and administrators; new systems of governance that give more authority to parents and teachers to run schools; schools programmed to serve more specialized missions than the common comprehensive secondary school; and increased school choice for students and parents.

Each of the above remedies appears reasonable at first glance and offers the potential for improving school culture, curriculum, and organization consistent with our conceptions of school membership and authentic work. But we can also imagine ways in which each of the above remedies could undermine the forms of engagement and achievement we propose. High-stakes testing by districts or states could continue to sanctify inauthentic reproduction of fragmented knowledge. School-based management can remain preoccupied with personnel and budget issues and neglect important matters of school culture, curriculum, and instruction (Malen, Ogawa, & Krantz, 1990). Specialized magnet schools and systems of choice can lead to deteriorating conditions for students who remain in conventional neighborhood schools (Moore & Davenport, 1989). It is impossible to assess the effects on student learning of most of the items above, because, as phrased here, they are silent on the specific commitments and competencies to be promoted. Our research found no clear systemic solutions about how to change hundreds or thousands of schools to enhance student engagement and achievement. But the research did suggest important questions that should guide evaluation of proposals for systemic change.

Are proposed systemic strategies consistent with what is known about human learning, social-cultural relations, and organizational functioning? We have learned much, for example, about the folly of trying to implement curriculum change simply by producing new curricula and mandating their use. Instead, the actual users of an innovation — teachers, administrators, parents — must be sufficiently involved in the process of adoption so they develop a sense of ownership. School-based ownership of innovation by participants closest to students and classrooms is widely endorsed. But will it be possible to nurture a sense of ownership among teachers within a system that may impose high-stakes accountability to performance standards set by distant state authorities?

The importance of local ownership may suggest an entirely new approach to systemic change. The traditional policy approach relies on top-down regulations that schools must meet to stay in operation. More recent thinking urges district and state bureaucracies to transform themselves from regulating agencies into those that instead offer services and support, based on needs of the schools. But who will set and enforce the purposes for which systemic support is offered — the local school or the state bureaucracy? A middle ground between these positions recommends that change might be pursued more effectively through thoughtful dialogue between people at the school site and state authorities. In this role, the education bureaucracy would function primarily neither as a regulator nor as a service provider. It would take on aspects of each, but its major mission would be to establish a constructive dialogue that, through a continuing dialectic, balances needs of individual schools and those of systemic reform.

Proposals for systemic change should be scrutinized for the extent to which they address the problem of loose-coupling and fragmentation within the system. Smith and O'Day (1991) described the vacuum of coordination among critical elements that influence education in schools. There is virtually no alignment among teacher education; local school curriculum; student performance standards set by schools, districts, or states; the preparation of commercial curriculum materials; criteria for teachers' professional advancement; and the nature of professional development activities. Given the failure to link critical elements in the system to reinforce one another, it should be no surprise that the system produces results of such low quality.

The costs and benefits of any single systemic intervention, such as national tests or school-based councils, can be debated. A more fundamental issue, however, is the extent to which discrete remedies can be integrated in ways that enhance systemic coordination. Taking this problem seriously leads to the question of scale. At what level — school, district, state, region, nation — would tighter, comprehensive coordination be desirable? Is it possible to work toward tighter linkages and still avoid the dangers of a monolithic system that does more harm than good? Tighter linkages will entail reductions in organizational autonomy from individual classrooms to university programs of teacher education. At what point should systemic responsibility for the education of children justify placing greater constraints on the variety of participants in that enterprise? If tighter linkages are desirable, what political, legal, and economic changes would make them happen? Unfortunately, most proposed systemic innovations have failed to address these problems of linkage and coordination.

## Schooling and Social Capital

Just as we concluded the reports of research by looking at adolescents beyond the classroom, in these final observations on choices for the future I try to put school in perspective. Parents, educators, researchers, and youth-serving professionals commonly acknowledge the enormous power of factors beyond formal schooling to affect the values, dispositions, skills, and knowledge of youth, and the likelihood that students will benefit from schooling. Economic resources, parenting styles, unique family and social-cultural history, and the media provide a wealth of "education," informally delivered. Educators typically feel overpowered by societal influences beyond their control. How can they educate students who come to school undernourished from homes filled with conflict or the emptiness of neglect? How can they teach children to cooperate, to live frugally to preserve the planet, or to participate in community affairs when the society bombards them with messages of individual competition, high material consumption, and civic powerlessness? How can they inspire students to take pride in doing their best work when they see so many examples of adults who take pride in doing only enough to get by?

Many educators answer such questions by abdicating responsibility for the engagement and achievement of students who don't seem to fit into conventional school routines. At the other extreme, parents, corporate leaders, and policy makers often expect educators to take far more responsibility for youth development than their resources permit. To the extent that major difficulties in educating students reflect fundamental deficits or dysfunctions in society, the improvement of education may depend on far more than technical advances or restructuring of schools. In addition, it may require restructuring of social, economic, and political life in the community at large. The problem is to clarify the extent to which schools might substantially enhance student engagement and achievement on their own, and the extent to which substantial school improvement requires prior or concurrent changes in institutions beyond schools.

Children cannot invest themselves in learning unless they have stable networks of social support beyond the school that provide basic material needs of food, clothing, shelter, and health care, and, most important, emotional bonding to adults who nurture trust, hope, and the self-confidence needed to develop intellectual and social competence. Traditionally these forms of support for children have been provided by families, adult friends, and the social, religious, and political organizations of neighborhoods and small communities. Increasingly, however, middle-class flight, a disintegrating economic base, deteriorating housing stock, and a general loss of stable institutions have weakened the ability of many urban neighborhoods to sustain constructive family life and other forms of social support (Wilson, 1987), including the political capability required for long-term fundamental school reform (Cohen, 1990). The problem seems most dramatic in urban areas, but recent investigations into the condition of children in the United States shows serious problems in diverse locations and social groups (Committee for Economic Development, 1987; Hodgkinson, 1991; O'Neil, 1991).

The human resources that provide support for children can be considered social capital (Coleman, 1988). Like fiscal or material capital, social capital is required for growth. Social capital is grounded in adults with important individual attributes such as the commitment and competence to care for children. Most important, however, social capital consists of an organizational fabric that provides collective adult support. The organizational fabric must offer opportunities to develop both formal and informal "institutions" that identify and solve collective problems. These may involve activities ranging from card games and bowling leagues to child care centers and drug rehabilitation programs.

The role of schools in the rebuilding of social capital is as yet unclear, but there should be little doubt that over the long term, education for many students will not improve substantially without advances in the social capital of their communities (Coleman & Hoffer, 1987; Schorr, 1988). Disparate efforts of churches, action organizations, social service agencies, unions, and businesses have attacked parts of the problem. Some education projects have launched major efforts to enhance parental involvement in schooling (e.g., James Comer's project in New Haven) and to coordinate social and health services in the school (San Diego's New Beginnings project). In general, however, both education reform and social welfare policy have failed to address the decline of social capital in American communities.

Most American secondary schools still have a long way to go to substantially improve the engagement and achievement of their students. We must not forget that in spite of all the talk about improving schools, most of the variation in students' school success across the system is due to differences between classes within schools, not between schools of different quality (Pauly, 1991). At the same time we did find schools and programs that distinguished themselves in the promotion of higher-order thinking, in developing effective programs for students at risk, and in maintaining high levels of teacher engagement with large proportions of economically disadvantaged students. These schools achieved success not primarily as a result of systemic policy pressure from external sources, but through a process of reflective dialogue within the school that, in some cases, benefitted substantially from the stimulation and support of external change agents. Whether these schools were accidental heroes or whether the lessons of their success can be generalized and harnessed toward more systemic improvement remains to be seen.

Many voices have recently urged an historically unique national agenda for education in the United States, and at this writing several initiatives have begun. Unfortunately, the press for school choice, national tests in six curriculum areas, school-based management, and new restructured schools leaves unresolved most of the issues just discussed. Unless proposed innovations attempt to tackle these issues explicitly, it will be difficult to predict their effects on student engagement and achievement.

## NOTES

1. In Chapter 2 Gamoran and Nystrand found that teachers of low-track students asked authentic, student-centered questions, but not about literature. Only when authentic questions were directed toward substantive content (as in high-track classes) did authenticity contribute to understanding of literature.

2. Elmore (1991) summarizes six emerging ideas about best teaching practice that call for depth of understanding as a central focus of learning. Porter, Archbald, and Tyree (1990) present the concept of "hard content" and discuss the extent to which state policies of curriculum control and empowerment have achieved it.

3. See Fullan and Stiegelbauer (1991) for a far-reaching synthesis of research on educational change in individuals, institutions, and systems.

4. Sarason (1990) offers one of the most comprehensive essays on the problem of educational change in the contemporary social context.

5. This material is taken from Wehlage, Lipman, and Smith (1990) and adapted to a high school setting. The scenes of students' instructional experiences were published in the National Center on Effective Secondary Schools *Newsletter*, 5(3) (Winter, 1990–91), p. 4.

6. I use the labels here only to draw general outlines of dispute, without representing their full complexity and varied interpretation over several decades of discussion. For a related set of persisting dilemmas, see Berlak and Berlak (1981). Along similar lines, Jackson (1986, Chapter 6) summarizes disputes on education dating back to the Greek sophist Protagoras. Jackson labels these two alternative outlooks on teaching "mimetic" and "transformative."

7. Controversies over education goals also center on the relative priority to give to preparation for work, for civic life, and for personal affairs. But regardless of how one settles these three priorities, tensions between traditional and progressive approaches remain.

8. For evidence on the dominance of traditional views see Cuban (1984); Kliebard (1986); and Rugg and Shumaker (c1928). Some reformers who historians consider progressive actually emphasized administrative efficiency or social reform without supporting a progressive vision of knowledge and learning (Tyack, 1974; Kliebard, 1986).

9. Directions for professional development are suggested in Lichtenstein, McLaughlin, and Knudsen (1991) and Levin (1991).

## REFERENCES

Bennett, S. (1987). *New dimensions in research on class size and academic achievement.* Madison, WI: National Center on Effective Secondary Schools.

Berlak, A., & Berlak, H. (1981). *Dilemmas of schooling: Teaching and social change.* New York: Methuen.

Brice Heath, S., & Magnolia, L. (1991). *Children of promise: Literate activity in linguistically and culturally diverse classrooms*. Washington, DC: National Education Association.

Brookover, W., Beady, C., Flood, P., Schweitzer, J., & Wisenbaker, J. (1979). *School social systems and student achievement: Schools can make a difference*. New York: Praeger.

Bryk, A. S., & Driscoll, M. E. (1988). *The high school as community: Contextual influences, and consequences for students and teachers*. Madison: National Center on Effective Secondary Schools, University of Wisconsin.

Bryk, A. S., Lee, V. E., & Smith, J. B. (1990). High school organization and its effects on teachers and students: An interpretive summary of the research. In W. H. Clune & J. F. Witte (Eds.), *Choice and control in American education: Vol. 1. The theory of choice and control in American education* (pp. 135–226). Philadelphia: Falmer Press.

Cohen, D. K. (1990). Governance and instruction: The promise of decentralization and choice. In W. H. Clune & J. F. Witte (Eds.), *Choice and control in American education: Vol. 1. The theory of choice and control in American education* (pp. 337–386). Philadelphia: Falmer Press.

Coleman, J. S. (1988). Social capital in the creation of human capital. *American Journal of Sociology, 94* (Supplement), 95–120.

Coleman, J. S., & Hoffer, T. (1987). *Public and private high schools: The impact of communities*. New York: Basic Books.

Committee for Economic Development. (1987). *Children in need: Investment strategies for the educationally disadvantaged*. New York: Author.

Cuban, L. (1984). *How teachers taught*. New York: Longman.

David, J. L., Purkey, S., & White, P. (1989). *Restructuring in progress: Lessons from pioneering districts*. Washington, DC: National Governors Association.

Edmonds, R. (1979). Effective schools for the urban poor. *Educational Leadership, 37*(1), 15–24.

Elam, S. M., Rose, L. C., & Gallup, A. M. (1991). The 23rd annual Gallup poll of the public's attitudes toward the public schools. *Phi Delta Kappan, 73*(1), 41–56.

Elmore, R. F. (1991). *Teaching, learning, and organization: School restructuring and the recurring dilemmas of reform*. Paper presented at the annual meeting of the American Educational Research Association, Chicago, April 1991.

Fullan, M. G., & Stiegelbauer, S. (1991). *The new meaning of educational change*. New York: Teachers College Press.

Gamoran, A. (1987). The stratification of high school learning opportunities. *Sociology of Education, 60,* 135–155.

Grant, G. (1988). *The world we created at Hamilton High*. Cambridge, MA: Harvard University Press.

Hodgkinson, H. (1991). Reform versus reality. *Phi Delta Kappan, 73*(1), 9–16.

Jackson, P. W. (1986). *The practice of teaching*. New York: Teachers College Press.

Keating, D. P. (1988). *Adolescents' ability to engage in critical thinking*. Madison, WI: National Center on Effective Secondary Schools.

Kliebard, H. M. (1986). *The struggle for the American curriculum, 1893–1958.* Boston: Routledge & Kegan Paul.

Levin, H. M. (1991). *Building school capacity for effective teacher empowerment: Applications to elementary schools with at-risk students.* New Brunswick, NJ: Center for Policy Research in Education, Rutgers University.

Lichtenstein, G., McLaughlin, M., & Knudsen, J. (1991). *Teacher empowerment and professional knowledge.* New Brunswick, NJ: Center for Policy Research in Education, Rutgers University

Lipsitz, J. (1984). *Successful schools for young adolescents.* New Brunswick, NJ: Transaction Books.

Louis, K. S., & Miles, M. B. (1990). *Improving the urban high school: What works and why.* New York: Teachers College Press.

Madden, N. A., Slavin, R. E., Karweit, N. L., Dolan, L., & Wasik, B. (1991). *Success for all: Multiyear effects of a school-wide elementary restructuring program.* Paper presented to American Educational Research Association, Chicago, April 1991.

Malen, B., Ogawa, R. T., & Kranz, J. (1990). What do we know about school-based management? A case study of the literature — A call for research. In W. H. Clune and J. F. Witte (Eds.), *Choice and control in American education: Vol. 2. The practice of choice, decentralization and school restructuring* (pp. 289–342). New York: Falmer Press.

Metz, M. H. (1986). *Different by design: The context and character of three magnet schools.* New York: Routledge & Kegan Paul.

Moore, D. R., & Davenport, S. (1989). High school choice and students at risk. *Equity and Choice, 5*(1), 5–10.

National Center on Effective Secondary Schools. (Winter 1990–91). Authentic work: Implications for curriculum knowledge and student participation. *Newsletter, 5*(3), 4.

Oakes, J. (1985). *Keeping track: How schools structure inequality.* New Haven: Yale University Press.

O'Neil, J. (1991). A generation adrift? *Educational Leadership, 49*(1), 4–10.

Pauly, E. (1991). *The classroom crucible: What really works, what doesn't and why.* New York: Basic Books.

Peterson, K. D. (1989). *Secondary principals and instructional leadership: Complexities in a diverse role.* Madison, WI: National Center on Effective Secondary Schools.

Porter, A. C., Archbald, D. A., & Tyree, A. K., Jr. (1990). Reforming the curriculum: Will empowerment policies replace control? In S. H. Fuhrman & B. Malen (Eds.), *The politics of curriculum and testing: The 1990 yearbook of the Politics of Education Association* (pp. 11–36). Philadelphia: Falmer Press.

Resnick, L. B. (1987). *Education and learning to think.* Washington, DC: National Academy Press.

Rugg, H. O. & Shumaker, A. (c1928). *The child-centered school: An appraisal of the new education.* Yonkers, NY: World Book Co.

Sarason, S. B. (1990). *The predictable failure of educational reform: Can we change before it's too late?* San Francisco: Jossey-Bass.

Schorr, L. (1988). *Within our reach: Breaking the cycle of disadvantage.* New York: Doubleday.

Slavin, R. E. (1990). Achievement effects of ability grouping in secondary schools: A best-evidence synthesis. *Review of Educational Research, 60*(3), 471–499.

Slavin, R. E., Karweit, N. L., & Madden, N. A. (1989). *Effective programs for students at-risk.* Boston: Allyn & Bacon.

Smith, M. S., & O'Day, J. (1991). Systemic school reform. In S. H. Fuhrman & B. Malen (Eds.), *The politics of curriculum and testing: The 1990 yearbook of the Politics of Education Association* (pp. 233–267). Philadelphia: Falmer Press.

Stedman, L. (1985). A new look at the effective schools literature. *Urban Education, 20,* 295–326.

Tyack, D. B. (1974). *The one best system: A history of American urban education.* Cambridge, MA: Harvard University Press.

U.S. Department of Education. (1987). *What works: Schools that work: Educating disadvantaged children.* Washington, DC: Author.

Wehlage, G. G., Lipman, P., & Smith, G. (1990). *A good school.* Madison, WI: National Center on Effective Secondary Schools.

Wehlage, G. G, Rutter, R. A., Smith, G. A., Lesko, N., & Fernandez, R. R. (1989). *Reducing the risk: Schools as communities of support.* Philadelphia: Falmer Press.

Wilson, W. J. (1987). *The truly disadvantaged: The inner city, the underclass, and public policy.* Chicago: University of Chicago Press.

# Index

219

# About the Contributors

**B. Bradford Brown** is a professor in the Department of Educational Psychology and a research scientist at the Wisconsin Center for Education Research at the University of Wisconsin–Madison. He received an A.B. in sociology from Princeton University and a Ph.D. in human development from the University of Chicago before joining the faculty of the University of Wisconsin in 1979. His publications focus on coping with stress in adulthood and on peer relations in adolescence.

**Adam Gamoran** is an associate professor of sociology and educational policy studies at the University of Wisconsin–Madison. He received a doctoral degree in education from the University of Chicago. His current research projects include studies of the organization of schooling in inner cities, the effects of ability grouping and curriculum tracking, and the allocation and effects of instruction in classrooms.

**Susie D. Lamborn** is currently a research scholar at the University of West Florida's Educational Research and Development Center. She received her B.A. from Pennsylvania State University in psychology and her Ph.D. in developmental psychology from the University of Denver. She has completed research on adolescent development in the family context, with a focus on normative issues of development for youth from differing cultural heritages. She has collaborated with program developers on the design and implementation of evaluation studies of education and adolescent development.

**Karen Seashore Louis** received her doctoral degree in sociology from Columbia University, and has worked in a variety of policy research and academic settings. She is currently an associate professor in the Department of Educational Policy and Administration at the University of Minnesota. Her research and consulting have focused on how to improve schools through organizational design and development, research utilization, and better planning and implementation processes. This includes evaluation and research on federal and state programs in the United States and work on school improvement with a variety of European and Canadian groups and the Organization for Economic Cooperation and Development.

Nina S. Mounts is currently a postdoctoral research fellow in developmental psychology at the University of Illinois at Urbana–Champaign. She received a doctoral degree in child and family studies at the University of Wisconsin–Madison, a master of science degree in child and family studies from Syracuse University, and a bachelor of arts degree in sociology from Saint Lawrence University, Canton, NY. Her research interests are in both peer and parent–child relationships during childhood and adolescence. She is especially interested in the linkages between parent–child and peer relationships.

Fred M. Newmann, professor of curriculum and instruction at the University of Wisconsin, directed the National Center on Effective Secondary Schools, and he now directs the Center on Organization and Restructuring of Schools. He majored in American studies at Amherst College and received master's and doctoral degrees in education at Harvard. His publications deal with curriculum for citizenship, higher-order thinking in social studies, education and the building of community, and alternatives to standardized testing.

Martin Nystrand is professor of English and a principal investigator at the Center on Organization and Restructuring of Schools, located in the Wisconsin Center for Education Research, the University of Wisconsin–Madison. His publications have explored the structure of written communication and language as a way of knowing. He is active in research on writing and on instructional discourse. He is also current president of the American Education Research Association Special Interest Group for Writing Research. His current research, with sociologist Adam Gamoran, concerns the effects of instructional discourse, including writing, reading, and talk, on achievement in high school English and social studies.

BetsAnn Smith is a doctoral candidate in the Department of Educational Policy and Administration, University of Minnesota. Her research interests are in the areas of teachers' work and school organization.

Gregory A. Smith is an assistant professor at the University of Alaska–Fairbanks where he is involved with an innovative secondary education program called Teachers for Alaska. He received his Ph.D. from the University of Wisconsin–Madison in educational policy studies. His research has addressed the development of effective schools for students at risk of academic failure, and education concerning environmental limits.

**Laurence Steinberg** is professor of psychology at Temple University. He received his Ph.D. in human development and family studies from Cornell University. A fellow of the American Psychological Association, his research focuses on adolescent development and behavior, with an emphasis on the role of family, peers, and community in young people's lives.

**Gary G. Wehlage** is Associate Director of the Center on Organization and Restructuring of Schools and a professor of curriculum and instruction at the University of Wisconsin–Madison. He is a graduate of Augustana College (SD) and received his master's and doctorate degrees from the University of Illinois–Urbana. His research has addressed the high school dropout problem, and the problem of restructuring schools for at-risk students. For several years he has worked with the Annie E. Casey Foundation's New Futures Initiative. His recent publications include (as co-author) *Reducing the Risk: Schools as Communities of Support* (1989).